VITAL
MINISTRY
ISSUES

THE VITAL ISSUES SERIES

VITAL MINISTRY ISSUES

*Examining Concerns &
Conflicts in Ministry*

ROY B. ZUCK
GENERAL EDITOR

kregel
RESOURCES

Grand Rapids, MI 49501

Vital Ministry Issues by Roy B. Zuck, general editor.

Copyright © 1994 by Dallas Theological Seminary.

Published by Kregel Resources, an imprint of Kregel Publications, P.O. Box 2607, Grand Rapids, MI 49501. Kregel Resources provides timely and relevant resources for Christian life and service. Your comments and suggestions are valued.

Cover Design: Sarah Slattery
Book Design: Alan G. Hartman

Library of Congress Cataloging-in-Publication Data
    Roy B. Zuck.
    Vital ministry issues: examining concerns & conflicts in ministry / Roy B. Zuck, gen. ed.
        p.   cm. (Vital Issues Series)
    1. Pastoral theology. 2. Clergy—Office. I. Zuck, Roy B.
II. Series: Zuck, Roy B. Vital Issues Series.
BV4011.V55   1994   253—dc20   94-6932
                                                            CIP
ISBN 0-8254-4068-8 (paperback)

1 2 3 4 5 Printing / Year 98 97 96 95 94

Printed in the United States of America

Contents

5

Contributors

Kenneth L. Barker
Executive Director, NIV Translation Center, Lewisville, Texas

Ann Bowman
Faculty, Department of Biblical Studies, International
School of Theology, San Bernardino, California

Earl V. Comfort
Senior Pastor, Jacksonville Chapel, Lincoln Park, New Jersey

Kenneth O. Gangel
Vice President for Academic Affairs, Academic Dean, and
Professor of Christian Education, Dallas Theological
Seminary, Dallas, Texas

Ed Glasscock
Assistant Professor, Moody Graduate School,
Chicago, Illinois

D. Edmond Hiebert
Late Professor of New Testament, Mennonite Brethren
Biblical Seminary, Fresno, California

J. Gary Inrig
Pastor, Trinity Evangelical Free Church, Redlands, California

Homer A. Kent, Sr.
Professor Emeritus of New Testament and Greek, Grace
Theological Seminary, Winona Lake, Indiana

Ted G. Kitchens
Senior Pastor, Christ Chapel Bible Church, Fort Worth, Texas

William D. Lawrence
Executive Director, Center for Christian Leadership and
Professor of Pastoral Ministries, Dallas Theological
Seminary, Dallas, Texas

A. Duane Litfin
President, Wheaton College, Wheaton, Illinois

Raymond C. Ortlund
  President, Renewal Ministries, Newport Beach, California

Jay A. Quine
  Associate Pastor, Jacksonville Chapel, Lincoln Park, New
  Jersey; Former Municipal Court Judge, Colfax, Washington;
  and Former Deputy Prosecutor, Whitman County,
  Washington

John R. W. Stott
  President, London Institute for Contemporary Christianity,
  London, England

Donald R. Sunukjian
  Pastor, Westlake Bible Church, Austin, Texas

Timothy S. Warren
  Professor of Pastoral Ministries, Dallas Theological
  Seminary, Dallas, Texas

Preface

Pastors and physicians share a number of traits—both are concerned about helping people improve, both offer prescriptions for people's problems, and both professions call for a high level of preparation and dedication. What is more, being in the ministry, like practicing medicine, means being on call, facing frequent interruptions, and having a demanding position of challenging responsibilities. Pastors are expected to lead and to serve, to preach and to equip, to challenge and to convert.

Vital Ministry Issues speaks to the multi-sided aspects of serving a local church as pastor: ministry standards, ideals, and obligations; credibility, communication, and concern; training elders and deacons, and leading congregations in worship and in growth; knowing the roles of women and men in ministry, the role of the small church, and the role of church discipline.

These are issues—vital, practical concerns—which church leaders must face and meet head on. Like a physician, a pastor is effective to the extent to which he serves people's needs. I trust these chapters will enhance the quality and impact of pastoral leadership in the United States and around the world.

ROY B. ZUCK

About *Bibliotheca Sacra*

A flood is rampant—an engulfing deluge of literature far beyond any one person's ability to read it all. Presses continue to churn out thousands of journals and magazines like a roiling, raging river.

Among these numberless publications, one stands tall and singular—*Bibliotheca Sacra*—a strange name (meaning "Sacred Library") but a journal familiar to many pastors, teachers, and Bible students.

How is *Bibliotheca Sacra* unique in the world of publishing? By being the oldest continuously published journal in the Western Hemisphere—1993 marked its 150th anniversary—and by being published by one school for sixty years—1994 marks its diamond anniversary of being released by Dallas Seminary.

Bib Sac, to use its shortened sobriquet, was founded in New York City in 1843 and was purchased by Dallas Theological Seminary in 1934, ten years after the school's founding. The quarterly's one-hundred and fifty year history boasts only nine editors. Through those years it has maintained a vibrant stance of biblical conservatism and a strong commitment to the Scriptures as God's infallible Word.

I am grateful to Kregel Publications for producing a series of volumes, being released this year and next, commemorating both the journal's sesquicentennial (1843–1993) and its diamond anniversary (1934–1994). Each volume in the Kregel *Vital Issues Series* includes carefully selected articles from the thirties to the present—articles of enduring quality, articles by leading evangelicals whose topics are as relevant today as when they were first produced. The chapters have been edited slightly to provide conformity of style. As Dallas Seminary and Kregel Publications jointly commemorate these anniversaries of *Bibliotheca Sacra*, we trust these anthologies will enrich the spiritual lives and Christian ministries of many more readers.

ROY B. ZUCK, EDITOR
Bibliotheca Sacra

For *Bibliotheca Sacra* subscription information, call Dallas Seminary, 1–800–992-0998.

CHAPTER 1

The World's Challenge to the Church

John R. W. Stott

One of the greatest needs in today's church is for a greater sensitivity to the world. As true servants of Jesus Christ, believers should keep their eyes open, as He did, to human need and their ears cocked to the world's cries of pain. They should respond, as again He did, with compassion to the real issues of the day.

This does not mean that in every respect believers allow "the world to set the agenda for the church" or that they trot like a little dog at the world's heels. To behave like that would be to confuse service, to which believers are called, with servility, to which they are not. It would be to interpret sensitivity, which is a virtue, in terms of conformity, which is a vice. No, Christians are first and foremost to declare and do what God has told them to declare and do. They are not to pay obsequious homage to the world.

At the same time, unless believers listen attentively to the voices of secular society and struggle to understand people's misunderstandings of the gospel, unless Christians feel with people in their frustration, alienation, and even despair, and weep with those who weep, they will lack authenticity as the disciples of Jesus of Nazareth. They will run the risk, as has often been said, of answering questions no one is asking, scratching where no one is itching, supplying goods for which there is no demand, in other words, of being totally irrelevant.

People today are engaged in a threefold quest. These are three human aspirations, which Jesus Himself arouses by His Spirit, which He alone can satisfy, and which challenge the church to proclaim Him in His fullness. These are the quest for transcendence, the quest for significance, and the quest for community.

The Quest for Transcendence

Until recently "transcendence" was regarded as a rather pedantic word. Its use was limited to institutions of higher theological learning in which students are introduced to the distinction between transcendence and immanence, between God above and beyond the created world, and God active within it.

Now, however, everyone has some notion of transcendence, for it has been popularized by the craze for Transcendental Meditation. The quest for transcendence is understood as the search for ultimate reality beyond the material universe. It is a protest against secularization, against the attempt to eliminate God from His own world. People are discovering that materialism does not satisfy the human spirit.

Four examples illustrate the current disenchantment with secularism.

The failure of Euro-Marxism. Marxism was originally offered as an ideological substitute for outworn religious belief. But converts to Marxist-Leninism have been very few because of its gross materialism. As Beeson has written in *Discretion and Valour,* "the basic doctrines of Communism have neither convinced the minds, nor satisfied the emotions of either the intelligentsia or the proletariat."[1] On the other hand, religion has displayed an unexpected resilience and has refused to wither away. Solzhenitsyn has drawn attention to this in many of his books and speeches.

The wasteland of Western materialism. Materialism is no more satisfying to the human spirit in its capitalistic than in its communistic guise. Roszak is an eloquent exponent of the emptiness of Western materialism. The subtitle of his book, *Where the Wasteland Ends,* is "Politics and Transcendence in Post-industrial Society." He bemoans what he calls the "Coco-colonisation of the world." People are suffering, he continues, from a "psychic claustrophobia within the scientific world view," in which the human spirit cannot breathe. He castigates science for its reductionist assault on human life, its arrogant claim to be able to explain everything, its "debunking spirit," its "undoing of the mysteries." For what science can measure is "only a portion of what man can know," and this materialistic world of objective science is not nearly "spacious enough" for man. Indeed without transcendence "the person shrivels."[2]

Roszak is right. Human beings know instinctively that reality cannot be confined to a test tube, smeared on a slide for microscopic examination, or apprehended by cool scientific detachment. Human beings are convinced that there is a spiritual dimension to life, a

Reality that is "awesomely vast," as Roszak puts it—in other words, Transcendence.

The proliferation of modern religious cults. According to Toffler, 1,000 new religious cults have won a following from about 3 million Americans.[3] This is another symptom of the quest for transcendence, another piece of evidence that materialism does not satisfy.

The world was shocked in November 1978 by the news that nearly 1,000 followers of Jim Jones, formerly of the People's Temple in San Francisco, had died in their jungle colony in Guyana, mostly in a mass poison-drinking suicide. In a leading article in *The Economist* its author wrote, "A groping has begun for new forms of spiritual experience . . . and in that search for God, it is all too easy to blunder into the arms of Satan instead."[4]

The epidemic of drug abuse. The phenomenon of drug abuse is interpreted differently. But Christians affirm that it is neither a purely innocent experimentation, nor always a protest against conventional mores, nor even an escape from the harsh realities of life, but also and specially a search for this other reality. This was clear from the writings of Castaneda in the late sixties and early seventies. He claimed that Don Juan, the Yaqui Indian, had explained to him that there are two worlds of equal reality, the "ordinary" world (of living humans) and the "nonordinary" world (of *diableros* or sorcerers): "The particular thing to learn is how to get to the crack between the worlds and how to enter the other world. . . . There is a place where the two worlds overlap. The crack is there. It opens and closes like a door in the wind."[5] Moreover, he said the only way for a human being to be transported beyond the boundaries of himself and to enter the realm of nonordinary reality is through drugs.

Here then are four contemporary evidences of the current disenchantment with materialism, of the rejection of it, and of the search by many people for another reality. They seek it everywhere—through yoga, Transcendental Meditation, and other forms of Eastern mysticism; through sex, which Malcolm Muggeridge calls "the mysticism of the materialist"; through music and other arts; through drug-taking and the "higher consciousness"; through modern religious cults and dangerous experiments with the occult; and through the fantasies of science fiction.

Christians understand what these people are doing. In the language of Paul in Athens (Acts 17:27), they are feeling after God, like blind people in the dark, groping after their Creator, who leaves them restless until they find their rest in Him (Augustine). They are recognizing the human need for transcendence.

This quest for transcendence constitutes a challenge to the quality of Christian public worship. Does it offer what people are seeking—the element of mystery, the sense of the numinous, in biblical language "the fear of God," in modern language "transcendence," so that they "bow down before the Infinitely Great"[6] in the mixture of awe, wonder, and joy called worship?

The answer to this question is "not often." The Christian church is not conspicuous for the profound reality of its worship. In particular, evangelicals do not know much how to worship. Evangelism is their specialty, not worship. They have little sense of the greatness and glory of Almighty God. The tendency is to be cocky, flippant, superficial, and proud. Little effort is made to prepare worship services, which are often slovenly, mechanical, perfunctory, and dull. No wonder those seeking reality pass the church by.

No book, not even by Marx and his followers, is more scathing of empty religion than the Bible. The eighth and seventh-century B.C. prophets were outspoken in their denunciation of the formalism and hypocrisy of Israelite religion. Jesus applied their critique to the Pharisees of His own day, saying, "This people honors Me with their lips, but their heart is far away from Me" (Matt. 15:8). And the indictment of religion by the prophets and by Jesus is uncomfortably applicable to contemporary churches. Too much of worship is ritual without reality, form without power, and religion without God.

What is needed, then? First, such a faithful reading and preaching of God's Word that through it the voice of the living God is heard, addressing His people today. Second, such a reverent and expectant administration of the Lord's Supper that there is a sense of Jesus' presence, not in the elements but among His people and at His table, Jesus Christ Himself coming to meet the believer, ready to make Himself known in the breaking of bread, anxious to give Himself to the believer, that he may feed on Him in his heart by faith. Third, such a sincere offering of praise and prayer that God's people say with Jacob, "Surely the Lord is in this place, and I did not know it. . . . This is none other than the house of God, and this is the gate of heaven" (Gen. 28:16–17). Moreover, unbelievers will fall down, exclaiming, "God is certainly among you" (1 Cor. 14:25).

In brief, it is tragic that people seeking transcendence should turn to drugs, sex, yoga, mysticism, and science fiction, instead of to the church, in whose worship services true transcendence should always be experienced and a "close encounter" with the living God enjoyed.

The Quest for Significance

Much in the modern world not only smothers a sense of transcendence, but also diminishes and even destroys an individual's sense of significance. The following are a few examples.

TECHNOLOGY

Technology can be liberating, insofar as it frees people from domestic and industrial drudgery. It is great to have a computer in one's kitchen, if you can afford one! But technology can also be dreadfully dehumanizing, as men and women feel themselves no longer persons with a name that expresses their unique dignity, but, in Toynbee's words, "serial numbers punched on a card designed to travel through the entrails of a computer."[7]

SCIENTIFIC REDUCTIONISM

Some scientists from various disciplines are arguing that a human being is nothing but an animal (to be more precise, a "naked ape" in Morris's famous phrase[8]) or a machine (programmed to make automatic responses to external stimuli). This prompted the late Donald Mackay to popularize the expression "nothing buttery" as a definition of "reductionism," and to protest against every tendency to reduce humans to a level lower than the fully personal.

To be sure, the human brain is a machine, a highly complex mechanism, and the human anatomy and physiology are those of an animal. But that is not a complete account of humanness. There is more to being human than having a body and a brain. When people affirm they are "nothing but" this or that, they make a serious and dangerous mistake.

EXISTENTIALISM

Existentialists may be said to differ from humanists by taking their atheism seriously and facing its terrible consequences. Because they say there is no God, they have no values or ideals, no moral laws or standards, no purposes or meanings. Though man exists and has to seek the courage to be, there is yet nothing that gives anyone any significance. This explains the increase of suicides due to existential despair.

Perhaps no one has expressed the quest for significance better than the late Frankl in his book *Man's Search for Meaning* (originally published in 1959 under the title *From Death Camp to Existentialism*). He noticed in the Auschwitz concentration camp that the prisoners most likely to survive their ordeal were those "who knew that there was a task waiting for them to fulfill."[9] So he quoted Nietzsche's dictum, "He who has a *why* to live for can bear almost any *how*." Frankl therefore postulated that in addition to Sigmund Freud's "will to pleasure" and Alfred Adler's "will to power," human beings have a "will to meaning." He wrote, "The striving to find a meaning in one's life is the primary motivational force in man."[10]

If the quest for transcendence was a challenge to the quality of Christian worship, the quest for significance is a challenge to the quality of Christian teaching. Millions of people do not know who they are or that they have any significance. Hence believers face the urgent challenge to tell them who they are, to enlighten them about their identity, and to teach the full biblical doctrine of their humanness.

Only Christians fully appreciate the intrinsic worth of human beings, because of the doctrines of creation and redemption. God made man male and female in His own image and gave them a responsible dominion over the earth and its creatures. He has endowed them with unique rational, moral, social, and creative faculties, which make them like Him and unlike the animals. Human beings are godlike beings! True, they are fallen from their sublime origin, and their godlikeness has been severely distorted. But it has not been destroyed. The Bible is clear on this.

Christian teaching on the dignity, nobility, and worth of human beings is of the utmost importance today, partly for the sake of their own self-image and partly for the welfare of society. When human beings are devalued, everything in society goes sour. Women and children are despised; the sick are regarded as a nuisance, and the elderly as a burden; ethnic minorities are discriminated against; capitalism displays its ugliest face; labor is exploited in the mines and factories; criminals are brutalized in prison; opposition opinions are stifled; unbelievers are left to die in their lostness; there is no freedom, dignity, or carefree joy; human life seems not worth living, because it is scarcely human any longer.

But when individuals are valued, because of their intrinsic worth, everything changes. Women and children are honored; the sick are cared for and the elderly allowed to live and die with dignity; dissidents are listened to; prisoners rehabilitated, and minorities protected; workers are given a fair wage, decent working conditions, and a measure of participation in the enterprise; and the gospel is taken to the ends of the earth. Why? Because people matter, because every man, woman, and child has significance as a person made in the image of God.

The Quest for Community

The modern technocratic society, which destroys transcendence and significance, is destructive of human community as well. The present age is an era of social disintegration. People are finding it increasingly difficult to relate to one another in love.

Mother Teresa is a witness of this fact. Though she was born in Albania and lived in Yugoslavia, she went to India at the age of 17, has long been an Indian citizen, and looks at the West through Third World eyes. She has said, "People today are hungry for love, for understanding love which is . . . the only answer to loneliness and great poverty. That is why we are able to go to countries like England and America and Australia where there is no hunger for bread. But there, people are suffering from terrible loneliness, terrible despair, terrible hatred, feeling unwanted, feeling helpless, feeling hopeless. They have forgotten how to smile, they have forgotten the beauty of human touch. They are forgetting what is human love. They need someone who will understand and respect them."

Love is indispensable to humanness, so people are seeking this too. Since the sixties some have been breaking from Western individualism in favor of communal styles of living; others are replacing the nuclear family (traditional in the West) with the extended family (traditional for centuries in Africa and Asia), Yet others are repudiating the institutions of marriage and the family in the false belief that they will find the spontaneity of love in freedom from them. Everybody is seeking genuine community and the authentic relationships of love. This was the dominant theme of Bergman's films in the sixties and seventies, as it is of

Woody Allen's films today. For instinctively, everyone knows that this is what life is all about and that the greatest thing in the world is love.

So the world's third challenge to the church concerns the quality of Christian fellowship. Jesus Christ offers true community. Christ's purpose is not to save isolated individuals and so perpetuate their loneliness, but to build a church, a new society in which racial, social, and sexual barriers have been transcended, which offers itself to the world as the true alternative society, and which challenges the values and standards of the world.

A 1979 study of the Jonestown tragedy in the Guyana jungle discovered that "Jones's victims were from our churches," but they did not find love there. Jean Mills, for example, a defector after seven years, said, "I was so turned off in every church I went to, because nobody cared." And Grace Stoen, whose lawyer husband Tim became the second most powerful man in the People's Temple, said, "I went to church until I was eighteen years old . . . and nobody ever befriended me." In the People's Temple, however, according to Jean Mills, "everyone seemed so caring and loving. They hugged us and made us welcome . . . and said they . . . wanted us to come back." This study concluded that all believers should resolve: I will do my best to help make my church a more loving community to our members and the strangers in our midst."[11]

Where true love flourishes, its magnetism is all but irresistible. As Stephen C. Neill has written,

> Within the fellowship of those who are bound together by personal loyalty to Jesus Christ, the relationship of love reaches an intimacy and intensity unknown elsewhere. Friendship between the friends of Jesus of Nazareth is unlike any other friendship. This ought to be the normal experience within the Christian community. . . . Where it is experienced, especially across the barriers of race, nationality and languages, it is one of the most convincing evidences of the continuing activity of Jesus among men.[12]

Conclusion

Here then are the three major quests in which many people are engaged today. Though they probably would not articulate them in this way, it may be said that looking for transcendence, they are trying to find God; looking for significance, they are trying to find themselves; looking for community, they are trying to find their neighbor. For this is humankind's universal search—for God, for one's neighbor, and for oneself. Moreover, Christians dare to claim that those who seek will find—in Christ and in His new society.

So this contemporary secular quest constitutes what is one of the greatest challenges—and opportunities—the church has ever faced. People are openly looking for the very things Christ is offering!

The only question is whether the church can be so radically renewed by the Word of God and the Spirit of God that it offers an experience of transcendence in its worship, significance through its teaching, and community through its fellowship. For if so, people will turn to it eagerly in their quest, and the proclamation of the good news will have a credibility that otherwise it would lack.

CHAPTER 2

Called to Serve: Toward a Philosophy of Ministry

J. Gary Inrig

The thing that you are doing is not good, You will surely wear out, both yourself and these people who are with you, for the task is too heavy for you; you cannot do it alone" (Ex. 18:17–18). Jethro's ancient warning to his son-in-law has lost none of its cogency in the present world. Faced with an onslaught of needs and a barrage of demands, the servant of God is tempted to jump, Moses-like, on a treadmill of activity. But as Thomas Carlyle observed a century ago, "Nothing is more terrible than activity without insight." Unless service for the Lord is guided by biblical insights, it will be frustrating and possibly even destructive. A biblical philosophy of ministry can help determine one's priorities and shape his activities.

According to *Webster's Collegiate Dictionary* "ministry" involves "the office, duties, or functions of a minister," who is, in turn, defined as "one officiating . . . in church worship" or "a clergyman especially of a Protestant communion." While this undoubtedly reflects popular usage, it severely distorts biblical truth. Ministry is not the activity of a spiritual aristocracy or the work of a professional class. Rather, it is the lifestyle, responsibility, and privilege of every believer. A philosophy of ministry that fails to recognize this fact cannot be truly biblical. On the other hand a rejection of a spiritual aristocracy must not lead to the opposite extreme: a spiritual anarchy that fails to recognize the differing gifts Christ has given to members of His body.

The New Testament uses several terms to express the concept of ministry. Every believer is a slave (δοῦλος) of the Lord Jesus.[1] People in the ancient world despised slaves since it meant living without freedom under the authority of another. Believers, however, rejoice in the dignity of being the Lord's slaves. As Hansen observed, "Only a few (Israelites) are distinguished by the title,

'My servant.' To be called 'my servant' by God was a great and exceptional honor."[2] Every Christian is privileged to be a "slave" of the Lord Jesus, living to please Him (Gal. 1:10) and to serve others (5:13).

The word ὑπηρετῆς ("helpers, assistants, officers, stewards") emphasizes the stewardship or accountable authority of a person who is under authority (Matt. 26:58; John 7:32; Acts 5:22; 13:5). A believer also offers to his Lord λατρεία, service that flows from prayerful dependence (John 16:2). Such service is the visible display of worshiping faith. Another vital aspect of ministry is embodied in the term λειτουργία. Its use in the Septuagint and in Hebrews (8:6; 9:21) describes the activity of Levitical priests, but the New Covenant ministry of λειτουργία ("spiritual service") and λειτουργός ("spiritual servant") is carried out by believer-priests in evangelism (Rom. 15:16), financial sharing (Rom. 15:27; 2 Cor. 9:12), and practical service (Phil. 2:17, 25, 30).

A full New Testament philosophy of ministry is enriched by each of these terms. However, the most comprehensive biblical word for ministry is διακονία.

The Meaning of Ministry: The Definition of Διακονία

The word used most frequently to describe the spiritual activity of believers differs radically from the world's value system. Διακονία refers to menial and mundane activities, such as waiting on tables or caring for household needs—activities without apparent dignity. Since such service necessarily involved dependence, submission, and constraints of time and freedom, the Greeks regarded διακονία as degrading and dishonorable. Service for the public good was honored, but "voluntary giving of oneself in service of one's fellow man is alien to Greek thought. The highest goal before a man was the development of his own personality."[3] That last sentence is strikingly contemporary, and is mindful of the fact that a culture that is focused on self-actualization and self-fulfillment will find little value in servanthood. Beyer's observation about Greek attitudes suggests some parallels to modern concepts:

> In Greek eyes, service is not very dignified. Ruling and not service is proper to a man. . . . The formula of the sophist: "How can a man be happy when he has to serve someone?" expresses the basic Greek attitude. . . . Service acquires a higher value only when it is rendered to the State. . . . For the Greek in his wisdom and freedom there can certainly be no question of existing to serve others.[4]

Judaism had no philosophy of ministry involving diakoniva. The eight occurrences of this word in the Septuagint are unimportant theologically. Judaism, however, adopted a philosophy of service not unlike that of the Greeks. If service was rendered at all, it was done as an act of social obligation or as an act to those more worthy. A superior would not stoop to become a servant! Such an attitude, which conforms so closely to man's natural prejudices, causes the Lord's example and teaching to stand out in brilliant contrast.

> Though Judaism in the time of Jesus knew and practiced its social responsibilities, e.g., to the poor, this was done mainly by alms, not by service (cf. Luke 10:30–35). Lowly service, e.g., waiting at tables, was beneath the dignity of a free man (cf. Luke 7:44ff). Sometimes, the greater would wait at tables, but this was unusual.[5]

The New Testament introduces a radically new attitude toward ministry. Diakoniva is not the activity of a lesser to a greater, but is the lifestyle of a follower of the Lord Jesus. "Serving" pervades the New Testament, not merely in the frequency of the word's usage[6] but in the constant recurrence of attitudes and examples of service. Diakoniva is modeled on the pattern and command of the Savior and represents the practical outworking of God's love, especially toward fellow believers. "Ministry" is not the activity of an elite class, but the mutual caring of a band of brothers. Such service is personal and practical, rather than institutional. A diavkono" is one who by choice and position has come to be under the authority of his Master and who therefore serves others in love and gratitude.

The Model of Ministry: The Pattern Servant

The Lord Jesus is the source of the entirely new attitude toward diakoniva found throughout the New Testament. By the way He lived and the words He spoke, He instituted a new attitude toward service, and His model provides the basic ingredients for a philosophy of ministry. Six passages speak of the principles of diakoniva that He taught His disciples.

THE AMBITION OF A SERVANT (Mark 9:33–37; cf. Matt. 18:1–5; Luke 9:46–48)

The disciples' discussion about "which one of them was the greatest" (Mark 9:34) strikes modern readers as rather bizarre, not because they do not think such thoughts, but because "sophistication" has led them to adopt more subtle ways of raising the issue. However, Jewish society raised the question of greatness more directly. As Schlatter observes, "At all points, in worship, in the administration of justice, at meals, in all dealings, there constantly arose the question of who was the greater and estimating the honor due to each was a task which had constantly to be filled and was felt to be very important."[7]

Jesus interrupted the disciples' argument with the declaration of a revolutionary principle: "If anyone wants to be first, he shall be last of all, and servant of all" (Mark 9:35). He did not rebuke their desire for greatness. Instead, He transformed the concept of greatness. God's approval, not men's applause, is the only adequate standard of evaluation. How believers serve others, not how others defer to them, is the measure of greatness.

Jesus illustrated this principle in two ways. First, He lovingly and gently reached out to embrace a child (v. 36). Children had little public status in Judaism and He thus modeled a sensitivity to the ignored and lowly, an act which would receive no acclaim from the power brokers of Israel. Second, He called His disciples to welcome such children in His name (v. 37).

> Now a child has no influence at all. A child cannot advance a man's career or enhance a man's prestige. A child cannot give us things. It is the other way around. A child needs things. A child must have things done for him. . . . The child is typical of the person who needs things and it is the society of the person who needs things that we must seek.[8]

The mark of a servant is that he serves not the influential but the needy, in the name and for the glory of the Lord Jesus. Ministry involves a choice of service in the lowest place out of an ambition to be great in God's eyes, and to know His approval.

THE CHOICE OF A SERVANT (Matt. 20:20–28; cf. Mark 10:35–45)

After the Lord's third prediction of His death and resurrection, the disciples again displayed their misguided concern for greatness. James, John, and their mother, inspired perhaps by dreams of glory in the kingdom, requested positions of prominence—a request that inspired the jealous anger of the others, who shared a similar preoccupation with rank and greatness.

The Lord's response was to teach His disciples three things about service. First, they must realize that greatness in His kingdom is not patterned after Gentile rule and domination

(Matt. 20:25). Concepts such as domination and power-wielding are inappropriate in Christian service: "It is (shall not be) so among you" (v. 26). Second, ministry and spiritual greatness involve doing the work of a servant (διάκονος, v. 26); and taking the role of a slave (δοῦλος, v. 27) is a position which is chosen, not imposed. The Lord was not merely saying that service is a way to greatness. Rather, in His kingdom, service is greatness. Third, He Himself is the model of service (v. 28). His purpose in His incarnation was not to have people serve Him, but to serve them. His διακονία extended even to death. The comparison "just as" links verse 28 to verse 27 to emphasize that the Lord's voluntary choice of service, which involves suffering and death, provides the pattern for all His servants. Thus, in one succinct sentence, He summarized not only His life, but also all Christian ministry.

THE RELATIONSHIPS OF A SERVANT (Matt. 23:8–12)

Jesus drew a dramatic contrast between the lifestyle of the Pharisees and that of His disciples. Having portrayed the Rabbis' love of position and prominence, He totally repudiated any such pattern for His people. The church can have only one Head, one Lord, one Teacher. All ministry ultimately comes from the Lord through believers who are brothers. Therefore disciples are to recognize that the greatest is a servant, and such service involves self-chosen humbling ("whoever will humble himself"). This is not ascetic self-abnegation, but spiritual self-giving for one's brothers. Self-humbling brings the promise of divine exaltation, but a person who chooses self-exaltation will experience the discipline of humility.

Christian ministry is thus to be the service of brothers to one another under the lordship of Christ. It is based on self-chosen humbling to service and repudiates any notion of self-exaltation.

THE NOBILITY OF A SERVANT (Luke 22:24–27)

The disciples apparently entered the Upper Room repeating a familiar argument—that of greatness. Behind their selfish argument were two assumptions of the ancient world: the right of authority and the privilege of age. Those in authority took titles such as "the august one" (Augustus), "benefactor" (Ptolemy III and Ptolemy VIII), "he who deserves adoration" (Augustus and Tiberias, as indicated by inscriptions on coins found at

Caesarea Philippi). The privilege of rank was to be served by all lesser men. The privilege of age was to be waited on by those who were younger.

The Lord, by serving His disciples and washing their feet, utterly rejected such assumptions, natural as they may seem. In His church, the older serves the younger and the leader becomes a servant. The Head of the church established the pattern. As Morris observes, "Jesus is not saying that if His followers wish to rise to great heights in the church, they must first prove themselves in a lowly place. He is saying that faithful service in a lowly place is itself true greatness."[9] Jesus taught the nobility of lowly service as a man surrenders all assumptions about rank and privilege. "In the kingdom of God, service is not a stepping stone to nobility, it is nobility, the only kind of nobility that is recognized."[10]

THE PARADOX OF SERVICE (John 12:23–26)

As the time of Jesus' death drew near (John 12:23), He said, "Unless a grain of wheat falls into the earth and dies, it remains by itself alone; but if it dies, it bears much fruit" (v. 24). That was the essential paradox of His life. He could not save the seed (His life) and still see fruit. To hoard one's life, to live selfishly seeking to save one's life is to waste and lose his life. To serve is to "hate one's life," to repudiate self-love as a life pattern. But it is, in fact, to invest life and to keep it for eternity.

In view of that principle, the Lord added, "If anyone serves Me, let him follow Me; and where I am, there shall My servant also be" (v. 26). An essential feature of a servant is that he follows his master. For a believer, this means obedience to a life of self-denying sacrifice. The paradox is that when a servant follows his Lord in suffering, he shares with Him in glory. Sacrificial service also involves honor from God, for "if anyone serves Me, the Father will honor him" (v. 26; cf. Luke 18:29–30).

Thus ministry is self-giving and sacrificial, involving "death" and "hating one's life," as a servant keeps following his Lord. But service is the secret of life, for it produces fruitfulness, an unwasted life, and divine honor.

THE REWARD OF SERVICE (Luke 12:37; 17:7–10)

Two neglected truths about ministry are stated by the Lord in these passages. First, service is obligatory and a disciple deserves no praise for doing his duty (Luke 17:7–10). Even the finest service establishes no claim on God since believers are at best unprofitable servants. But God is gracious. In fact, He is so gracious that besides receiving the service of faithful, alert servants, He even reverses roles and actually serves His servants (12:37). This is the second idea—service is graciously rewarded by God. Nothing could more clearly underline the truth that grace and love lie at the heart of Christian service.

A number of basic truths about Christian ministry emerge from these statements of the Lord.

1. All ministry is the Lord's ministry. Believers serve Him. He is doing the work as the Model Servant (Rom. 15:8), and the disciples must therefore model and follow Him. Service is intrinsic to discipleship (Matt. 20:28; Luke 22:26; John 12:26).
2. The key to servanthood is a voluntary act of humbling. Διακονία is chosen, not imposed, and involves a repudiation of self-centered living (Matt. 23:11–12; John 12:24–26).
3. Service done to others in the Lord's name is service to the Lord Himself. The motive of such service is love for Christ; the manner in which the service is performed involves sensitivity to those in need (Matt. 25:44; Mark 9:36).
4. The supreme value is not a position of influence or gifts of prominence, but a servant heart which sees the needs of individuals (Matt. 20:26–27; Mark 9:37).
5. The task of a servant is to do his Master's will. He is to follow his Lord in carrying out instructions with faithfulness and diligence (Luke 12:37; 17:8; John 12:26).
6. The reward of a servant is certain but not necessarily immediate. It comes from God, not men (Luke 12:37; John 12:26).

The Manner of Ministry: The Expression of Διακονία

After the Gospels, the rest of the New Testament enlarges on the pattern of ministry embodied by the Lord Jesus. At least seven principles foundational to a biblical philosophy of ministry can be discovered in the apostolic description of διακονία (and the related verb διακονέω).

ALL MINISTRY SHARES A COMMON PATTERN

Three occurrences of διάκονος in Colossians 1 provide a useful framework for considering the essential components of ministry. Epaphras was a "faithful διάκονος of Christ" (Col. 1:7), a statement emphasizing that the Lord Jesus, as Head of the church, is the Source of ministry. Paul spoke of "the hope of the gospel . . . of which [he] was made a διάκονος" (v. 23). The gospel, the Word of God, determines the shape of ministry. Then Paul wrote about "His body (which is the church) . . . of which [he] was made a διάκονος" (vv. 24–25). The church provides the sphere of ministry.

Christ: the Source of ministry. Every believer enjoys a unique ministry given by the risen Head of the church. Thus while their gifts come from the indwelling Spirit (1 Cor. 12:4) and their effectiveness comes from the sovereign will of God the Father (1 Cor. 12:6), their ministry is from the Lord, for "there are varieties of ministries, and the same Lord" (1 Cor. 12:5). In other words, an individual believer fits into the body and functions as the Head intends. As Torrance observes, "The διάκονος is one who has been given a task by his Master, and who does only what is commanded by Him, not what he thinks out for himself."[11]

Because every believer possesses a God-given ministry, each can speak with Paul of "the ministry which I received from the Lord Jesus" (Acts 20:24). Ministry is both from Him and for Him, and a believer's motive should be to please Him in all things. The Christian thus serves with a sense of liberty and dignity. He ministers by divine calling as a fellow-worker of God (1 Cor. 3:5), sharing in the ministry of Christ. Such an exalted yet humbling perspective on service produces both rejoicing (Rom. 11:13) and endurance. As a result, suffering becomes an authenticating mark of a true servant of Christ (2 Cor. 11:23–28), a reflection of the principle that a servant is not greater than his Lord. Since Jesus in His life of service knew suffering, opposition, and humiliation, His disciples must not expect exemption. Furthermore a God-given ministry requires faithfulness, such as Tychicus modeled (Eph. 6:21; Col. 4:7). This quality, which is required before the Lord entrusts a person with a significant responsibility (1 Tim. 1:12), will be seen particularly by obedience to the truth of God (1 Tim. 4:6).

Christ, then, is the Source of ministry, the One to whom believers owe allegiance and who puts them into service. Ministry requires loyalty to the Lord Jesus in whatever sphere He assigns, and a recognition that He alone is the Source of strength and enablement for service. Graciously He sets forth the pattern of service and also strengthens those He calls.

The gospel: the shape of ministry. As a servant of Christ, a believer is a servant of the gospel of Christ (Col. 1:23). Because a true servant seeks to bring glory to his Master, Paul could ask, "What, after all, is Apollos? And what is Paul? Only servants, through whom you came to believe—as the Lord has assigned to each his task" (1 Cor. 3:5, NIV). To exalt personalities is wrong for no glory is due mere servants. What matters is the message and ultimately the Master. As Stott perceptively comments,

> The preposition *through*, in the context of these early chapters of 1 Corinthians, has an important significance. We are not servants, "from whom you believed," as if preachers were the authors of men's faith, quickening and evoking it. Nor are we servants *in* whom you believed, as if preachers were the objects of men's faith. . . . Instead, we are "servants *through* whom you believed," the agents through whom God works, or the instruments by which He arouses faith in the hearers of the Word. . . . Each servant has a different task assigned to him, but the Lord works through each.[12]

A servant of the gospel recognizes that he has no right to alter or reshape the message. Nor is his function to impress people with his wisdom. Rather, he is to convey and exalt the message (1 Cor. 2:1–5) since he has been entrusted with "the ministry of reconciliation" and stands in the world as an ambassador of Christ (2 Cor. 5:18–20). To fulfill his ministry, he must preach the Word and do the work of an evangelist (2 Tim. 4:2, 5). Therefore a good servant is one who is controlled by God's truth and communicates it to others (1 Tim. 4:6).

Every believer should be able to say with Paul, "I became a servant of this gospel by the gift of God's grace given me through the working of his power" (Eph. 3:7, NIV). Servanthood means an absolute loyalty to God's revealed truth, a recognition that all ministry must be based on God's Word, and a commitment to share God's Word. It also means a determination that all glory go to the Master, "for we do not preach ourselves, but Jesus Christ as Lord, and ourselves as your servants for Jesus' sake" (2 Cor. 4:5, NIV). In such servanthood there is true authority, for it is the authority of the Lord.

The church: the sphere of ministry. Service is carried out within the Master's house, to the Master's people, for the Christian is a servant of the church (Col. 1:25). This produced in Paul an overwhelming desire to bring every believer to maturity in Christ by proclaiming Christ and pouring himself into the lives of fellow believers (Col. 1:28–29). True ministry is intensely people-centered. Thus the household of Stephanas is held up as a model to follow since "they have devoted themselves for ministry to the saints" (1 Cor. 16:15). Their authority came, not from achievement or status, but because they joined in the work and they labored at it (1 Cor. 16:16). A leader worthy of recognition has a servant's heart. Even servants possess genuine authority, to which others are to submit. But servants do lead by demanding respect not for their position but by their character. Authority thus flows from service, a truth embodied in the fact that deacons, key leaders in the early church, received the unadorned title "servants" (διάκονοι, Phil. 1:1; 1 Tim. 3:8).

Besides being the sphere of service, the church is based on "the work of service" (Eph. 4:12). Ministry is not something carried on by a select few for the benefit of others, nor is it merely an occupational task. Saints do the work of service and every believer is part of the ministry. Nor is the ministry limited to certain tasks (preaching, counseling, administering). Ministry is all that believers do for one another in obedience to the Lord.

ALL MINISTRY IS NEW COVENANT MINISTRY

Second Corinthians, the most autobiographical of Paul's epistles, provides indispensable material for a biblical philosophy of ministry. Most of the epistle presents an exposition of the nature and implications of the New Covenant ministry. To participate in the New Covenant as God's new creation is to be servants (διακόνους) of the covenant (2 Cor. 3:6). New Covenant ministry, the theme of 2 Corinthians 2:14–7:4, involves at least five major ideas.

A ministry of the Spirit. New Covenant ministry does not depend on human resources or enablement. The flesh cannot carry out a spiritual ministry. "Not that we are adequate in ourselves to consider anything as coming from ourselves, but our adequacy is from God, who also made us adequate as servants of a new covenant, not of the letter, but of the Spirit; for the letter kills, but the Spirit gives life" (2 Cor. 3:5–6). "But we have this treasure in earthen vessels, that the surpassing greatness of the power may be of God and not from ourselves" (4:7). The indwelling and enabling of the Holy Spirit is essential for ministry and provides the basis of a servant's confidence (3:4; 4:1). As Griffith Thomas observed, "In all Christian work, there are three elements absolutely indispensable: the Spirit of God as the power, the Word of God as the message, and the man of God as the instrument. The Spirit of God uses the message by means of the man."[13]

A ministry of grace. The New Covenant transcends the Old (Mosaic) Covenant, as the sun outshines the moon. Paul contrasted the two covenants in 2 Corinthians 3:7–18, to show that New Covenant ministry is motivated by grace, not by law or legalism. The power for such a ministry is God's gracious provision, and the message believers bring to others is one of grace, not law. Ministry must be controlled by God's grace or it is not Christian ministry at all.

A Christ-centered ministry. The essence of the New Covenant is intimate fellowship with the Lord Jesus. With unveiled face, the believer sees the glory of God in the face of Christ (2 Cor. 3:18; 4:6), a glory seen through the mirror of the Word of God (3:12-18). The essence of ministry is spending time in the presence of the Lord, being transformed by the Holy Spirit (3:18), and proclaiming to others "the glory of Christ" and "Christ Jesus as Lord" (4:4–5). People are converted by turning to Christ (3:16), changed by beholding Him (3:18), and commissioned to proclaim Him (4:5). This Christ-centeredness also produces divine enablement to live above circumstances, since believers recognize that their goal is that "the life of Jesus also may be manifested in [their] body" (4:10). The supreme motivation of all New Covenant service is "to be pleasing to Him" (5:9).

A ministry of reconciliation. New Covenant ministry is concerned with the world, for the believer has received "the ministry of reconciliation" (2 Cor. 5:18) by which he stands in the world as Christ's ambassador, beseeching people to be reconciled to God. Denney describes the unique character of this ministry.

> Most observers note the amazing contrast between πρεσβευομεν ("we are ambassadors") and δεόμεθα ("we beseech you"). The ambassador, as a rule, stands upon his dignity; he maintains the greatness of the person whom he represents. But Paul, in this lowly passionate entreaty, is not false to his Master; he is preaching the gospel in the spirit of the gospel; he shows that he has really learned of Christ.[14]

Ministry must not become introverted. The church does not exist for its own convenience, but for the promotion of the glory of Christ in the world. Thus service in the church must ultimately promote ministry in the world by announcing God's work of reconciliation in Christ.

A ministry of integrity. New Covenant ministry is consistent with the character of Christ. It repudiates unworthy methods and refuses to accept pragmatic results as justification for illicit means. The New Covenant ministry is supernatural, not manipulative. This determines the way believers handle God's Word. "For we are not like many, peddling the word of God, but as from sincerity, but as from God, we speak in Christ in the sight of God" (2 Cor. 2:17). This also determines the way believers handle people. "But we have renounced the things hidden because of shame, not walking in craftiness or adulterating the word of God, but by the manifestation of truth commending ourselves to every man's conscience in the sight of God" (2 Cor. 4:2). The New Covenant ministry also influences the way believers handle circumstances. "Giving no cause for offense in anything, in order that the ministry be not discredited, but in everything commending ourselves as servants [διάκονοι] of God, in much endurance, in afflictions, in hardships, in distresses" (2 Cor. 6:3–4).

ALL MINISTRY IS BASED ON SPIRITUAL GIFTS

The fact that Christ, the Head of the church, has given believers spiritual gifts through His indwelling Spirit is of crucial importance to the biblical concept of ministry. The New Testament does not depict ministry as a specialized position, occupied by a select few. Gifts are God's provision for serving each other (1 Peter 4:10). In fact Peter divided gifts into major categories of speaking and serving gifts (1 Peter 4:11), and Paul spoke of a particular gift of service (Rom. 12.7). Service takes place by means of spiritual gifts, which shape and define one's ministry.

Spiritual gifts are a stewardship for which believers are accountable to God. Peter indicated that believers are to use gifts "as good stewards of the manifold grace of God" (1 Peter 4:10). Not to exercise gifts properly is to fail one's stewardship. This fact inspired Paul's exhortation to Archippus, "Take heed to the ministry which you have received in the Lord, that you may fulfill it" (Col. 4:17).

ALL MINISTRY IS TO EQUIP THE SAINTS FOR MUTUAL EDIFICATION

While every believer is gifted for the work of service, God has also given certain individuals (Eph. 4:11) to the church "for the equipping of the saints for the work of service" (Eph. 4:12). The goal is not that some "do the ministry," but rather that they equip and enlist all believers in ministry.

This has great strategic importance for the functioning of an assembly of believers. A ministry does not exist for its own sake and no elite class should carry on a ministry while others passively observe. Every believer is divinely gifted, and certain people are called by the Lord to function as enablers and equippers. All ministry is mutual ministry and the body of Christ grows only by "the proper working of each individual part" (Eph. 4:16). The goal of gifted men must therefore be the involvement of others by instruction in the Word and the development of spiritual gifts.

ALL MINISTRY IS TO BE LOVING SERVICE

Because the Lord Jesus is the Model of ministry, love is essential. "When we speak of service, we imply work done for another either voluntarily or compulsorily, the benefit of which will accrue to the one for whom it has been done."[15] The New Testament is filled with examples of individuals who served in practical ways, lovingly caring for the needs of others: Timothy and Erastus (Acts 19:22), the house of Stephanas (1 Cor. 16:15), Tychicus (Eph. 6:21; Col. 4:7), Onesiphorus (2 Tim. 1:16–18), Mark (2 Tim. 4:11), and Onesimus (Philem. 13). In each case Paul was the recipient. His ministry could never have had the impact it did if they had not served him. They were thus fellow-workers with Paul and the Lord in the gospel. All service in love is valued by the Lord.

ALL MINISTRY IS TO BE TO THE WHOLE PERSON

In the New Testament διακονία is often used in connection with financial contributions to believers. It describes Paul and Barnabas' journey to Jerusalem with a collection from Antioch (Acts 11:29; 12:25). Later Paul made the collection for the believers in Jerusalem such a priority that he invested years of time and risked his life in the process. This activity is a ministry "to the saints" (Rom. 15:25, 31; cf. 2 Cor. 8:14, 19–20; 9:12–13). The care of widows is described as ministry ("daily serving," Acts 6:1). Also caring for Paul's physical needs was a ministry (2 Tim. 1:18; Philem. 13).

For Paul to break away from his ministry of church planting to devote himself to meeting financial needs of believers gives an important balance to a biblical concept of ministry. Nothing could more clearly indicate that ministry is not confined to preaching and teaching. Ministry must be controlled by the Word, but it must be concerned with the whole person, not just with a "soul."

FAITHFUL SERVICE IS THE KEY TO EXPANDED MINISTRY

Speaking of deacons, Paul wrote, "And let these also first be tested; then let them serve as deacons (διακονείτωσαν) if they are beyond reproach" (1 Tim. 3:10). If a servant is faithful in his present involvement, he may then receive greater responsibility. An individual ought not be involved at a high level of responsibility till he has proved himself. This is based on the fact that character is the key to service.

Conclusion

Stating a complete philosophy of ministry involves more than a study of διακονία and διακονέω. But the truths related to these words are essential to a fully biblical concept and provide the framework for a dynamic ministry. Above all else, the believer in Jesus Christ is to be a servant—for the Lord, of His Word, and to His people.

The concept of servanthood also determines the ultimate purpose of ministry. A servant's goal is not to enlarge his sphere of influence or to achieve his personal goals. The goal of ministry is to be useful to the Master in such a way that His glory is increased and His work is extended.

"For the ministry of this service is not only fully supplying the needs of the saints, but is also overflowing through many thanksgivings to God. Because of the proof given by this ministry, they will glorify God for your obedience to your confession of the gospel of Christ" (2 Cor. 9:12–13). "As each one has received a special gift, employ it in serving one another . . . so that in all things God may be glorified through Jesus Christ, to whom belongs the glory and dominion forever and ever. Amen" (1 Peter 4:10–11).

A believer, willing to be a servant and committed to doing the will of his Lord and declaring His glory, can rest in the certainty that God will supply his needs. "For God is not unjust so as to forget your work and the love which you have shown toward His name, in having ministered and in still ministering to the saints" (Heb. 6:10).

CHAPTER 3

Distinctives of Christian Leadership

William D. Lawrence

What makes Christian leadership unique? In what distinctive ways does following Christ mark leadership? There is a kind of leadership which is Christian and which unbelievers can talk about but never accomplish. The distinctively Christian marks of leadership form the foundation for Christian thinking about this subject, as Eims emphasized when he wrote, "We need to look at leadership from the standpoint of the Bible."[1]

The aim of this chapter is to discuss seven aspects that are unique to *Christian* leadership, that is, leadership that seeks to pursue the purposes of the Lord Jesus Christ.

Christian Leadership Is Distinctive As to Its Position

Christian leadership is different from other kinds of leadership because no Christian leader can assume the position of being "number one," that is, *the* leader. This is true because those who believe in Christ know there is only one "Number One," namely, the Lord Jesus Christ.

Therefore a Christian leader must know who the Leader is. He must know who is in control and that he is not in control. Jesus commended His disciples for calling Him Teacher and Lord (John 13:13), titles that show Him to be their superior in knowledge and authority. These titles show that He was the One to whom they were accountable, the One they were to follow. There was no confusion as to who the Leader was.

The chief characteristic of a Christian leader must be submission to Christ, and only those who have learned that submission is the key to power[2] can be effective Christian leaders. "The crown of . . . Christian leadership is a crown of thorns."[3] It is when the leader learns to submit to Christ as the Leader, that is, when he learns to fly "the white flag of victory,"[4] that he becomes an authoritative *Christian* leader. The Apostle

34

Paul demonstrated this throughout his ministry, as Butt observes.

> Christ's authority gave authority to Paul! Of his authority Paul had no doubt; he exercised it decisively and continuously. . . . This is no namby-pamby egalitarianism, no wishy washy leaderless group. Paul had a magnificent sense of command. Slave to Christ acting like a general! He showed us leadership up close; he was in charge and he knew it: his power to lead breathed strength.[5]

Paul's ability to lead grew out of his submission to Christ as Leader. Thus a significant element in leadership is the ability to show others which way the Leader is going. This principle has specific implications for leadership.

First, a leader must have a clearly defined awareness of the Lord's revealed purposes. He must know what the Leader wants. He must be aware of the place God's Word has in all of life and must be aware that God seeks to accomplish His truth, love, and righteousness in His followers.

Second, this truth, love, and righteousness must be evident in the Christian leader's character, behavior, and relationships if he is to expect other believers to respond to him as their leader. Paradoxically the Christian leader must be the ultimate follower, a follower of the Leader Himself. The chief prerequisite for being recognized as a leader in the body of Christ is to be a proven follower of the Head of the body. When this prerequisite is present, people will follow him even when they are uncertain about his wisdom; when this prerequisite is present, the Lord will stand by him even when others will not.

The purpose of each Christian leader should be to go guide others in following Christ. His aim should be to focus on Him and to show others how to do this.

Hendricks has defined a leader as "someone who knows where he's going and can get others to follow him."[6] This definition may be expanded to say that a Christian leader is someone who knows where the Lord is going and can get others to follow him as he follows the Lord. Hendricks observes that such a leader will have biblical objectives and spiritual motives. The Bible determines what he wants to do and the Holy Spirit determines why he wants to do it. This means that a Christian leader will have goals in keeping with his Leader's goals, and motives that are in keeping with his Leader's motives.[7]

Christian Leadership Is Distinctive in Its Character Requirements

Christian leadership is unique in that it teaches Christian character. Other kinds of leadership speak ideally of the leader's character but none of them requires *Christian* character. Though business puts a value on the family (a large number of successful executives have never been divorced[8]), it is sadly true that many leaders in business, politics, education, and other fields of life lack self-control, are lovers of money, and have lost the respect of their children. The standards stressed in 1 Timothy 3:1–7 deny leadership to any believer who does not exhibit Christian character. The marks found in this list must be in place *before* the position of elder can be assumed, which means that the individual in view has demonstrated these qualities previously. In fact it is through previous service that the character needed for ultimate leadership is developed. Christian character must be in place before leadership is assumed.

Leadership requires authenticity and authority. Authenticity of commitment to Christ's lordship, recognizing Him as "Number One," enables the leader to carry out one of his major tasks, that of being a model of Christlike maturity for those whom he leads. This authenticity makes the leader a living statement of all God wants His people to be.

Authority is also required and grows out of authentic Christian character. Such character means congruence between attitude, word, and action, a congruence that speaks of integrity and serves as a magnet to draw others who listen and respond to the leader. Sanders observes that "Paul never lacked followers. His qualities of character irresistibly lifted him above his colleagues and associates."[9] What was true of Paul must be true of all Christian leaders.

Christian Leadership Is Distinctive As to Its Source

The debate about whether leaders are born or made continues on,[10] but there can be little doubt about the source of the raw materials for Christian leadership ability: Christian leadership is a gift from the Holy Spirit. Romans 12:6 states, "And since we have gifts that differ according to the grace given to us, let each exercise them." And in writing of the gift of leadership, Paul wrote that "he who leads" should do so "with diligence" (v. 8). Spiritual gifts come from the Holy Spirit, as 1 Corinthians 12:7

declares: "But to each one is given the manifestation of the Spirit." "Manifestation" refers to spiritual gifts. Leadership then is more than a skill to be learned, though it certainly includes this. Unless the basic capacity to lead is present as a gift from the Holy Spirit, one cannot be a Christian leader. Later the point will be made that a Christian leader must be controlled by the Spirit; however, one must have a capacity for leadership from the Spirit in the first place or no amount of control will produce the skill necessary for spiritual leadership.

This gift, like other spiritual gifts, is sovereignly distributed by the Spirit at salvation and is not a matter of human choice or human effort. Believers can neither choose their gifts, take credit for their spiritual gifts, nor assume that their gifts make them superior people. "Gifts are shared out among Christians; all do not receive the same gifts but all the gifts come from the Spirit, so that there is no room for rivalry, discontent, or a feeling of superiority."[11] The fact that the Holy Spirit is the source of leadership capacity and that leaders are chosen sovereignly by Him produces freedom from pride and arrogance among those who are responsive to Him.

The gift of leadership is not a matter of a certain personality type. Peter was a leader by virtue of personal strength (Acts 4:8–12), James by virtue of practical wisdom (Acts 15:12–21), Paul by virtue of intellectual capacity (as seen in his sermons and epistles), Timothy by virtue of sacrificial service (Phil. 2:19–21), and John by virtue of his heart for God and man (as seen in his writings). All these leaders shared all these virtues, but each of them had a distinct personality strength that uniquely marked him. This demonstrates the fact that leadership is not a matter of human personality but of divine sovereignty. Just as the Spirit's gifts are not reserved for a few outstanding people,[12] so the Spirit's gift of leadership is not reserved for a particular kind of personality.

The gift of leadership is discovered and developed in the same way as other spiritual gifts, that is, through life experience, training, and the maturing process. Even though it is the product of the Spirit's presence and God's grace, this gift requires diligence, faithfulness, hard work, and commitment if it is to be exercised effectively.

Christian Leadership Is Distinctive As to Its Enablement

Christian leadership is empowered by the Holy Spirit, and only believers can count on His presence and power. Christians who possess this gift may exercise it in secular settings such as business, politics, or education, but non-Christian leaders in those areas cannot claim the Spirit's power. This truth is one of the most unique elements in Christian leadership. Christian leaders have many things in common with non-Christian leaders: both must provide vision for their followers; both must earn the trust of their followers; both must communicate to their followers; both must use their abilities effectively in providing leadership.[13] But only Christian leaders can count on the Holy Spirit to accomplish their purpose of affecting and changing others in the spiritual realm. The Spirit's power will not make their leadership perfect,[14] but it will guide them in a model of growing Christian maturity as well as enable them to have a spiritual impact that cannot be acquired in any other way or by any other kind of leader.

However, without dependence on the Spirit, Christian leaders become avenues of the flesh, just like unredeemed leaders. By its very nature Christian leadership demands the Spirit's power to accomplish God's purposes. Sanders states, "Leadership is influence, the ability of one person to influence others."[15] Influence is the ability to cause others to respond to the direction the leader gives, the ability to cause them to think, act, and live the way the leader encourages. From a Christian perspective, it would be unthinkable to believe this can or should occur apart from the enabling of the Holy Spirit. Again Sanders notes, "The spiritual leader . . . influences others not by the power of his own personality alone but by that personality irradiated and interpenetrated and empowered by the Holy Spirit. . . . Spiritual leadership is a matter of superior spiritual power, and that can never be self-generated."[16]

One of the most distinctive marks, then, of Christian leadership is that it is empowered by spiritual resources. Obviously leadership training must include a strong emphasis on the Spirit's ministry in the life of the believer or the gift will be misused. A person gifted in leadership who occupies a leadership position cannot fulfill the leader's function of godly influence apart from the Spirit's enablement. Leadership is not so much a position as it is a function. "*Leader* is not a title but a role. You only become a leader by functioning as one."[17] A Christian leader, then, must follow *the* Leader by exercising his gift in the power of the Holy Spirit.

Christian Leadership Is Distinctive As to Its Ambition

Few characteristics generate more reaction among Christians than ambition. This is because many people think of ambition as a self-centered seeking for more power and authority. There is no place for this attitude in any kind of leadership, least of all in Christian leadership.

But ambition is a desirable attribute when understood and exercised properly, though many miss the proper perspective of ambition and equate all expressions of it with ego and arrogance. Ambition is essential in a leader for it provides the drive and the desire necessary to carry the burdens and responsibilities of leadership; ambition is the fuel of leadership. There is no problem with ambition in itself; the problem with ambition lies in its aim, not in its strength and its presence, as Mark 10:35–45 makes clear.

This passage shows ambition at its worst and its best. In James, John, and the other disciples, all of whom sought the highest position for themselves, ambition is seen as self-centered, competitive, assertive, thoughtless, arrogant, proud, and blind (Mark 10:35–39, 41). "Their ambitious request was foolish because they did not know what was involved in it. They spoke in ignorance."[18] Nothing could be uglier than the attitudes found here. But nothing could be more surprising than Christ's response to these attitudes; He did not attack them for being ambitious, nor did He reject them for having drive and desire. Instead He redefined ambition and turned it into service for others without taking away any of its drive for achievement. Ambition is transformed into a humility directed toward serving others rather than a proud serving of self. Ambition is redefined from self-service to self-sacrifice (Mark 10:43–45), and included in this is instruction in how to be first. It is accomplished through the holy ambition of slavery in accord with the model of the Lord Jesus Christ Himself. [19] He demonstrated ambition at its best as the One who willingly sacrificed Himself for the sake of others.

Christian ambition, then, is the burning, even driving, desire to make a name for Christ, not self, which results in a constructive rather than destructive impact. In contrast to Christian ambition is the ambition of James 3:14, the selfish ambition that is earthly, fleshly, and devilish. There is no place for such ambition in spiritual leadership, but there must be a place for proper ambition in Christian leadership or there will be no leadership. The key to determining whether the ambition being expressed is Christian or not lies in the answer to the question raised by Fred Smith, "We must ask, *What is my purpose?* *Am I satisfying my ego through this ministry or sacrificing my ego to it?"*[20]

Christian ambition must be understood as the redirection of aim, not the denial of desire. Proper ambition is not the loss of ego (this will never happen until the believer at death or the rapture is ultimately separated from the flesh), but ego redirected according to God's purpose. Biblical ambition is not the lack of ego (again this will occur only when the believer is separated from the flesh through physical death or the rapture), but ego under the control of God's Spirit. Proper ambition is not the love of ego, but ego redeemed and used as God's redeeming force. Though "ego" is a negative concept, Paul's distinction in Romans 7:18 must be remembered: "For I know that nothing good dwells in me, that is, in my flesh." Only the flesh part of "me" is negative; there is a positive side about "me" (Christ living in me, Gal. 2:20), which is the product of the grace of God.

There is no place for the self-seeking ambition of those who reach for positions of honor on the right and the left of the Savior in Christian leadership. But there is no Christian leadership without the self-sacrificing ambition of those who follow the Savior in reaching for the redemption of others at great cost to themselves. The fact that there can be no leadership without ambition is obvious from the Lord's choice of disciples. He chose only men who had the raw material of ambition and rivalry[21] because no other kind of men could accomplish His task. But He refined that raw ambition and rivalry into holy ambition and humility. Christian leadership must be marked by ambition: redeemed, redirected, self-sacrificing ambition, but ambition nonetheless. Without it, no leadership will occur.

Christian Leadership Is Distinctive in Its Motivation

Ask someone for the marks of leadership and somewhere in the response may be the characteristics of dominance, control, and power. Such attributes are often synonymous with leadership, but never with Christian leadership. Once again, Christian leadership is different, this time in the area of motivation. True, Christian leaders are seen to be up front, at the head, in the lead, but not in a domineering power play. When ambition is redefined and redirected, the entire nature of leadership is affected.

Christian leadership is motivated by love and concern, not

power and position, as seen from the use of προΐστημι ("to lead") in Romans 12:8. In almost every occurrence of this word in Greek literature it is used figuratively in the sense of "to surpass, to preside." Synonymous meanings in Greek literature are "to lead, conduct, direct, govern, take over the direction of the people, and stand or go before someone or something in protection." This usage can be summarized as "to assist, to join with, to protect."[22]

The New Testament meaning of the word is to lead, but it also includes an emphasis on being concerned about, caring for, and giving aid to others.[23] This emphasis adds a uniquely Christian dimension to the word. Whenever the term is used in the New Testament the context demands the connotation of "to care for" as well as "to lead" (cf. Rom. 12:8; 1 Thess. 5:12; 1 Tim. 3:4–5, 12; 5:17; Titus 3:8, 14). "This is explained by the fact that caring was the obligation of leading members of the infant Church."[24]

For example the context of 1 Thessalonians 5:12 shows that the task of the leader is in large measure that of pastoral care and the emphasis is not on rank or authority but on the leader's efforts on behalf of these who follow him.[25] The references in 1 Timothy show again that the ideas of caring and guiding are both present.[26]

"In all these instances . . . the verb has in the NT the primary sense of both 'to lead' and 'to care for,' and this agrees with the distinctive nature of the office in the NT, since according to Luke 22:20 the one who is chief . . . is to be as he who serves."[27]

Leadership, then, is the developed gift of giving direction to others out of care and concern for them and their needs and is not the result of position or title, a point made by contemporary writers as well.[28] Thus leadership is not taken or given, but is earned through service that puts the needs of others first. This must be one of the key marks of the Christian leader. His leadership is empowered by the Holy Spirit through a gift He has given, and it is also the product of care for others at the sacrifice of self. The regeneration of ambition into self-sacrifice produces a love that is others-centered.

Christian Leadership Is Distinctive As to Its Authority

A seventh distinguishing mark is the nature of the authority of Christian leadership. The Christian leader is a *servant* leader. This is the inevitable result of the other characteristics, particularly as it relates to the unique aspects of ambition and motivation. Self-sacrificial, others-centered leadership must be servant leadership. It can be nothing else.

Many people find the concept of servanthood repulsive, since it seems to be demeaning and undignified. True, a servant is limited by the will of his master, a servant is dependent on his master for all his life needs, and he has no freedom to do anything except what his master desires. But there is another perspective concerning the role of a servant, at least a servant of God.

> The word צֶבֶד ("servant") ranges in meaning from a slave to a vassal king but always refers to one characterized by dependence and servitude. Royal officials and personal representatives of a king were thus designated "servants." The term "servant" indicated a degree of honor, depending on the position of the one served. To be the "servant of God" denoted the highest honor.[29]

This means that to be a servant leader under the Lord Jesus Christ is to gain the highest honor since it enables the one who occupies the position to share in the very glory and prestige of the Lord of the universe. The following definition conveys the concept of servant leadership: A servant is someone under the authority of another who voluntarily serves for that one's benefit with a spirit of humble dependence and who finds his freedom, fulfillment, and significance in the limits of his service.

But how can a servant leader exercise authority? Many have the impression that because a servant is subject to his master, he cannot exercise authority over those who are under him. In other words, how can a servant leader serve others and still exercise authority over them as necessary when providing leadership for them? This is a significant issue because a failure to exercise necessary authority is one of the major problems of leadership. "Problems in organization seldom come from 'the excessive desire of individuals to assume responsibility.' Just the contrary. The difficulties spring from 'their reluctance to *take* responsibility.'"[30] This is a very critical issue, therefore, because a misunderstanding of the servant concept of leadership has disastrous results.

A key passage in helping resolve this tension is 2 Corinthians 4:5: "For we do not preach ourselves but Christ Jesus as Lord, and ourselves as your bond-servants [δοῦλοι] for Jesus' sake." The servant leader is enslaved to those whom he serves, but not to do their will; he is enslaved to them for Jesus' sake—that is, out of concern for Christ's interests. Thus he serves others not to do for them what they want but to do for them what Christ wants; the servant leader serves others out of an interest in seeing Christ's purposes accomplished in their lives. And what are Christ's interests in the lives of others? Consider the list below:

1. Christ is interested in God's glory (John 17:4).
2. Christ is interested in proper worship (Matt. 21:12–17; John 2:13–22; 4:24).
3. Christ is interested in discipling (Matt. 28:16–20; Mark 1:16–17; John 17:6).
4. Christ is interested in the Great Commission (Matt. 28:16–20; Mark 16:14–15; Luke 24:44–49; John 20:19–23; Acts 1:8).
5. Christ is interested in restoring sinning saints (Matt. 18:15–20).
6. Christ is interested in confronting sin (Matt. 18:15–20).
7. Christ is interested in disciplining rebellious saints to maintain the purity of the church (Matt. 18:15–20).
8. Christ is interested in correcting competitive leadership (Mark 10:43–45).
9. Christ is interested in stable marriages (Matt. 5:31–32; 19:3–12).
10. Christ is interested in having authoritative leadership (Matt. 18:18–20; 28:20; Mark 6:7; John 20:21–23).

From this list of Christ's interests in the lives of His followers it is clear that servant leaders must have and exercise authority if they are to provide true leadership. The difference between secular leadership and Christian leadership does not lie in the absence of authority but in the attitude that motivates authority, the sanctified nature of ambition and motivation, and the holy character mentioned earlier. Servant leaders must exercise authority if Christian churches and organizations are to develop and grow. They are needed to model godliness, make policies, manage finances, give direction, hold the group accountable for its purpose and actions, and provide the human layer of security under Christ which is needed if unity is to be maintained. How can anyone participate in the practice of church discipline without exercising authority, as Paul demonstrated in 1 Corinthians 5:1–8 and 2 Corinthians 7:8–13? "Had Paul not faithfully fulfilled his painful duty of writing in stern terms to them, and had they not responded with repentance, they would have suffered loss . . . as a result of his negligence."[31]

The servant leader under the Lord Jesus Christ cannot be negligent if he is to represent the interests of his Lord responsibly. However, his authority does not come from his position or his power or his dominance, but from his commitment to *the* Leader, his reflection of the Leader's glory, his redirected ambition, his motivating love, and his faithful exercise of authority. In essence, the servant leader serves by leading,[32] by providing direction, by holding others accountable, by planning, by organizing, and by equipping others to do the same.

Conclusion

This article has focused on the distinctives of Christian leadership. Yet much of leadership literature today suggests that this kind of leadership is what all want, both Christian and non-Christian. *The One Minute Manager,*[33] *In Search of Excellence,*[34] and *Leaders*[35] are full of Christian leadership concepts.

> What is most interesting is that the leadership style which has evolved from multi-million dollars of research . . . is not far removed from the leadership style which Scripture delineates from the start! It is a style which recognizes the inherent value of the individual and the worth of human relations not only as a means to an end but as an end in itself.[36]

Perhaps the thing that makes Christian leadership most distinctive is the fact that so many want it but so few have it.

This then is the Christian leader: a follower of Christ, *the* Leader, who possesses the Leader's character, and who is gifted and enabled by the Holy Spirit, marked by self-sacrificial ambition, motivated by an others-centered love, and a pursuer of servant authority. This kind of leadership produces the kind of impact made by first-century leaders when "Christ turned straw into bricks, nobodies into somebodies, recruits into generals."[37] This is the dream of all who exercise leadership, but especially of those who seek distinctive Christian leadership.

CHAPTER 4

Pauline Images of the Christian Leader

D. Edmond Hiebert

W hen seeking to trace the biblical portrayal of the qualities of Christian leadership, one's thoughts naturally turn to the Apostle Paul, one of the most effective leaders in the entire history of the Christian church. The Scriptures record the challenging example of his own grand achievements, while his epistles contain ample information concerning his concept of the character and work of a Christian leader. His views of the nature and function of the Christian leader are delineated especially in the Pastoral Epistles. These letters were directed to Timothy and Titus who, when Paul wrote, occupied important leadership positions in the churches.

Although the common designation "the Pastoral Epistles" is somewhat misleading, these letters do offer valuable guidance to men in the pastoral office. But since neither Timothy nor Titus were pastors in the modern sense of that term, it is fully justifiable to use these letters in seeking to ascertain the qualifications of leaders who may not be directly involved in the pastoral office. In the Lord's work the precise office does not materially alter the needed qualifications of those engaged in varied types of Christian service. (This statement may be supported by comparing the similarity of the qualifications for elders and deacons in 1 Timothy 3:1–10.)

The purpose of this article is to discover the biblical qualifications for leadership positions in the church. This goal is attempted through an exegetical study of the seven images of the Christian leader Paul employed in the second chapter of his last letter, 2 Timothy.

A Teacher

"And the things which you have heard from me in the presence of many witnesses, these entrust to faithful men, who will be able to teach others also" (2 Tim. 2:2).

45

Though the noun "teacher" does not appear in this verse, the contents of the verse as well as the infinitive διδάξαι ("to teach") unmistakably establish the fact that Paul had the image of a teacher in mind. The fact that this image stands first in Paul's series indicates his recognition of the importance of the teaching function in the furtherance of the Christian faith. It was part of his own apostolic work in relation to the gospel (2 Tim. 1:11). In both of his epistles to Timothy, Paul stipulated that the Christian worker must be "able to teach" (1 Tim. 3:2; 2 Tim. 2:24).

The Christian teacher must first be a diligent student, having faithfully received and assimilated the instruction given him. This is implied in Paul's words, "the things which you have heard from me." The words παρ' ἐμοῦ ("from me") reminded Timothy of the authoritative source of the instruction he had received. The things he had heard from Paul are best taken as referring to the totality of the preaching and teaching he had listened to on numerous occasions. And he had heard these things set forth by Paul διά πολλῶν μαρτύρων ("in the presence of many witnesses"). These witnesses not only confirmed that Paul had taught these things, but they also bore witness with Paul that it was indeed the truth of God he had proclaimed. Timothy's confidence in his teachers had confirmed his own conviction that these things were indeed the truth of God (2 Tim. 3:14–15).

The mention of these many witnesses who had heard Paul's teaching indicates that the teachings Timothy had received from Paul were not esoteric doctrines taught only to an inner circle of select followers. The Gnostic teachers, whose heretical teachings were beginning to trouble the church, claimed to possess such secret apostolic traditions on which they based their own dissenting views. But the orthodox church denied the existence of such esoteric teachings and insisted that Christian teachings were public and open to all believers alike. The Christian leaders emphatically repudiated the Gnostic claims to teachings that had been privately communicated to the believers. There is nothing secret and restrictive about the message the Christian teacher is to communicate. The gospel is a precious revelation from God which is intended for and suitable to all. The Pastoral Epistles place strong emphasis on the need for sound doctrine (1 Tim. 1:10; 2 Tim. 1:13; 4:3; Titus 1:9–13; 2:1). Any teacher who brings a contrary message is to be rejected.

Timothy's diligence as a student qualified him to be a teacher of new workers. The things he learned, Paul wrote, "these entrust to faithful men." The word ταῦτα ("these"; literally, "these things") stressed that he was to teach others the message he himself had been taught. His duty was not to develop a new and different teaching but faithfully to transmit the message received. According to 2 Timothy 1:14, that message is τὴν καλὴν παραθήκην ("the treasure"; literally "the good deposit"), which had been entrusted to Timothy. Any message contrary to that precious treasure cannot be the true message. Lenski aptly remarks, "The apostle evidently did not expect the future teachers of the Church to produce new or different teaching. The Gospel is changeless in all ages."[1]

This changeless gospel message Timothy must "entrust to faithful men." The verb παράθου ("entrust") carries the picture of a precious treasure being deposited as a trust into the hands of other persons. Those to be entrusted with the message must be "faithful" persons (πιστοῖς), reliable and trustworthy. They must be individuals "who will not swerve aside because of fear or favor, who will not compromise with the spirit of the age through which they are passing."[2] They must not handle the message recklessly.

Those taughted must be "able to teach others also." The essential task of Timothy was the multiplication of gospel workers. The very nature of Christianity demands that it be propagated, and this demands trained workers who, having been entrusted with the divine message, are able and willing to pass it on to others. "Others" (ἑτέρου) certainly includes the officially appointed teachers in the churches but is not restricted to them. These others in turn are to communicate the message to still others. "The torch of heavenly light must be transmitted unquenched from one generation to another."[3]

Here is the picture of Christianity being perpetuated through a successful teaching ministry, maintaining from age to age the apostolic message in faith and practice. This is true "apostolic succession." The faithful Christian teacher is this, as Barclay observes, "a link in the living chain which stretches unbroken from this present moment back to Jesus Christ."[4] As a teacher of the gospel the Christian leader stands in a glorious tradition; he has a tremendous responsibility to be true to the redemptive message of God entrusted to him.

This first Pauline image of the Christian leader sets forth at least three essential qualities: (1) He must be a diligent student of the biblical message and be thoroughly conversant with its teachings. (2) He must be loyal and faithful to the divine message entrusted to God's church. (3) He must be actively involved in the training and equipping of additional workers, a step essential to the successful progress of the church.

A Soldier

"Suffer hardship with me, as a good soldier of Christ Jesus. No soldier in active service entangles himself in the affairs of everyday life, so that he may please the one who enlisted him as a soldier" (2 Tim. 2:3–4).

The soldier image was a favorite with the Apostle Paul, and its use was widespread in the early church. While the figure may be applied to all Christians, Paul felt it especially appropriate in setting before Timothy the demands on the Christian leader.

The exhortation, "suffer hardship with me, as a good soldier of Christ Jesus," calls on Timothy to assume a willing attitude of readiness to share the hardship involved in being a Christian leader. Not always is the Christian soldier called on to endure hardship, but "as a good soldier of Christ Jesus" he must be willing and ready to do so, since he has pledged undivided loyalty to his Savior and Lord.

However, as a good soldier he knows that he is not alone in the Lord's battle; he has joined "the company of the committed," that noble band of soldiers united under the banner of their victorious Leader. Paul indicated this fellowship in suffering by his use of the compound verb, συγκακοπάθησον, which means "to suffer in treatment with." Kelly renders it, "Take your share of rough treatment."[5] The term expresses the fact that the work of the Christian leader is not an easy, self-indulgent activity. Rather, as Plummer remarks, it "involves self-sacrifice, endurance, discipline, vigilance, obedience, ready cooperation with others, sympathy, enthusiasm, loyalty."[6] A willingness to accept such an assignment is the sure mark of a dedicated man.

Paul also noted that the position of the soldier demands detachment from all that would hinder his wholehearted obedience to the call of his commander (v. 4). The words "no soldier in active service" (more literally, "no one soldiering," οὐδεὶς στρατευόμενος) picture the soldier, not on furlough or in winter quarters, but on active duty in the fighting line. Well aware that the Christian leader's life is a constant battle, Paul's picture stresses not the vicious enemies to be faced but the unreserved dedication to his task needed by the soldier.

As a soldier under arms his duty is not to "entangle himself in the affairs of everyday life." The Roman soldier avoided all preoccupation with the daily affairs of the marketplace in order to be free to obey without hindrance the orders of his commander. Engaged in a spiritual battle, the Christian soldier likewise must concentrate on his work; he must not devote his time and interests to a business on the side which hinders his faithful performance of his primary responsibility. Paul's language does not mean that a Christian worker must never engage in any secular work or tentmaking (Acts 18:3). Rather, he must be on guard against becoming so involved in such pursuits that he no longer feels free to give himself fully to the call of Christian service. As a loyal soldier of Christ he may "feel compelled to lay aside certain things, certain habits, certain amusements, certain pursuits, certain methods in business, and even certain friends—not because any of these may necessarily be wrong in themselves as such, but because they are a snare and entanglement"[7] to him.

The effective Christian leader will deliberately avoid such entanglements "so that he may please him who enrolled him as a soldier." His supreme ambition must ever be to win the commendation of his heavenly Captain. In the original, the words rendered "the one who enlisted him as a soldier" stand emphatically before the verb, thus stressing that Paul's concern was to please Him, rather than any human beings. And this effort to "please" Him whose initiative made him a soldier implies "pleasing by good service."[8] To gain the heavenly approbation, "well-done," is an exalted goal that demands "his soul, his life, his all." Men may live to please themselves or others; but the supreme motive of the Christian leader must be to please Christ.

In summarizing the teaching latent in this second image, at least three other qualities come into view: (1) The Christian leader is one who has heard the Lord's call to service and has wholeheartedly aligned himself with the battle of the Lord. (2) The spiritual leader is willing to accept the hardship and suffering involved in his high calling. (3) His chief concern is to gain Christ's approval on his service in His cause.

An Athlete

"And also if any man competes as an athlete, he does not win the prize unless he competes according to the rules" (2 Tim. 2:5).

Paul's third image of the Christian leader is drawn from the athletic contests which were a prominent feature of Greco-Roman life. This image of a competitor in the games was another favorite with Paul. While elsewhere the figure is used of all believers (1 Cor. 9:25), here Paul employed it specifically of the Christian leader. Based on a comparison of Paul's language in this verse with that of the ancient writer Galen (d. A.D. 201), Simpson suggests that Paul was thinking of the professional athlete, not an amateur.[9] The figure, which suggests the thought of serious struggle and effort, is thus significant for the Christian leader. Like a professional athlete who is wholly absorbed in his pursuit in order to be successful, the Christian leader cannot engage in his task in a listless and indifferent manner but must concentrate on his work.

Paul said nothing here about the fierce competitors to be overcome, since his emphasis was on the necessary self-discipline of the contestant himself. The participant in the games could not win the prize unless he competed according to the rules. He had to adhere to all the prescribed conditions in connection with the contest. The contestants in the games had to meet rigorous training rules before being admitted to the contest, and then had to compete in full compliance with the regulations of the contest. It has been debated whether here Paul was thinking of the preparatory demands as well, or only of the regulations imposed for the actual contest. Both views have been maintained, but from the context it seems that Paul here was not thinking about the preparatory requirements but of the grueling contest itself. Even though a contestant finished as the apparent victor, if he had violated any of the regulations he was disqualified and fined.

Paul's figure stresses that, like the athlete, the Christian leader must be a person of rigid self-discipline, adhering strictly to all the regulations governing his work. He must faithfully adhere to the prescribed regulations, whatever self-sacrifice may be involved. In the words of Van Oosterzee, the Christian worker "dare not arbitrarily exempt himself from this or that portion of his task, or even direct his activities according to his own discretion; not the bias of his own heart, but the will of the Lord alone must be his standard."[10] He must rigidly discipline himself to use methods that are straight and true and must do nothing which the searching test of the divine Umpire would condemn. He must perform his task "not only for God-approved ends in view, but by way of God-approved means."[11]

The contestants in the athletic games willingly endured the rigid demands imposed on them in hope of winning the prize. The needed self-discipline qualified them to perform victoriously in the contest. Likewise, the Christian leader gladly endures hardships and struggles in order to complete the contest victoriously and win the heavenly prize. The hope of the future reward must be for him a sustaining and invigorating reality. A certain minister who had endured unusual persecution and unjust charges was asked by a friend how he was able to bear it. He replied, "I always live in view of eternity."

Two significant qualities for the Christian leader emerge from this image of the athlete. First, he must be a person with strong self-discipline, willing and able to conform his activities to the demands of truth and justice. Second, he must be motivated by the hope of future reward for present faithful service.

A Farmer

"The hard-working farmer ought to be the first to receive his share of the crops" (2 Tim. 2:6).

The word γεωργὸν, translated "farmer," means "a tiller of the soil." (The King James Version renders the "husbandman.") Farming is an essential occupation but it has no spectacular appeal or exciting glamour. Paul makes the hard work of the farmer central in his picture. The participle κοπιῶντα ("hardworking") denotes toiling to the point of weariness and exhaustion. Some innocent souls may harbor the illusion that the farmer simply sits under his vine or fig tree and lets the ripe fruit fall into his lap. But anyone having any acquaintance with farming knows that if there is to be fruit, there must first be hard, exhausting toil.

This image gives emphasis to the fact that Christian service is hard work. Stott makes this remark: "This notion that Christian service is hard work is so unpopular in some happy-go-lucky Christian circles today that I feel the need to underline it."[12] Clearly Paul expected the willingness to work hard to be a normal characteristic of the Christian leader. Human hearts are the soil where the Christian leader sows the seed of the Word of God and where the fruits of his labors are produced. While never easy work, it is for the sake of the harvest that the Lord's husbandman gladly engages in the demanding toil.

But the intended point in Paul's figure of the farmer is the fact that the toil of the Christian worker has its present rewards. Because of his persistent toil, the farmer "ought to be the first to receive his share of the crops." "Ought" ($\delta\epsilon\hat{\iota}$) indicates that his partaking of the fruit is a moral necessity. By the very nature of his occupation the farmer toils to produce food for others. But if he does not himself profit from the harvest produced, he will soon cease farming. The Christian worker toils to produce food for others through his study and teaching of the Word. But to remain spiritually effective, he must first nourish his own spiritual life with the food he produces.

In 1 Timothy 4:16 Paul urged Timothy, "Pay close attention to yourself and to your teaching." The order is significant: "yourself . . . your teaching." So the Christian worker has the duty and privilege of being the first to partake of the fruit produced. He must be willing to engage in hard and difficult toil in fulfilling his duty.

But he also has the rewarding privilege of first nurturing his own spiritual life from the results of his labors. Faithful toil in the Lord's service has its rewards for the worker both here and hereafter. The faithful Christian worker experiences blessings from his work now vastly more rewarding than anything the world has to offer.

Paul's fourth figure, that of the hardworking farmer, sets forth two qualities needed by the Christian leader. He must be willing to engage in difficult and exhausting toil in fulfillment of his assignment. But he must also be sure to nurture his own spiritual life from the results of his toil.

A Workman

"Be diligent to present yourself approved to God, as a workman who does not need to be ashamed, handling accurately the word of truth" (2 Tim. 2:15).

This figure of the workman appears in a context that stresses the need to check the inroads of false teaching in the Christian community. If the false teaching is to be checked, Timothy by his own example must show what a true Christian workman is and does. He is set in contrast to the quibblers about unprofitable words whom Paul had mentioned in the preceding verse. In opposing these quibblers the Christian workman must use the influence of positive personal example.

What occupation Paul had in mind when using this figure of a "workman" is not certain. The basic meaning of the word ἐργάτην is "one who works for hire"; it thus conveys the thought that he works under the direction of another and is subject to the employer's inspection of his work. The term was commonly used of agricultural workers, but it was also applied to those who engaged in fishing, building, or the production of some artifact. In Paul's picture the stress is not on the needed skill of the workman but rather on his diligence to assure that his work is approved by his employer. The hortatory form of the verse makes clear that such approval will require serious and persistent effort. The words "give diligence to present yourself approved unto God" summarize what the life-business of the workman is to be. The aorist imperative σπούδασον, rendered "be diligent," summarizes all the needed efforts as a unit. This high goal requires ceaseless, serious, earnest effort.

In all his activity the workman's aim is to be "approved to God." Plummer observes that this high aim will secure "diligence without fussiness, and enthusiasm without fanaticism."[13] He will not be indifferent to the approval of men, but his governing concern will be divine approval. The word σεαυτὸν ("yourself") stands emphatically forward and implies that the character of the approved workman will be established by the nature of his work. The adjective δόκιμον ("approved") denotes that as a workman he "has done his job well and can therefore submit it to his employer without qualms or embarrassment."[14] Thus the Christian leader must live under the consciousness that all his work is subject to God's inspection. God is always aware of the quality of work the believer does.

From the thought of the divine approval of his work, Paul's thought turns to the workman himself who comes under the divine inspection. For himself, his concern must be to be found "a workman who does no need to be ashamed." He is concerned to avoid the embarrassment of having his work rejected. Stott remarks, "There can be no worse shame than to be proved incompetent in your own proper work, and this applies to the Christian teacher as to every other workman."[15]

"Handling accurately the word of truth" states the workman's activity which will assure the divine approval. "The word of truth" is the whole gospel message as embodied in the Scriptures.

"The modifier 'of the truth,'" Hendriksen observes, "emphasizes the contrast between God's unshakable special revelation, on the one hand, and the Ephesian errorists' worthless chatter on the other."[16] The nature and function of "the word of truth" Paul explicitly stated in 2 Timothy 3:16–17. Its divine nature demands that it be handled aright. "As the subject-matter is trustworthy, let it be trustily handled."[18]

"Handling accurately" renders the participle ὀρθοτομοῦντα, which has been the occasion for much discussion. It is a compound form having the primary meaning of "cutting straight." The intended figure behind the term has been variously held to be that of a farmer plowing a straight furrow, a mason cutting a straight edge on a stone, a workman cutting a straight road, and even a priest's proper dissection of a sacrificial animal. The suggestion that the figure was drawn from Paul's own trade of tentmaking seems plausible. The word occurs only here in the New Testament, but in the Septuagint it occurs twice in Proverbs, both times in connection with the word "path" or "road." Proverbs 11:5 says, "Righteousness cuts out blameless paths." (Cf. also Prov. 3:6.) Thus the lexicographers Bauer, Arndt, and Gingrich suggest that the probable meaning here is to "guide the word of truth along a straight path (like a road that goes straight to its goal), without being turned aside by wordy debates or impious talk."[18]

It is probable that in Paul's usage the idea of cutting recedes into the background, with the emphasis falling on the adjective ὀρθός ("straight"), indicating that the Scriptures must be handled in a straight and true way. This view underlies the rendering "handling aright the word." The demand is for

> a fair and conscientious or straightforward handling of the word itself. This, as opposed to all kinds of tortuous interpretations, or by-plays of ingenuity for sinister purposes, is pre-eminently what becomes the teacher who would stand approved in the judgment of God: . . . he must go right on in his use of the word, maintaining it in its integrity, and applying it to the great spiritual ends for which it has been given.[19]

The Christian leader recognizes that the Word of God has its proper division and applies it according to the divine intention. All deceitful handling of the Word will surely receive divine condemnation in the day of judgment.

Two needed qualifications of the Christian leader stand out in this picture of the Lord's workman. He must ever remember that he is accountable to God and must seek His approval on his work. He must handle God's Word, which is so central in his work, with due care and without change, mutilation, or distortion.

A Vessel

"Therefore, if a man cleanses himself from these things, he will be a vessel for honor, sanctified, useful to the Master, prepared for every good work" (2 Tim. 2:21).

In this image the stress falls on the character qualification of the leader for usefulness in the Lord's service. Personal separation from pollution and inner holiness are essential for acceptable service in Christ's cause. This necessity arises out of the mixed condition existing within Christendom, which Paul pictured in verse 20 as "a great house" with its many vessels of mixed value and destiny. This mixed condition was obvious from the heretical activities of Hymenaeus and Philetus, who claimed to be Christian teachers in the church. This mixed condition Jesus had already foretold in His parable of the wheat and the tares (Matt. 13:24–30, 36–43).

The word σκεῦος, rendered "vessel," can mean a jar, vessel, or dish; but the term has a wider meaning and can denote any household utensil. The image need not be confined to a hollow container. In Paul's picture the two sets of utensils are clearly meant to represent true and false teachers in the professing Christian church. Since both classes professed allegiance to the Lord of the church, in the eyes of the world both were part of the church. These conditions demanded, therefore, that the Christian leader "cleanse himself from these" (2 Tim. 2:21), the vessels "to dishonor" (v. 20), with their heretical teachings and polluting influence.

For usefulness and approval the Christian leader under these conditions must as a definite act "cleanse himself," by separating himself from these heretical teachers and their doctrines. The verb ἐκκαθάρῃ stresses the thoroughness of the needed separation. An inward moral withdrawal is involved, but the full picture includes a separation that refuses to have mutual fellowship with such enemies of the basic truths of the faith. The conditional form of Paul's statement leaves undetermined the individual's response but implies an expectancy that it will be fulfilled.

Such purging of himself will assure that the Christian leader will be "a vessel for honor." He will be a vessel whom the Lord of the house can employ for noble ends. "For honor" (εἰς τιμήν) refers to the Lord's evaluation of the vessel, not the self-evaluation of the vessel. Barclay declares, "No Christian should ever think of fitting himself for honor; every Christian must always think of himself as fitting himself for service."[20]

Paul added three elucidating predicates to describe further such a usable vessel. First, he or she will be "sanctified" (ἡγιασμένον), set apart and fully consecrated to the service of his Lord. The perfect tense in the original speaks of his permanent condition. Through the operation of the indwelling Spirit he will be a saint in position and experience.

Second, he will be "useful to the Master." The adjective εὔχρηστον ("useful") means "well-usable, easy to be used." The master finds him or her a vessel that is readily available and fit for his use. The word δεσπότης ("master") denotes one who has undisputed ownership and control. It speaks of the sovereign Lord who is the sole owner of His servants and who determines what use He will make of the vessels.

Third, the Lord's vessel will be "prepared (ἡτοιμασμένον) for every good work," fully equipped and ready to take advantage of each opportunity for service which presents itself. He or she holds himself in a state of readiness for every kind of beneficial activity in the Lord's cause.

Two specific qualities of the Christian leader are conveyed by this image of a vessel. First, he or she must be realistically aware of the fact of apostasy in Christendom and realize its polluting power. Second, being separated from contamination, the Christian leader must desire to be fully available for the service of his sovereign Lord.

A Slave

"And the Lord's bondservant must not be quarrelsome, but be kind to all, able to teach, patient when wronged, with gentleness correcting those who are in opposition" (2 Tim. 2: 24–25a).

In this final image the picture is again that of a human being, but his status is lowly, that of a "bondservant." The δοῦλον is the common Greek term for a slave. The absence of a definite article here with the term indicates his qualitative status as revealing a servant character. But the restrictive genitive κυρίου ("the Lord's") makes clear that this is his Godward relationship, not his manward position. There is no implication here that the Christian leader must be the slave of the people to whom he ministers. As the

Lord's slave he freely acknowledges that he belongs wholly to his Master. He must personally manifest the fact that is true of all believers, "you are not your own . . . you have been bought with a price" (1 Cor. 6:19b–20). Furthermore, as the Lord's slave he is committed not to do his own will but to govern all his activities by the Lord's will. In view of what follows, it is probable that Paul's selection of this image was inspired by the "servant of the Lord" passage in Isaiah 53.

The Christian worker's status as the Lord's bondservant must be revealed in his conduct, both negatively and positively. Negatively, he "must not be quarrelsome." "Must" (δεῖ) indicates that this is necessary in view of what he is. He has the moral obligation not to become characterized as a battler, one who is of a contentious and combative disposition. He must not involve himself in unprofitable and senseless controversies. But this does not mean that he must never engage in controversy when the truth of the gospel is at stake. It is his duty to "contend earnestly for the faith" (Jude 3), but he must not do so as a lover and seeker of contention.

Over against this negative demand Paul set forth a fourfold positive description of the proper demeanor of the Lord's servant. First, the worker must "be kind to all," the opposite of harsh and irritable. One must be affable and mild in his dealings with "all," not only with loyal followers but also with those who are unfriendly and antagonistic. In the words of Woychuk, he must continually be "cultivating a spirit of habitual courtesy, while using the strongest arguments from the armory of truth."[21]

Second, in one's dealings with others the servant must be διδακτικόν ("able to teach"), capable and willing to impart instruction and counsel whenever the opportunity arises. In the words of Barclay, "He must not only know the truth, but he must also be able to communicate the truth."[22]

Third, he must be ἀνεξίκακον ("patient when wronged"; literally, "patient under injury"). Lenski renders this word, "putting up with what is bad."[23] Whenever his efforts to impart instruction are met with rejection or hostile scorn and ridicule, he must patiently bear those injuries without anger or resentment. Barclay makes the significant observation, "There may be greater sins than touchiness, but there is none which does greater damage in the Christian Church."[24]

Fourth, he must be mild in dealing with opponents, "with

gentleness (πραΰτητι) correcting them who are in opposition."
This is the needed attitude in seeking to win opponents away from
their hostility and the devil's snare and to lead them to the
knowledge of God's truth and salvation.

In this final image of the Christian leader two basic qualities
are indicated. As the Lord's bondsman he must accept and work
in full submission to the will of his heavenly Master. And he must
also exhibit a becoming disposition and pleasing conduct in his
endeavor to help others spiritually.

Summary

Paul's portrayal of the Christian leader in 2 Timothy 2 has been
considered under the images of a teacher, soldier, an athlete, a
farmer, a workman, a vessel, and a slave. These seven images
present a challenging composite picture of the essential nature
and function of the godly leader in the Christian community. This
discussion of the qualities depicted in these images has not been
exhaustive; neither should it be assumed that these give a total
picture of all the qualities desirable in a God-chosen Christian
leader. But it is obvious that they do provide a clear picture of the
essential qualities for effectiveness in the Lord's work. These
qualifications relate to four relationships of the Christian leader.

Fundamental to most of these images is the thought of the
leader's *relationship to God*. Called and commissioned by his
Lord, he knows that he is not his own but that he belongs wholly
to his heavenly Master. His Master has enlisted him in the battle
against sin and evil and expects him to be yielded, prepared, and
ready to carry out His assignments. Called to further the work of
the Lord, an essential part of his task is the training and equipping
of additional workers. He stands accountable to his Lord for all he
does and he desires to win the Lord's full approval.

The God-approved leader has a close, positive *relationship to
the Scriptures*. He maintains an unswerving loyalty to the divinely
revealed message therein and nurtures his own spiritual life by
feeding on that message. He has a strong concern to handle the
Scriptures accurately without change, mutilation, or distortion.
His own loyalty to the inspired Word makes him keenly aware of
the evil of perverting the revealed message. He is opposed to all
apostasy and is keenly sensitive to the dangers inherent in any
departure from or repudiation of the divine Word.

As a God-called leader he realizes the importance of his

relationship to others. He endeavors to use the influence of personal example as well as faithful instruction in dealing with others. He seeks to lead and instruct faithful followers, but he is also seriously concerned about seeking to rescue those who have become entangled in error. From among those who receive his guidance and instruction he is concerned about calling forth and training further leaders.

In *relationship to himself,* the Christian leader must be a person of strong self-discipline. He must be willing to accept hard work as a natural part of his assignment and be prepared to face opposition and suffering in his work of opposing the forces of evil. He is wholly committed to carrying out the will of God and willing to pay the cost involved in his high assignment. In thus fulfilling his duties he knows the joy of faithful service now and is inspired by the prospects of future reward after completing his work here on earth. Keenly aware of the privileges and responsibilities of his assignment, it is his constant desire to present himself to God as a workman who has no need of being ashamed.

CHAPTER 5

Jeremiah's Ministry and Ours

Kenneth L. Barker

T he Word of the Lord came to Jeremiah (cf. Jer. 1:4) in a period of history when conditions were strikingly similar to those in today's Western society.[1] Politically it was a time of upheaval in the ancient Near Eastern world—an upheaval involving the great world powers of Assyria, Egypt, and Babylonia, and also involving such momentous events as the fall of Nineveh in 612 B.C., the Battle of Carchemish in 605 (in which Babylon was victorious over Egypt), and the fall of Judah and the destruction of Jerusalem, including Solomon's temple, in 587 or 586. Religiously there was moral and spiritual decay. Even in little Judah, society was terribly rotten.

The ultimate reason for this appalling condition was given by God Himself in Jeremiah 2:13: "For My people have committed two evils: They have forsaken Me, the fountain of living waters, to hew for themselves cisterns, broken cisterns, that can hold no water." This indicates that Josiah's reform was apparently only superficial, external, and temporary. No real repentance or inner change in the national character had resulted from it. Many were foolishly and erroneously reasoning that because of these outward religious reforms, Judah would now be secure and exempt from divine judgment. The reform itself, then, seems to have actually contributed to the general attitude of complacency, along with the dangerous notion of the people that the presence of the temple, the house of God, in Jerusalem automatically brought security with it. All this meant that judgment was now certain, that Judah as a country or separate national entity was soon to die.

At such a time, then, God called a man who is known as both the weeping prophet and the prophet of loneliness. He was a weeping prophet because he was a man of pathos, feeling, and compassion. This aspect of the nature, personality, and emotion of this man of God may be ascertained from such references as 9:1 and 14:17, and the entire Book of Lamentations. He was the prophet of loneliness because God Himself commanded him never to marry as a sign of the impending disruption of the whole social life of Judah (16:2–4). Thus he was never to know the joys of home and family. Then, too, any person who faithfully proclaims the Word of God will at times find himself standing virtually alone. This was certainly true in Jeremiah's case, so much so that he was even accused of being unpatriotic—a traitor! His life became a veritable history of persecution. But above all else Jeremiah was a man who, though tempted to relinquish his prophetic work, nevertheless continued faithfully to proclaim the Word of God, and who, in the face of mounting pressure from all sides, refused to temper the message God had given him, refused even to water it down a bit, and refused to be silent. The Word of God was like a fire shut up in his bones which, try as he might, he could not hold in (20:9).

The Preface

These verses (Jer. 1:1–3) present the preface, superscription, or title page to the whole book. The meaning of Jeremiah's name is uncertain. Possibly it means "the Lord throws," that is, "the Lord throws down," which would be appropriate to his message of judgment.[2] Jeremiah was a priest, for he wrote, "The words of Jeremiah, the son of Hilkiah, of the priests who were in Anathoth in the land of Benjamin" (v. 1). Prophets came from practically all walks of life. The real stamp that marked a prophet was not what he was before his call, but the fact that he had received a supernatural call from God to his prophetic office and ministry. The word "Anathoth" is modern Anata, and it includes the name of the Phoenician or Canaanite goddess, Anat. This town is three miles northeast of Jerusalem. Being from the land of Benjamin, Jeremiah was from the same tribe or territory as both the Old and New Testament Sauls.

"To whom the word of the LORD came in the days of Josiah, the son of Amon, king of Judah, in the thirteenth year of his reign [approximately 626 B.C.] [The Word of the Lord] came also in the days of Jehoiakim, the son of Josiah, king of Judah" (1:2–3a). Josiah was the last good and godly king of Judah. Actually before Jehoiakim, Jehoahaz reigned for three months. Perhaps his name is omitted because his reign was so brief and not particularly significant. "Until the end of the eleventh year of Zedekiah, the son of Josiah, king of Judah" (1:3b). Again, before the reign of

Zedekiah, Jehoiachin reigned for the short space of three months. "Until the exile of Jerusalem in the fifth month" (1:3*c*). This catastrophic event occurred in 587 or 586 B.C. This means Jeremiah's public ministry covered a period of about 40 years, not counting his ministry in Jerusalem and Judah after 586 and his ministry in Egypt. If those are included, another five to ten years should be added.

Jeremiah's Call and Appointment (1:4–5)

From the human standpoint Jeremiah's call and appointment to the prophetic office occurred in 626 B.C. Verse 5 indicates when Jeremiah was called from the divine viewpoint, and appointed to the prophetic office. "Before I formed you in the womb, I knew you, and before you were born I consecrated you; I have appointed you a prophet to the nations." In the synonymous parallelism of the beautiful poetry of this verse, God informed Jeremiah that before he was born and even before he was formed, shaped, or fashioned in the womb, God did three things: He knew, sanctified, and ordained. Because of the parallelism, these three words are roughly synonymous. But at the same time it is possible to make certain distinctions between them.

First, God declared, "I knew you." In the Old Testament and, for that matter, in all Semitic usage, "knowing" implies a personal relationship, indeed a very personal inward relation.[3] When used of God toward an individual or nation, it is tantamount to such a close personal relationship or interest in the person or nation that it is virtually the same as other words such as "selection," "singling out," or "choice," and that would not be a bad translation here: "I chose you." This usage is clear in several other references. In Amos 3:2 God said of the nation of Israel, "You only have I known of all the families of the earth" (literal translation). That is to say, "I entered into a very close personal covenant relationship with you," or, "I had such a personal interest in you that I singled you out, I selected you, I chose you" (cf. Ex. 33:12; Ps. 144:3).

Second, God said, "I consecrated (or sanctified) you." To paraphrase, stressing the root idea of "sanctified,"[4] "I separated you to Me," that is, "I set you apart for the service or ministry of the prophetic office."

Third, God said to Jeremiah, "I appointed (or I ordained) you." Actually the word used here means "to give." But the best translation would be "I appointed you."[5] Implied in the meaning also is an appointment that carries with it the importation of spiritual gifts, the necessary gifts for the office. Then, "I have appointed you a prophet [i.e., 'as one called to be my spokesman'[6]] to the nations." The nations are referred to because Jeremiah's ministry was not restricted to Judah (cf. chaps. 25, 46–51). His ministry encompassed many great nations.

In Jeremiah 1:5 the reader confronts the doctrine of divine sovereign election. This is a puzzling and disconcerting doctrine to some, but actually it ought to be a comforting and encouraging doctrine. If a minister of God today has a similar consciousness that before he was born or even fashioned in the womb, God in His eternal counsels sovereignly elected or chose him, set him apart for the work of the gospel ministry, and appointed him to His service—if he has that kind of conviction, assurance, or consciousness, then this will comfort him more than anything else. It will anchor him, as it did Jeremiah, through all the testings and onslaughts of Satan and will make him a faithful servant of God with unshakable convictions. All servants of Christ need to keep the knowledge and awareness of this constantly before them.

Jeremiah's Reticence (1:6)

Verse 6 reports Jeremiah's reticence on receiving this call. "Then [or perhaps 'But'] I said, Alas, Lord God! Behold, I do not know how to speak, because I am a youth." Jeremiah did what other servants of God have done. In the face of such an awesome responsibility and task, he hesitated. He recognized his weaknesses and lack of qualifications; so he shrank back. In saying, "I do not know how to speak," the word "know" often means "to be skilled or experienced in doing something."[7] The idea here then is, "I am not experienced in speaking, for I am a "youth" or "young man."[8] Perhaps Jeremiah at that time was 19 or 20 years of age. In this expression he was pleading immaturity, the fact that he was a novice. In this verse there is a cry of weakness on the part of Jeremiah before such an awesome responsibility, but not necessarily a cry of unwillingness. He pleaded his immaturity and inexperience, but he needed to discover that God never calls a man to any work without imparting the necessary gifts and enablement for performing it.

An interesting question could be raised at this point. Why does God often choose the weak (or those who are cognizant of their weakness and who cry out in their hearts, "Who is sufficient for

these things?")? The answer is given in 1 Corinthians 1:26–31.
God often chooses the weak (in the eyes of people) so that no one
"should boast before God" (v. 29). God will not share His glory
with another. The reason is also stressed in 2 Corinthians 4:7:
"But we have this treasure in earthen vessels, that the surpassing
greatness of the power may be of God, and not from ourselves."
He must receive all the credit, glory, and honor for what is
accomplished.

Paul was such an individual. Physically he was weak and felt
inadequate and insufficient. In one of those moments of weakness,
when he was praying that God would deliver him from whatever
physical malady or abnormality plagued him, Christ reassured
him with these words: "My grace is sufficient for you; for [My]
power is perfected in weakness" (2 Cor. 12:9). Every believer
needs his or her strength daily from God by faith, so that they can
constantly experience the truth of Ephesians 3:16, "strengthened
with power through His Spirit in the inner man."

Jeremiah's Revelation (1:7–10)

Concerning his ministry (vv. 7–8). In response to Jeremiah's
hesitation God was pleased to give him a revelation concerning
his ministry, particularly the nature of his ministry. "But the LORD
said to me, 'Do not say "I am a youth."'" Why? "Because
everywhere I send you, you shall go, and all that I command you,
you shall speak." Essentially God declared, "Go where I command
and speak what I say." In other words speak the Word of God. The
Word of God was to be central in his ministry. There is too little of
this kind of preaching and teaching today. The typical speaker
reads a few verses and then merely uses them as a takeoff for
whatever he wants to say, instead of reading a passage from the
Word of God and then sharing with the people what God says
from that passage of Scripture to them and their needs. From this
verse, then, it is clear that the Word of God was to be central in
Jeremiah's ministry.

The motto of Dallas Theological Seminary, "Preach the Word,"
is taken from 2 Timothy 4:2. This means that even in the sometimes
necessary changing, adapting, or adjusting of methods and
approaches to meet the needs of a changing society, the preacher
still adheres to the truths of the Word of God. Just how seriously is
this motto taken in the teaching and preaching of today's ministers?
It is possible to discuss some topic, tell some interesting stories,

issue an appeal or challenge, and still not preach the Word! Today's ministers must never forget that God has promised to bless only His own Word.

The Lord said to Jeremiah, "I am watching over My word to perform it" (Jer. 1:12). In Isaiah 55:11 God promised, "So shall My word be which goes forth from My mouth; it [my Word] shall not return to me empty, without accomplishing what I desire; and without succeeding in the matter for which I sent it." This is surely one of the goals or objectives of seminary professors, namely, to help equip called and gifted individuals to expound the Scriptures, and to do it accurately, effectively, and in terms relevant to today. Many people are hungry for a word from God, who want to hear someone open the Scriptures to them and tell them what God has to say. Ministers today ought not disappoint them. Like Jeremiah, pastors should be people of the Book.

Next, God reassured His prophet. "Be not afraid of them, for I am with you to deliver you" (Jer. 1:8). God spoke similar words to Moses, Joshua, and many others. Regardless of the nature of the problems, obstacles, or difficulties a servant of God may encounter in his ministry, these words, "I am with you," should give him courage and cause him to cry out triumphantly, "If God is for us, who is against us?" (Rom. 8:31). On several occasions, men actually sought to have Jeremiah executed, but God kept His promise and rescued him.

Concerning his message (v. 9–10). First, God was pleased to give Jeremiah a revelation concerning the general content of his message. "Then the LORD stretched out His hand and touched my mouth, and the LORD said to me, 'Behold, I have put My words in your mouth.'" This statement by the Lord is an explanation of the symbolic act in the first part of the verse. That is, the touching of Jeremiah's mouth by God's hand symbolized the fact that God had placed His words in his mouth. This points back to verse 6, where Jeremiah had said, in essence, "I am not an experienced speaker." God's answer was, "I have put my words in your mouth." This, then, is to be the general content of his message: "My words." Of course this verse also has bearing on the doctrine of inspiration—these are inspired words.

Then Jeremiah received a word concerning the somewhat more specific content of his message. The specific content is twofold. First, it was to be a message of destruction—that is the negative aspect; then it was to be a message of construction—that is the positive aspect. "See, I have appointed you this day over the nations and over the kingdoms, to pluck up [a figure of planting], and to break down [a figure of building], to destroy [referring back to 'pluck up' and the figure of planting], and to overthrow [referring back to 'break down' and the figure of building]." These verbs point to the energy or power of the Word of God, for the ministry of the Word is in view here. He who utters it destroys and builds with it. In this same book God said, "Is not My word like a fire . . . and like a hammer which shatters a rock?" (23:29). The reason four words are used in 1:10 in the negative sense, while only two are employed in the positive sense, is evidently because the prophecies threatening destruction and judgment in the book far outnumber those promising construction, hope, and salvation. But verse 10 ends with a positive emphasis: "to build and to plant." From 31:28 it is clear that these words of construction will find their primary fulfillment and application in the New Covenant.

Preaching or teaching the Word of God is much like building and planting. These same two figures are used in the New Testament. In 1 Corinthians 3:11 Paul wrote, "For no man can lay a foundation other than the one which is laid . . . Jesus Christ." Again, "Let each man be careful how he builds upon it" (3:10). The building is done primarily through the ministry of the Word of God. In 1 Corinthians 3:5–8 the figure of planting is used. There Paul stated that if one faithfully sows or plants the good seed of the Word of God, then someone else, or perhaps even the sower again, will water it, and God will ultimately give the increase, fruit, or harvest.

God is still calling individuals to a mission similar to that of Jeremiah. The question is, Will they be as faithful to God and His Word as Jeremiah was? Just how committed are today's Christian servants in their adherence to the Word, both in their personal lives and in their public ministry? As one submits to the Word, he or she will be planted and built up. But if one rebels and refuses to bow to the authority of Scripture, he or she may be uprooted and torn down. This writer heartily commends to today's ministers a ministry of the Word of God. Study it diligently, believe it implicitly, obey it completely, and expound it faithfully!

CHAPTER 6

Ideals of Pastoral Ministry

John R. W. Stott

One feature of the contemporary church is its uncertainty about the role of its professional ministers. Are pastors primarily social workers, psychiatrists, educators, facilitators, administrators, or what? Since the ministry involves all believers, are professional clergy superfluous and even inhibiting? Would the church be healthier without them? Should someone establish a Society for the Abolition of the Clergy?

Throughout its long history the church has oscillated unsteadily between extreme clericalism and extreme anticlericalism. There has seldom been any clear consensus about what ordained clergy are for.

Huckleberry Finn was conversing with Mary Jane, the redheaded daughter of Peter Wilks. Huck told her that in the church of the Reverend Harvey Wilks, her uncle from Sheffield, there were "no less than 17 clergy." But, he added, "they don't all of 'em preach the same day—only one of 'em." "Well, then," asked Mary Jane, "what does the rest of 'em do." "Oh, nothing much," said Muck. "They loll around, pass the plate, and one thing or another. But mainly they don't do nothing." "Well then, what are they for?" asked Mary Jane in astonishment, to which Huck replied, "Why, they are for *style*. Don't you know nothing?"[1]

Against this background of contemporary uncertainty or malaise about the ministry, Acts 20, the valedictory address Paul delivered to the Ephesian elders, is an appropriate passage for consideration.

It was a memorable speech. For one thing, Luke was there to hear it (Acts 21:1). For another, it is the only speech Luke recorded in Acts which is addressed to elders, indeed to a Christian audience; all the other speeches are either evangelistic sermons or judicial defenses.

In addition this speech gives insight into the warm heart of the Apostle Paul. For three years he had labored among the Ephesians.

Now, he told them, imprisonment awaited him in Jerusalem, and they would not see him again. So he reflected on his ministry among them and delivered a solemn farewell speech or pastoral charge. It was a very poignant situation.

The Ministry of the Ephesian Elders

IT WAS A PASTORAL OVERSIGHT; THEY WERE SHEPHERDS

Luke called them πρεσβύτεροι ("elders"), a word borrowed from the Jewish synagogue (Acts 20:17), while Paul called them ἐπίσκοποι ("overseers or guardians"), a word borrowed from a Greek context (v. 28). The two titles evidently described the same people.

Their function was pastoral, caring for God's flock. The Greek verb ποιμαίνειν means "to do the work of a shepherd or tend a flock," and in particular "to lead a flock to pasture, and so to feed it." This is the first duty of shepherds. "Should not the shepherds feed the flock?" (Ezek. 34:2). Translating the metaphor, the first duty of pastors is to teach the Word of God to the people of God. Whether preaching from the pulpit, training a group, or counseling an individual, the pastoral ministry is a ministry of the Word.

IT WAS A PLURAL MINISTRY; THERE WERE SEVERAL ELDERS

There is no biblical warrant either for the one-man band (a single pastor playing all the instruments of the orchestra himself) or for a hierarchical or pyramidal structure in the local church (a single pastor perched at the apex of the pyramid). On the contrary, the church had a plural oversight from the beginning. During their first missionary journey Paul and Barnabas ordained elders (in the plural) in every church (Acts 14:23). In Miletus Paul sent for the elders of the church of Ephesus (again plural, Acts 20:17). Later he instructed Titus to select and appoint elders (once more plural) in the churches he superintended (Titus 1:5). So today the concept of a pastoral team is needed—including full-time and part-time people, salaried and voluntary, or ordained and lay.

In developing the pastoral metaphor, Paul described his own teaching ministry among them as their shepherd, warned them of the rise of false teachers, whom he called "wolves," and affirmed the value of the people, who are God's sheep. So the example of the shepherd, the danger of the wolves, and the value of the sheep are the three topics of his valedictory speech.

The Example of the Apostle Paul (The Shepherd)

In Acts 20:18–27 Paul looked back on his ministry and reminded the elders of his example. Without doubt they had watched him closely. Yet he was able to say that he had no misgivings or regrets about his ministry among them. There had been a degree of thoroughness about it, which left his conscience clear.

PAUL HAD BEEN THOROUGH IN HIS MESSAGE

What had he proclaimed to them? He called it "the gospel of the grace of God" (v. 24) and of "the kingdom of God" (v. 25). He had also taught the necessity of both "repentance toward God and faith in Jesus Christ" (v. 21). The great related gospel themes of grace and faith, divine rule and human repentance had been spelled out.

Twice Paul said that he did not "shrink" from his teaching responsibility. He did not "hesitate" (NIV) to declare anything profitable to them (v. 20), the whole counsel (or plan) of God (v. 27). Perhaps these phrases refer to the same thing, since all Scripture is God-breathed and profitable (2 Tim. 3:16). What was this "whole purpose of God"? Doubtless it included the great doctrines of creation by God (as Paul unfolded this in Athens), redemption by Christ, and regeneration by the Spirit; the bringing into being of the church; the ethical standards of Christian discipleship; together with final salvation and final judgment. Much of contemporary preaching appears very thin in contrast to the whole purpose of God Paul unfolded.

PAUL HAD BEEN THOROUGH IN HIS MINISTRY

Paul was as concerned to reach the whole population of Ephesus as he was to teach the whole purpose of God. He wanted to teach everything to everybody! So he had a ministry to both Jews and Greeks (Acts 20:21). In fact Luke described this in the previous chapter (Acts 19). He wrote that Paul first spent three months speaking boldly to Jews in the synagogue, and then for two years he rented the lecture hall of Tyrannus, where he argued the gospel daily (vv. 8–10), the Bezan text adding "from the fifth hour to the tenth," from 11:00 A.M. to 4:00 P.M. A daily five-hour lecture, six days a week for two years would represent 3,120 hours of gospel argument! It is not surprising that Luke immediatcly commented that "all who lived in [the province of] Asia heard the Word of the Lord." For everyone in the province came to Ephesus, the capital city, on some occasion, perhaps on market day, or to visit a relative or a politician, or do some shopping. And one of the sights of the town was to listen to this lecturer Paul, for he was at it five hours every day. Many dropped in, listened, were converted, and returned to their villages born again. It is a great strategy for the city center, which is needed today.

Paul set forth a challenging example in his resolve to reach everyone with the gospel. For pastors too should be concerned not only for the flock of God already gathered in, but for those "other sheep" whom Jesus mentioned, who are still lost. Must believers not go out into the secular wilderness in order to seek and to save them? How can Christian leaders be content until every soul in their district has heard the gospel?

PAUL HAD BEEN THOROUGH IN HIS METHODS

Paul threw himself into his ministry with his whole heart and soul. He talked to people both publicly in the synagogue and in the hall of Tyrannus, and privately "from house to house" (Acts 20:20). He also continued day and night (v. 31). He was absolutely indefatigable. Nothing could stop him, not even the "tears and trials" (v. 19) he experienced through the plots of the Jews. He did not consider his life to be of value, for he was quite ready to lay it down (v. 24), to die in the service of the gospel. His only ambition, like his Master before him, was to finish the race and to complete the task he had been given to do.

In all this the sincerity of Paul's commitment was obvious. He had no ulterior motives. He was not seeking his own power or prestige. He had coveted no one's money or possessions (v. 33). On the contrary he had supported himself and his colleagues by working with his own hands (v. 34). His whole ministry, both manual and pastoral, had exemplified the words of the Lord Jesus that "it is more blessed to give than to receive" (v. 35).

Such was the thoroughness of Paul's ministry in Ephesus. In modern terms it was a fine example of "evangelism in depth." Paul omitted no part of God's revealed message. He neglected no section of the local community. He left no stone unturned in devising means to reach the people. He permitted himself no relaxation of his high standards of life and ministry.

He shared all possible truth with all possible people in all possible ways. He taught the whole gospel to the whole city with his whole strength. Only then could he make the solemn and daring claim that he was innocent of the blood of all people (v. 6). Perhaps he was consciously echoing God's instruction to Ezekiel. God appointed the prophet a watchman over the house of Israel, telling him to warn the people and that if he failed to do so, their blood would be required at his hand (Ezek. 33:1–9). Paul had been a faithful watchman. He had been conscientious in both teaching and warning the people. So he was innocent; no one's blood would be required at his hand.

Paul's example must have been an unfailing inspiration to the Ephesian elders, and his thoroughness and devotion remain a standing challenge. The church needs Christian leaders of the same dedication today, who are determined with their whole heart to bring the whole gospel to their whole city or neighborhood.

The Rise of False Teachers (The Wolves)

In Acts 20:28 Paul spoke of the sheep and their shepherd. Now in verse 29 he spoke of the wolves. The exhortation of verse 28 is based on the knowledge of verse 29. Because Paul knew that after his departure false teachers would enter the church, he begged the Ephesian elders to be diligent in teaching the people. Their care of God's sheep must be all the more diligent because of the danger from the wolves. In the ancient Near East, wolves were the chief enemy of sheep. Sheep were defenseless against them, so that shepherds could not afford to relax their vigilance.

It is not difficult to interpret what Paul was referring to. In fact he supplied his own interpretation in verse 30. For he moved from the metaphor of wolves not sparing the flock to the rise of men who would distort the truth and draw away disciples after them, some entering the flock from without, and others rising from within.

This prophecy came true. 1 Timothy 4:1–3; 2 Timothy 3:1–9; and Christ's later letter to Ephesus (Rev. 2:1–7) show that this happened. Jesus Himself had issued the same warning in general terms. "Beware of false prophets," He had said. He had also warned that they would come in disguise, insinuating their way into the unwary flock as "wolves in sheep's clothing" (Matt. 7:15).

Therefore "be on your guard!" Paul urged (Acts 20:31). Good shepherds, like those in the fields near Bethlehem, are to "keep watch over their flock by night," and by day as well. Good shepherds are concerned to guard their people from false teachers.

The shepherds of Christ's flock have a double duty: to feed the sheep, and to protect them from wolves. The shepherds' first duty is to teach the truth, and their second is to warn of error. Paul later emphasized this in his letter to Titus, when writing about candidates for elders. They must hold firm the sure word according to the apostolic teaching, he said, so that they would be able both to give instruction "in sound doctrine and [also] to refute those who contradict" it (Titus 1:9).

This emphasis is unpopular today. It is frequently said that pastors must always be positive in their teaching, never negative. But those who say this have either not read the New Testament or, having read it, they disagree with it. For the Lord Jesus and His apostles gave the example and even set forth the obligation to be negative in refuting error. Is it possible that the neglect of this ministry is one of the major causes of theological confusion in the church today? To be sure, theological controversy is distasteful to sensitive spirits and has its spiritual dangers. Woe to those who enjoy it! But it cannot conscientiously be avoided. If, when false teaching arises, Christian leaders sit idly by and do nothing or turn tail and flee, they will earn the terrible epithet "hirelings" who care nothing for Christ's flock. Is it right to abandon His sheep and leave them defenseless against the wolves, to be like "sheep without a shepherd"? Is it right to be content to see the flock scattered and individual sheep torn to pieces? Is it to be said of believers today, as it was of Israel, that "they were scattered for lack of a shepherd, and they became food for every beast of the field" (Ezek. 34:5)? Today even some of the fundamental doctrines of historic Christianity are being denied by some church leaders, including the infinite personality of the living God, the eternal deity, virgin birth, atoning death, and bodily resurrection of Jesus, the Trinity, and the gospel of justification by grace alone through faith alone without any meritorious works. Pastors are to protect God's flock from error and seek to establish them in the truth.

The Value of the People (The Sheep)

Implicit in Acts 20:28 is the truth that the pastoral oversight of the church belongs ultimately to God Himself. He is the supreme Overseer of all things, and especially of His people. Each of the three persons of the Trinity has some share in this oversight.

It is not clear whether verse 28 should read "the church of God" (as in RSV and NIV) or "the church of the Lord" (as in NEB). In either case it is plain that the church is God's church; it belongs ultimately to God the Father.

It is also not clear whether verse 28 should read that He purchased the church "with His own blood" (NIV) or "with the blood of His own" (RSV), referring to His only Son. In either case it is plain that the blood with which the church has been bought is the blood of Christ, the Son of God. And in this church, which belongs to God and has been bought by Christ, the Holy Spirit appoints overseers. So the oversight is His too.

This splendid truth, that the pastoral oversight of the church belongs to God (Father, Son, and Holy Spirit), should have a profound influence on one's ministry.

IT SHOULD HUMBLE THE OVERSEERS

The church does not belong to the overseers. They have no proprietary rights over it. They should therefore be extremely cautious in their use of possessive adjectives. It may be appropriate for kings and queens to talk of "My people," but it is unbecoming for pastors to do so. When the Corinthians were arguing that they belonged to Paul, Apollos, or Cephas (1 Cor. 1:12; cf. 3:4), Paul reversed the sentiment and wrote, "All things belong to you, whether Paul or Apollos or Cephas" (3:21–22). In addition the people are God's people, not the pastors', and the oversight of them is God's, even after it has been delegated to the pastors.

IT SHOULD ENCOURAGE THE OVERSEERS

For, although God delegates a part of the pastoral oversight of the church to elders, He does not relinquish His responsibilities. The church is still His church, and the oversight is still His. He created the church, bought it, owns it, indwells it, and supervises it. He will never allow it to wither away or die. Though individual sheep may suffer from bad pastors, yet God will preserve His church from destruction and bring to completion the work He has begun. Even the gates of Hades (the power of death) will not be able to destroy it (Matt. 16:18). It is a great encouragement to remember this.

IT SHOULD INSPIRE THE OVERSEERS

Pastors always need to remember their privilege in being shepherds of the flock of God. Sheep are not at all the clean and cuddly creatures they sometimes appear. In fact they are dirty, subject to unpleasant pests, and regularly need to be dipped in chemicals to rid them of lice, ticks, and worms! They are also unintelligent, wayward, and obstinate. Naturally one should hesitate to apply the metaphor too closely or to call the people of God dirty, lousy, or stupid! But some Christian ministers find some church members a great trial, even as some members find some ministers a great trial. People can be extremely perverse and aggravating.

How can Christian leaders persevere in caring for such people? They must remember how precious they are, how valuable they are in the sight of God. They are so precious that the whole Trinity is involved in caring for them. They are the flock of God the Father. They were purchased by the precious blood of God the Son. And they are supervised by pastors appointed by God the Holy Spirit. If the three Persons of the eternal Godhead are this concerned for the well-being of the flock, should not pastors be also? In particular this is the emphasis here: If the Good Shepherd died for the sheep, should not the undershepherds be willing to live for them? The Son of God shed His blood for them; the Apostle Paul shed his tears for them; should not others be willing to spend their lives in their service?

As Baxter wrote,

> Oh then, let us hear these arguments of Christ, whenever we feel ourselves grow dull and careless: "Did I die for them, and wilt not thou look after them? Were they worth my blood and are they not worth thy labor? Did I come down from heaven to earth, to seek and to save that which was lost; and wilt thou not go to the next door or street or village to seek them? How small is thy labor and condescension as to Mine? I debased Myself to this, but it is thy honor to be so employed. Have I done and suffered so much for their salvation; and was I willing to make thee a coworker with Me, and wilt thou refuse that little that lieth upon thy hands."[2]

Reminding the Ephesian elders that they were shepherds, Paul invited them to look first at himself, the apostolic shepherd, who had set them an example; second at the wolves, soon to rise; and third at the sheep, infinitely precious because they were bought by the blood of Christ.

Conclusion

Two lessons may be learned from this passage. First, pray that the Holy Spirit will appoint *more pastors* in the church. One must not follow the unbiblical tendency to despise the office and work of a pastor or to declare clergy to be redundant. No—pastoral oversight is a permanent feature of the church. Though the New Testament gives no detailed blueprint for the pastorate, yet the ascended Christ still gives pastors and teachers to his church.

And they are greatly needed today. As the sheep multiply in many parts of the world, there is an urgent need for more pastors to feed or teach them. And as the wolves multiply, there is an equally urgent need for more pastors to rout them by giving their minds to the refutation of error. So the more sheep there are, and the more wolves there are, the more shepherds are needed to feed and protect the flock.

Second, pray not only for more pastors but also for *better pastors*. As Paul wrote, "Be on guard for yourselves and for all the flock" (Acts 20:28). Pastors have a duty to themselves as well as to their flocks. In fact their duty to themselves takes precedence over their duty to the flock, since they cannot serve others if they neglect themselves. So it is important that they "keep watch over" (NIV) themselves, guarding their devotional life, maintaining the discipline of daily prayer and Bible meditation, and conforming their lives in thought, word, and deed to the high and holy standards of Scripture.

Only if pastors first guard themselves, will they be able to guard the sheep. Only if pastors first tend their own spiritual life, will they be able to tend the flock of God.

> If God would but reform the ministry, and set them on their duties zealously and faithfully, the people would certainly be reformed. All churches either rise or fall as the ministry doth rise or fall, not in riches or wealthy grandeur, but in knowledge, zeal, and ability for their work.[3]

CHAPTER 7

The Nature of the Pastoral Role: The Leader as Completer

A. Duane Litfin

There are few vocations that splinter a man like the pastoral ministry. The average pastor is expected to be "all things to all men" in a way quite beyond what the Apostle Paul intended. Several humorous paragraphs have circulated in recent years, masquerading as ministerial want ads, which were designed to make this very point. Everyone expects a pastor to be at once an effective scholar, administrator, communicator, counselor, motivator, educator, and a host of other things as well.

Unfortunately, few can fulfill such expectations. The result is a rash of frustrated and confused ministers. In fact those who counsel pastors suggest that the ministerial identity crisis is a familiar problem among clergymen, which has prompted many to leave the pastorate altogether. In the midst of all the bulletin preparation, the janitor-hiring, the Sunday school teacher-motivating, the babysitting which passes for counseling, the delivery of half-prepared sermons, the shuffling of paper, the organizing of meetings, the planning of events, the often interrupted study times, the visitation, the placating, the public relations—in the midst of it all the ministry can easily get lost in the shuffle. What, the pastor asks himself, is this all about?

Seeking a Theory

A pastor needs some way to consolidate all these diverse activities into a comprehensive *theory of his role as leader in the congregation*, a theory that will enable him to sort through the muddle and evaluate what he is doing. Only in this way can a pastor face the complexity of his ministry without losing himself and his sense of purpose. To attempt to function without such an overall theory is to court the disaster of directionlessness that seems to afflict so many pastors.

One must not apologize, of course, in calling for a theory of pastoral leadership. Nothing is quite so useful as a good theory. It informs one's behavior at every turn. Without a sound theory by which to operate, a person's steps are often random, lacking a cohesive purpose and overall direction. There is no such thing as a theory that is good on paper but does not work in practice. A theory is by definition a bad theory if it does not work in practice. A theory is a good theory only if it corresponds to and helps one understand, organize, and respond to reality in an effective way.

In looking for a comprehensive theory of the pastoral role, what is being sought is a "model," as that term is used in scientific parlance. In this sense a model is a picture borrowed or constructed so as to give a synthetic view of the whole. For instance, those who study mental disorders often borrow a "medical model," and speak in terms of "disease," "symptoms," "illness," "health," and so on.

"Shepherd" as Model

Such a model is precisely what the Bible provides by discussing the congregational leader's role in terms of "shepherding" or "pastoring." The former term is derived from Anglo-Saxon and the latter from Latin, but both hearken back to the relationship between a flock of sheep and the one who keeps them. This shepherding image is regularly used in the New Testament to speak of the relationship between a congregation and its leaders (Acts 20:28–29; 1 Cor. 9:7; Eph. 4:11; 1 Peter 5:1–4).

One might ask, then, since a model for the ministry is already provided, why look for another? The answer is that the model of the shepherd is not intended to be a complete model for the pastoral ministry. That is why the term "pastor" is buttressed by other terms such as "elder" (1 Tim. 5:1, 17; Titus 1:5; James 5:14; 1 Peter 5:l) and "overseer" (Acts 20:28; Phil. 1:l; 1 Tim. 3:1; Titus 1:7).

The model of the shepherd does not provide a comprehensive picture of the relationship of the congregation to its leaders; indeed, in some ways the image of the shepherd can be pushed so far as to be downright misleading. For example, though the disparity between the knowledge, wisdom, and intelligence of the shepherd and that of the sheep may usefully portray the disparity between the Good Shepherd and His people, it does not accurately picture the gap between the average minister and his congregation. While some such gap will often exist in a church (if it does not, does the pastor qualify biblically to serve as a pastor?), it is highly patronizing to suggest that this gap approaches anywhere near the disparity between a reasonably intelligent shepherd and his very stupid sheep. Yet many pastors have pushed the model just this far, with the result that their congregational leadership is overbearing and quite contrary to the larger picture the Scriptures portray.

Hence the biblical image of the shepherd is insufficient as a comprehensive model of the minister's role in the local church. It is evocative, but imprecise; instructive, but incomplete. And so is the oft-used managerial model of a business executive or the player-coach model of an athletic team. These and other such images partially capture the role of the leader in the congregation but do not adequately convey the entire picture. In fact it is questionable whether any single model borrowed from everyday life can capture the complexity of the pastoral ministry, for there is nothing else quite like it.

A Secular Model

Yet another source of useful models is available, namely, the secular world of research and writing in the area of leadership in groups. Here too those who have attempted to understand the phenomenon of leadership have found no single picture from everyday life to be adequate. Inevitably, such models are too simplistic to account for the complexity of their subject. So researchers have cast about for an invented model which is powerful and sophisticated enough to serve their purpose, and they have done so in a rigorous and thorough manner.

Curiously these secular researchers have come up with an overall concept of leadership that can help pastors in thinking about their role in the church. And the reason it can help pastors is that it is a view of leadership that corresponds in a striking way to the particulars of that concept of the pastoral ministry set forth in the pages of Scripture. In other words many secular researchers are coming to a view of leadership that in significant ways corresponds to what the Bible has said all along. Thus such theories measured critically against the plumb line of Scripture can help pastors understand more clearly the Bible's teaching on their pastoral role. In this way they may see the biblical teachings in a light in which they had not seen them before; or perhaps they may even discover what they had previously missed altogether.

Modern Theories of Leadership

In seeking to understand leadership, secular researchers looked for many years down a blind alley. They assumed that all true leaders possessed certain traits or characteristics. Originally such traits were considered to be inborn; later it was agreed that they could be learned. But in either case the assumption was that leadership traits existed and could be isolated by research.

Only after many failures did researchers begin to concede that the phenomena of leadership were much more complicated than any trait theory could explain. Many of the studies discovered that leadership requirements changed from situation to situation, and that leaders who were effective in one situation were not automatically effective in another. Thus the trait theory was eventually eclipsed by a more mature and sophisticated view of leadership which prevails today.

Modern theorists often begin by distinguishing between "leadership" and "leader." "Leadership" is broadly defined as any behavior that helps the group meet its stated goals or fulfills its purpose, while "leader" refers to anyone who is assigned to provide such behavior or who emerges in an extraordinary way to do so on his or her own.

This is a useful distinction because it allows one to focus on and isolate those leadership behaviors or functions a group needs in order for it to prosper. These behaviors or functions are commonly divided into two categories: *task* and *maintenance*. The *task behaviors* are those that help the group reach its specified goals; the *maintenance behaviors* are those that enhance the group's interpersonal relationships in such a way as to enable it to function as an effective social unit.

It is important to note that the *task* and *maintenance functions* can be fulfilled by anyone in the group. In this sense leadership can be shared fully among group members. It is not necessary or even desirable that "the leader" fulfill all these leadership acts. The research suggests that the healthiest groups are those wherein the various leadership contributions are widely dispersed throughout the group.

This does not mean, of course, that everyone in the group

is equally capable of supplying any given leadership function. Typically some people are better at supplying certain functions than others. Thus group members tend to develop specialties based on their abilities, and they come to be relied on by other members to contribute in those areas where they are most capable.

Leadership in the Congregation

So far the above is merely a simplified summary of a contemporary view of leadership. But several similarities exist between this view of leadership in groups and the biblical view of the congregation, particularly as the latter is seen in Ephesians 4; 1 Corinthians 12, and Romans 12. A congregation consists of a group of people, each of whom is uniquely gifted for some work of service (1 Cor. 12:7, 11; Eph. 4:7). Each one has a function or behavior to contribute, a role to play in the overall life of the group (Rom. 12:6–8). This role grows out of the special God-given abilities for service (spiritual gifts) the Spirit of God has distributed to each one. Thus each member supplies a different aspect of the group's needs, based on the member's abilities (1 Cor. 12:4–31). These contributions must all be made with a view to furthering the purposes and welfare of the group (1 Cor. 12:7; 14:22, 26; Eph. 4:12; 1 Peter 4:10), which by definition is leadership behavior. What is more, each of these contributions can be viewed from the perspective of the task and maintenance categories. Some gifts are designed to further the congregation's "task" while others are designed to maintain and enhance the interpersonal relationships within the group itself. Perhaps most of the gifts involve some aspects of both. The healthiest congregations are those in which these "leadership" acts are widely dispersed, with "every joint supplying, according to the working of each individual part" (Eph. 4:16) what each is designed to contribute.

The Leader as Completer

If leadership is thus spread throughout the congregation, what then is the role of the designated leader, the pastor? An elegantly simple concept has the potential of serving as a comprehensive "model" for the pastor. It is called, simply, *the leader as completer*.

The concept of the leader as completer was first introduced by William C. Schutz, a well-known social psychologist. This view of leadership springs from that branch of psychoanalytic theory called ego psychology. In essence Schutz argued that the functions of leadership in a group are essentially the same as the functions of the ego in the individual personality. In other words, "an individual is assumed to have a group within him"[1] that functions in the same way as a group made up of several individuals. Thus what is known about individual personalities will also be true in a corresponding way of a group. Specifically the ego of the personality will function like the leader of the group, and vice versa.[2]

Evangelicals may legitimately remain wary of the parallel Schutz establishes, and the psychoanalytic theory on which it is based, without tossing aside the concept of the leader as completer, for the concept itself is sound. It is both consonant with the view of groups explained above and remarkably heuristic. Several aspects of Schutz's concept shed light on the role of the pastor.

According to Schutz the leader's task is to complete what is lacking in the group. "The best a leader can do is to observe which functions are not being performed by a segment of the group and enable this part to accomplish them. In this way he minimizes the areas of inadequacy of the group."[3] But then Schutz also notes that this concept "also implies that when the group is fulfilling all its functions adequately, the most appropriate behavior for the leader is inaction."[4]

Schutz makes a point of the fact that sometimes the role of the leader can be unpleasant, for it entails putting the welfare of the group before his own. Schutz specifically mentions the need for the leader sometimes to allow himself unfairly to become a scapegoat for the hostility of the group. Then he summarizes the role of the leader.

> One implication of this conception is that for some people, fulfilling these particular leadership functions would not be gratifying to their own interpersonal needs. For some, being the scapegoat voluntarily is not a pleasant way to interact in a group. Hence, the prime requisites for a leader are: 1) to know what functions a group needs; 2) to have the sensitivity and flexibility to sense what functions the group is not fulfilling; 3) to have the ability to get the things needed by his group accomplished; and 4) to have the willingness to do what is necessary to satisfy these needs, even though it may be personally displeasing. This whole conception of leadership is reminiscent of an old saying that "the good king is one whose subjects prosper."[5]

Pastoral Parallels

Several parallels between Schutz's concept and the role of the pastor are evident. The pastor's primary role is not in the final analysis to do the work of the ministry on his own; it is rather to function as a facilitator, to "equip the saints for the work of service, to the building up of the body of Christ" (Eph. 4:12). Five qualifications are necessary.

1. A pastor must understand the leadership requirements of the local church, both task and maintenance behaviors. What are the congregation's tasks, and what are the leadership behaviors required to accomplish these tasks effectively and to maintain within the congregation harmonious interpersonal relationships all the while? The New Testament addresses both of these issues at length.

2. A pastor must have the sensitivity to diagnose in his congregation which of these leadership requirements are and are not being met by members of the group. Where is the congregation smoothly functioning, and in what areas is it lacking? What leadership functions are needed to supply this lack?

3. A pastor must be able to help members of the congregation step in and fulfill those leadership behaviors that are lacking and they are capable of supplying. This requires that the shepherd know his sheep (as does the Good Shepherd, John 10:14)—their abilities and gifts as well as their weaknesses—and that he know how to enable them to fulfill their potential. Here the pastor's role as "example" plays an important part (Titus 1:7; 1 Peter 1:3).

4. Until others are "equipped" to fulfill the needed leadership functions, however, a pastor must be willing to step into the breach to fulfill the needed leadership behaviors himself, as a stopgap means of completing what is lacking in the group. But he must view such measures as temporary, lasting only until he can equip others to exercise their gifts.

5. A pastor must bring to all of this a selfless devotion to the welfare of the group, even though he may be involved in things that are personally displeasing. There is

no room in the pastorate for grasping power or pumping one's own ego. A pastor must come to relish and delight in seeing members of the congregation mature to the point where they take leadership activities on themselves and off the pastor. The good pastor is the one whose congregation prospers.

A Comprehensive Model

The concept of the leader as completer thus seems to capture the many aspects of the pastoral ministry and summarize them into one comprehensive whole. The pastor's goal is to work himself out of a job, so to speak. While at the outset he may have to do virtually everything, the thrust of his ministry is always to facilitate the ministry of others in the congregation. Since Christians today do not typically see themselves as providers of leadership in the church, a pastor may have before him a lifetime of enabling, encouraging, and edifying, repeating again and again the words, "Yes, you can do it—sure you can!" Such a belief in God's people stems from a belief in God, and the sanctifying and enabling power of His Spirit.

The pastor must remember, of course, that he is also a member of the congregation, and as such he must also exercise his own gifts in the service of Christ just like anyone else. Thus the pastor will never so completely work himself out of a job in the congregation as to be idle, even in the best of situations. Ultimately perhaps the ideal is that a pastor should supply only that proportion of the overall leadership needs of the congregation as his gifts and available time, relative to that of the rest of the congregation, dictate.

Such a situation is probably idealistic in most cases or may at best be long in coming. The average pastor will no doubt have to continue in the meantime to complete what is lacking, either by supplying it himself, or better yet, by working to enable some other gifted members of the congregation to supply it. This is the pastor's role in the congregation.

Some Implications

This concept of the pastor's role suggests at least four practical implications.

First, a pastor ought never to do anything in the congregation that someone else can (and will) do. Jay Adams writes,

> It ought to be a rule for every pastor not to do anything himself that a member of his congregation can do (or can be taught to do) as well as (or

better than) himself. Of course, there will be times (in emergencies, in brand new mission churches, etc.) when a pastor must do such things, but he will not make it a practice.[6]

Second, the concept of the leader as completer also suggests that if the pastor, after an extended period of ministry, is still supplying virtually all the leadership in the congregation, then his ministry is failing in a crucial way. The pastor's primary task is to equip the saints for the work of ministry, completing for his part only what is lacking. If after a period of time the congregation continues to depend solely or largely on the pastor for leadership behavior, the pastor's ministry is not succeeding in its central goal.

Third, the concept of the leader as completer also enables the pastor to involve others in the ministry without feeling like a shirker. The goal is not simply to get out of work (in the average congregation there will always be more than enough to do) but to enable others to become involved in the ministry. It is *inherent* in the pastor's job that he seek to prompt others to take leadership, as defined here. If both the congregation and the pastor understand the pastor's role in this way, the pastor need no longer feel twinges of guilt about providing less of the congregation's leadership needs this year than last. Equipping others to provide leadership in the congregation is a mark of success in the pastorate, not failure.

Fourth, this concept of the pastoral ministry could be of use to seminaries and Bible colleges in training pastors. Once these young ministers come to understand their central role as *completer*, then they must be taught the *task* and *maintenance* needs of the church. What is the church to be doing, and has God ordained methods of doing it? What then are the task needs of the church and how can they be met? What are the maintenance needs of the congregation and how can they be met? These are questions young ministers need to grapple with.

Pastors in training also need to be taught how to diagnose a congregation to find in any given situation which leadership functions are being met and which are lacking. They need to be taught how to step in and fulfill these needs and, more important still, how to train and motivate others to fulfill them. And perhaps most important of all, students need to be taught what it means to have a pastor's heart, a heart that delights in the successful service of God's people rather than hoarding power and leadership in himself. A true pastor must always say of his people, "They, as members of Christ's body, must increase; I must decrease. I am here to serve them, not them to serve me."

Conclusion

The concept of the leader as completer will not eliminate all the frustrations of the pastorate, but as an overall conceptualization or "model" of the ministry it can perhaps alleviate the identity crisis that seems to plague so many parsonages. The average pastor may still be unduly splintered in his daily activities, but every day he should become a little less so, as he successfully enables others to fill up what is lacking in the church's leadership needs. Moreover, through it all the pastor will have a broad understanding of what each of these diverse activities *mean*. They are all part of a pattern that he understands, a pattern that will ultimately lead to a fully functioning congregation with each member supplying that for which he or she has been gifted, "until we all attain to the unity of the faith, and of the knowledge of the Son of God, to a mature man, to the measure of the stature which belongs to the fullness of Christ" (Eph. 4:13).

CHAPTER 8

Priorities for the Local Church

Raymond C. Ortlund

Peter Drucker, management expert, has consulted with many churches and Christian organizations. He says the first question he always asks them is this: "What are you trying to accomplish?" And often he finds that they are in a crisis of objectives, not a crisis of organization.[1]

The problem most churches face is not that they do not do anything; they do plenty. The problem is that they are not doing the right things.

A pilot announced to his passengers over his intercom system, "Ladies and gentlemen, I have good news and bad news. The good news is that we have a tail wind, and we are making excellent time. The bad news is that our compass is broken, and we have no idea where we are going." A similar situation is true of many churches.

The issue is not that God's promises to the church are inadequate. Dods expands on God's statement, "I am the Almighty God," with these words:

> I am the Almighty God, able to fulfill your highest hopes and accomplish for you the brightest ideal that ever My words set before you. There is no need for paring down the promise until it squares with human probabilities, no need of adopting some interpretation of it which may make it seem easier to fulfill, and no need of striving to fulfill it in any second-rate way. All possibility lies in this: I am the Almighty God.[2]

God's promises to His church are vast. The church is equipped with the power to fulfill every objective God has for it. Certainly its expectation should be to accomplish every goal carved out by God.

Spurgeon said to a young preacher, "Young man, you don't really expect to see high and wonderful things happen in your life, do you?" The fellow said, "Well no . . ." And Spurgeon almost exploded, "Then you won't see them happen, either!"

Genuine expectation is part of the key. But for churches today perhaps a problem greater than low expectation is simply not knowing what their goals should be.

86

Biblical Priorities

What should be a church's biblical priorities? What should its overall objectives include?

Unless these questions are asked, churches will aim at nothing and hit it every time! Many a pastor thinks he has served a church five years or ten years, when actually he has repeated a one-year pastorate five times over, or ten times over. He has no sense of direction for himself or for his people.

Churches must have a philosophy of ministry, a direction, a sense of where they are going. "What is needed today are congregations that understand their unique purpose as a church and concentrate on fulfilling that function."[3]

A decade ago this writer asked the leaders of the congregation he was pastoring, "What should be a church's biblical priorities? What is a church basically to be, whether it is in Africa or South Dakota, whether existing in the year A.D. 200 or 2000?"

After working on a philosophy of ministry for several months, the congregation concluded that it is to be committed first to Jesus Christ, then to one another in Christ, and then to the world Christ died to save.

These three priorities must be kept in proper order. A church must not let its ministry to the world—its evangelism and good works—become of first importance.

Some churches are primarily "evangelistic centers." Most of what is done during the week and on Sunday mornings leads up to one exciting moment: the altar call. That is the focus of the entire life of the church; and it is wonderful to see people walk the aisle to the altar and acknowledge a decision of some kind. But that is not to be the *primary* focus of the church.

Some churches consider themselves "mission centers." These churches raise an extensive amount of money for missions, they have world maps in prominent places with lights twinkling on them, and the people talk a lot about "50–50 budgets" and hear numerous missionary reports from their pulpits. It is wonderful that local churches can help spread the good news in far-off places. But that is not to be the *primary* focus of the church.

Some churches, as "information centers," have as their main purpose the pouring out of biblical material. The people eagerly fill their notebooks, and the one with the fullest notebook and the fullest head is often considered the most spiritual. The pastor of this kind of church is primarily a dispenser of information. But that is not to be the *primary* purpose of the church. Other churches are "program centers." They present one extravaganza after another—gospel magicians, singing groups, ventriloquists, and others. Some churches are "building centered," acquiring an "edifice complex." Their distinctive is only in their buildings. But neither is that to be the *primary* purpose of the church. Still other churches are primarily "fellowship centers," where the emphasis is on "body life," relational theology, discipling, small groups, and the function of gifts. Relationships are exciting and beneficial, but that is not to be the *primary* purpose of the church.

Primarily—first and foremost—the church is to be for the Lord. He is the Head, and He must be the focus, the first priority.

Churches—and individual believers—are to be committed first to Christ, then to one another in Christ, and then to the world. These three are not to be "done" chronologically, one at a time, but they are to be part of churches' and believers' lives all at the same time.

The Bible repeatedly spells out these three priorities, both generally and specifically. In John 15 Jesus wove these into His teaching on the vine and the branches. Verses 1–11 stress the admonition, "Abide in me." That is the first priority. Verses 12–15 focus on the command, "Love each other." That is the second priority. And verses 16–27 say, in essence, "Testify about me." That pertains to the third priority.

In John 17 the prayer of the Lord Jesus to His Father reveals His own personal priorities. In verses 1–5, the emphasis is on God the Father. "Glorify your Son, that your Son may glorify you" (v. 1, NIV). Then in verses 6–19, He prayed for "those whom you gave me out of the world" (v. 6). He prayed for their protection (vv. 11, 15) and their joy (v. 13). And in verses 20–26 His praying extended to the world ("that the world may believe," [v. 21], "to let the world know" [v. 23]).

In Jesus' ministry on earth, these three priorities are clearly evident. He often withdrew from the disciples to be alone with His Father. But then He also gave much time to His inner circle of followers. And he gave Himself in preaching and healing to the people at large.

The Epistles also are heavily loaded with these three elements. In Colossians, for instance, Paul announced that Christ is preeminent (1:16–18). And therefore since Christ is supreme over all believers, His lordship is to be evident in loving relationships with each other (3:12–4:2). And based on the preeminence of Christ and believers' family relationships with each other, Paul gave urgent words: "And pray for us, too, that God may open a door for our message, so that we may proclaim the mystery of Christ, for which I am in chains. Pray that I may proclaim it clearly, as I should. Be wise in the way you act toward outsiders; make the most of every opportunity. Let your conversation be always full of grace, seasoned with salt, so that you may know how to answer everyone" (4:3–6, NIV).

One should not suppose that these three priorities are always given in this order throughout the Scriptures, for they are not. But they *are* in these passages cited, and they help to provide balance for church ministries.

The First Priority: The Lordship of Christ

The Scriptures cry out that at the top, at the center, in the front, and underneath, all that believers are and have is Christ. Paul told the Christians in Colossae that Jesus Christ is supreme (Col. 1:18). All creation is His work and exists for Him (vv. 15–17a). He holds it all together (v. 17b). He is the Head and source of the church (v. 18).

The lordship of Christ, however, is not some truth a Christian can leave as he goes on to deeper teaching. No believer ever outgrows this relationship to Christ. Every aspect of life is to be carried out continually in the light of this truth.

Many churches state in some way in their doctrinal statement that Christ is Lord and Head over all that the people are and do. But often there is a gap between a church's theology and its practice because of a failure to discern fully the implications of His lordship. Believers must learn to acknowledge Him "in all [their] ways" (Prov. 3:6).

Acknowledging the lordship of Christ takes constant attention (and an entire lifetime) to live out and experience. Christians are to be humble enough to admit the possibility that in some areas of their lives He indeed is not preeminent. Thus they need to spend time adjusting to Him and His supremacy. With Christ at the center there is movement, rearrangement, empowering.

Christ is in a class by Himself. Believers are to worship Him. They are to bow in reverence to *Him* and no other. "God was pleased to have all His fullness dwell in *Him*" (Col. 1:19). Christ is Lord!

How easy it is to let someone or something else become central. But nothing else works well at the center of a Christian's life. One's wife or husband cannot be central. At death a husband and wife must let go of each other's hands; they must each move into eternity alone. He or she can only be a companion on the way. Nor can one's children be first in life. Eventually they will bolt from home to escape that kind of pressure. Scholarship cannot be central. Some have made the symbols of scholarship—the degrees and letters after their names—so important that almost all of life is absorbed in and for scholarship. Nor should a believer make himself preeminent. Each believer was regenerated in order that Jesus may be exalted. "Seek [continually] first his kingdom and his righteousness, and all these things will be given to you as well" (Matt. 6:33).

Fromke expressed this point when he wrote,

> Believers may not often realize it, but even as believers we are either centered on man, or centered on God. There is no alternative. Either God is the center of our universe and we have become rightly adjusted to Him, or we have made ourselves the center and are attempting to make all else orbit around us and for us![4]

Balance in one's life comes from making sure that Christ is supreme. This is equally true in the corporate lives of churches. If a church is centered on anything, any person, any doctrine, any project, anything but Christ, it is off balance. Such churches are prone to rush here and there after every new program or gimmick that comes along. Eventually such patterns of behavior become deeply entrenched and the church focuses on activities rather than Christ.

The truth that Jesus Christ must be central may seem trite; but if it is taken seriously, its ramifications in a local church will be exciting, creative, and fresh.

> I have learned that there is only one truth that can motivate man simply through life: Christ. Before we can consider ourselves Christians we must have believed in Christ and accepted all the consequences of a radically altered life. Without this first basic commitment, growth in Christ through any church structure is impossible.[5]

Lancelot Andrews prayed so beautifully,

> Be, Lord,
> within me to strengthen me,
> without me to guard me,
> over me to shelter me,

> beneath me to establish me,
> before me to guide me,
> after me to forward me,
> round me to secure me.[6]

The Second Priority: The Body of Christ

People come to Christ individually; but as soon as they are inside the door of faith, they are surrounded by spiritual brothers and sisters. And this new family of God is to be held in high regard.

Paul was amazed that the Macedonian churches had their priorities right. "And they did not do as we expected, but they gave themselves first to the Lord and then to us in keeping with God's will" (2 Cor. 8:5, NIV). Christ was first, but that was not the end of it. They also loved and cared for others in Christ.

The Epistles command believers to unite together on the basis of their new family relationship in Christ. Over and over come the instructions: suffer together (1 Cor. 12:26), rejoice together (Rom. 12:15), carry each other's burdens (Gal. 6:2), restore each other (Gal. 6:1), pray for each other (Rom. 15:30), teach and admonish each other (Col. 3:16), refresh each other (Rom. 15:32), encourage each other (Rom. 1:12), forgive each other (Eph. 4:32), confess to each other (James 5:16), be truthful with each other (Eph. 4:25), spur each other to good deeds (Heb. 10:24), and give to each other (Phil. 4:14–15).

The great emphasis of the New Testament Epistles is clearly that believers are to give themselves generously to each other— in building up each other, in caring for each other, in loving each other, and in keeping peace among themselves. The last phrase of Galatians 6:10 spells out this special priority: "Therefore, as we have opportunity, let us do good to all people, especially to those who belong to the family of believers." Fellow believers are to have a higher priority than those outside of Christ.

How should this "priority two" be carried out? Certainly Christ's followers are to love the entire church by the power of the Holy Spirit's gift of love (Rom. 5:5). They must never make fun of any segment of the church or disparage it in any way. The church is God's redeemed, and each believer is a member of Christ's body. This truth is strongly affirmed in Christ's rebuke to Saul for persecuting believers: "I am Jesus, whom you are persecuting" (Acts 9:5). Christ, as the Head of the universal church, is intimately associated with it. Believers should thus speak well of the church, and should praise God for the whole body of Christ and all its parts.

All believers need to associate with and come under the authority of a local body of Christians. Younger Christians need to learn from older believers who have a wealth of experience in Christ. Adults need the vitality and vision supplied by children and youth. To be well acquainted with the whole spread of ages in a local church is a joyful experience.

Beyond one's participation in a local church one should be related to a select number of Christians in a deeper fellowship. Christ loved all the world and all His many hundreds of followers, but He spent much of His time with His inner circle of Twelve.[7] Paul always traveled with and had around him a small group of encouraging brothers. Paul included several of them in the greetings with which he opened many of his epistles: "Paul . . . and our brother Sosthenes" (1 Cor. 1:1); "Paul . . . and Timothy our brother" (2 Cor. 1:1); "Paul and Timothy, servants of Christ Jesus" (Phil. 1:1); "Paul . . . and Timothy our brother" (Col. 1:1); "Paul, Silas, and Timothy" (1 Thess. 1:1; 2 Thess. 1:1).

Both the Lord Jesus and the Apostle Paul, as they were leaving this life, were careful to say, in essence, "Now don't be the end of the line! You turn around and go make disciples, teaching them everything I've taught you" (Matt. 28:18–20), and "The things you have heard me say pass on to reliable men who will also be qualified to teach others" (2 Tim. 2:2). In other words, they both encouraged others to keep the chain of discipling going.

This writer's life was enriched and deeply changed when in the pastorate he began to meet with a small group of men. He had always had groups around him: but some years ago, as his local church was seeking to take more seriously the models of Christ and of the Apostle Paul, he realized his need to be obedient to the biblical pattern. He called in a few close friends in the church and stressed that he was exhausted because he had not been ministering in full accord with biblical methods. He pointed out, "Jesus worked through a small band of men, and for at least a year I would like you to become that group within our church. I would like two hours a week of your time for us to be together as a fellowship group."

They all with one accord began to make excuse! Understandably they were busy men. Finally one of them said, "This is not a discussion group. This is an altar call." And he went from one to the other saying, "Will you? Will you? Will you?" They all said yes, and that year of fellowship with those brothers provided a new beginning in this writer's life. He learned that he could not live without contact with other believers, at close range.

The Third Priority: The World

Out of one's commitment to Christ and to the church must flow a concern for the world which Christ died to redeem. This logical sequence is seen in John 15: " Abide in me" (v. 4), "love one another" (v. 12), and "go and bear fruit" (v. 16).

If believers put their ministry to the world above their ministry to each other, they are likely to injure each other in the process. This writer has often seen missionaries certainly dedicated to God (priority one) and certainly dedicated to their work (priority three) who have completely overlooked priority two and are lonely Christians, bottled up with their fears and frustrations, not deeply knowing or being known. And this is true of many Christians in this country as well.

If followers of Christ look at their local church as basically an *organization*, they will see the people in it according to their *function*. There is George the choir director, and there is Mrs. Murphy who keeps the Sunday school attendance records. There is Charlie who does not teach his third-grade boys very well, and there is Susie, a student behind in paying her tuition. When people in the church are seen as workers, as producers, they quickly begin to judge each other.

On the other hand, if believers view the local church as basically an *organism*, they will see the people in it as brothers and sisters, as members of the body of Christ, as what they are more than what they do.

Out of commitment to each other must come commitment to the world. This eliminates the mind-set of "God-bless-us-four-and-no-more" exclusivism, Together, in teams, in cooperative strategy, through prayer and through tears, believers are to reach out to the world.

Jesus said that the unity or togetherness of believers is in itself a witness to the world. It proves that they are genuine and that their faith is valid.[8] "A new commandment I give you: Love one another. As I have loved you, so you must love one another. All men will know that you are my disciples if you love one another" (John 13:34–35, NIV).

With those words Jesus began His Upper Room Discourse. And after that discourse He prayed in a similar vein: "I pray also for those who will believe in me through their message, that all of them may be one, Father, just as you are in me and I am in you. May they also be in us so that the world may believe that you have sent me. . . . May they be brought to complete unity to let the world know that you sent me and have loved them even as you have loved me" (John 17:20–21, 23, NIV).

In a sense the unity of believers in Christ is evangelistic, for it gives proof to the world that Christ is the Son sent from God and that God loves them as much as He loves His Son. Love for each other actually helps to teach unbelievers the gospel.

Immediately before His ascension the Lord Jesus said, "As the Father has sent me, I am sending you" (John 20:21). Jesus had come to bring to the world the full-orbed compassion of the Father. He commissioned the Twelve, and He has commissioned all believers with that same ministry.

The early church quickly got the picture. They went out in compassion to the needy world, and they went in teams. As Jesus had sent out the Twelve and the Seventy, so the first believers went out two by two, or in small groups.

Peter and John teamed up, showing their unity in Christ. Such an unlikely pair! It is interesting that in the early chapters of Acts their names were frequently linked in service and in preaching (Acts 3:1, 3–4, 11; 4:13, 19; 8:14).

Paul, Barnabas, and John Mark teamed up. On other occasions Paul was joined by Silas, Timothy, Luke, or others. Only in an emergency situation because of persecution did Philip minister alone in Samaria (Acts 8:4–13), but the apostles in Jerusalem heard about it and quickly sent along Peter and John (8:14–17).

These three priorities form a measurement by which Christians can test whether they are balanced. Is Christ being put first? Or is His preeminence merely a theological truth? Is there joy in fellowshiping with God's family as a local church, and with a few select believers on a deeper level? And is there a genuine, heartfelt reaching to the world? Only when these three priorities are operative and in their proper order is a believer—and a local church—balanced, whole, and biblical.

CHAPTER 9

Obligations of Pastor and Congregation to Each Other

Homer A. Kent, Sr.

In an exhortation to the "good minister of Jesus Christ," the Apostle Paul wrote, "But flee from these things, you man of God; and pursue righteousness, godliness, faith, love, perseverance and gentleness" (1 Tim. 6:11). The pastor in a special sense is a man of God. Therefore the church has a right to expect the things of him that are in conformity with such a designation.

What a Congregation Has a Right to Expect of Its Pastor

1. The church has a right to expect that its pastor will preach the Word of God. If he is a man of God, he ought to proclaim the message of the One whose name he bears. This is his supreme responsibility.

Jesus said to Peter, "Feed my sheep" (John 21:15–17). Paul wrote to Timothy in a most solemn charge, "Preach the Word" (2 Tim. 4:2). He already had said to the elders of Ephesus as he was taking his departure from them for the last time: "Be on guard for yourselves and for all the flock of God, among which the Holy Spirit has made you overseers, to shepherd the church of God which He purchased with His own blood" (Acts 20:28). This is what a congregation has a right to expect—to be fed with the manna from heaven. To engage in such a ministry is a holy and incomparable privilege.

When Andrew Jackson became president of the United States in 1829, he was overwhelmed with office seekers. Among them was a minister of the gospel. Mr. Jackson said to him, "And what do you do here?" He replied, "I am a minister of the gospel," whereupon Jackson said, "Then go home, my dear man, and preach for I have no office so high as that." The man of God must preach the Word. Let there be no hunger in the pew for lack of it.

2. The church has a right to expect its pastor to have a shepherd's

heart. The word "pastor" means shepherd. It is taken from the sheepfold with all the close contacts the shepherd has with his flock. To be a good pastor the man of God must have a heart of compassion, an intense desire to minister to needy individuals. In this respect he ought to be like the Good Shepherd whom he represents. Christ, as a Shepherd, looked on the multitudes with all their sin and need, and longed to help them, and did.

The minister must love people, the little children, the vivacious youth, those of mature years who bare so many of life's burdens, and older people as well. He must be sympathetic with those who are ill and depressed. He must seek through love and personal contact to win the erring back to fellowship with God.

The day for old-fashioned pastoral visits is not past. The complexities of modern life may often make it difficult, but the good pastor will not fail to enter the homes of his parishioners in time of need. He will follow the example of the apostle who ministered "publicly and from house to house" (Acts 20:20). The church has a right to expect that its pastor will develop skill in ministering to their hearts and homes.

3. The church has a right to expect that its minister will be free from reproach in his personal life and habits. A favorite word of Paul in his Pastoral Epistles is "godliness." It appears 10 times in the three letters. In one brief exhortation he wrote to Timothy, "Discipline yourself for the purpose of godliness" (1 Tim. 4:7). This is a matter about which every minister should be greatly concerned lest he fail to maintain a high standard of godly living. Therefore in harmony with the Word of God every congregation has a right to expect its leader to lead a life beyond reproach, free from bad or questionable habits, a life of good report, "a vessel for honor, sanctified, useful to the Master" (2 Tim. 2:21).

4. The congregation has a right to expect that its pastor will keep his own spirit under control. Often he will see things that will arouse his ire. But a part of the fruit of the Spirit is self-control. A minister who loses his temper and speaks in a rage will lose his influence. In a church business meeting things may not go according to his desire, and words may be spoken that will meet with his disapproval. Then is the time to manifest self-control. It will win in the end. At the Leipzig debate of 1519 between Martin Luther and Johann Eck, Luther held a bunch of flowers in his hand and when bitter words were spoken he would smell them. It seemed to ease the tension.[1]

5. The church has a right to expect its pastor to be generous in his giving to the Lord's work. It would be inconsistent for him to stress the grace for giving if he is stingy in his own giving. He ought to be liberal for the sake of his example as well as for the blessing it will bring to his own soul. Let the pastor not only preach the responsibility of stewardship; let him also be an honest steward himself (1 Cor. 4:2).

6. The church has a right to expect its minister to be a student. He cannot neglect his study and expect to keep fresh and interesting. The quickest way for a minister to fossilize is to neglect studying. This is a matter of life and death to his usefulness. He must always be a student of the Word, using every available means to make his study more meaningful. He must seek to become more effective in presenting the life-giving Word to others. He must also be a student of the times and of human nature, to be better equipped to relate the Word to particular needs.

Interestingly even when Paul was in prison and soon to be executed he was still a student. He made request for his "books" and "parchments" (2 Tim. 4:13). There would be more long and fruitful pastorates if all ministers would follow Paul's example.

7. The church has a right to expect the pastor to be filled with the Spirit of God. To be filled with the Holy Spirit is the privilege of every Christian. But who needs this filling so much as a pastor? With the message of God to declare and the life of godliness to be exemplified, he must have an emptying of self and a filling of the Spirit if he is to fulfill his task and bear the likeness of his Master. There can be no substitute for this.

What the Pastor Has a Right to Expect of His Congregation

Besides a church expecting certain things of its pastor, the pastor has a right to expect certain things of his church. The pastoral relationship is a two-sided affair, if the work of the church is to prosper. No pastor can do his best without the cooperation of his members. Neither can a church perform its best ministry without the cooperation of its pastor. Complete harmony between pastor and congregation is essential if the work of God is to prosper.

1. The pastor has a right to expect a growth in Christian experience on the part of his congregation. Paul was "confident of this very thing, that He who began a good work in you will perfect it until the day of Christ Jesus" (Phil. 1:6). In other words he

expected to see evidences of spiritual growth on the part of God's children. They should not always be babies feeding on the bottle of spiritual immaturity.

God expects believers to grow. "But grow in the grace and knowledge of our Lord and Savior Jesus Christ" (2 Peter 5:18). Unless His children permit things to come into their lives that cause spiritual disease or fail to partake of proper spiritual food, there will be growth. These two things inhibit spiritual growth, and it is the believer's fault if they are present to stunt development in the things of God. When a pastor faithfully proclaims God's Word, he has a right to expect that his members will apply it to their lives and thus become separated from the diseases of the soul that retard spiritual growth. He also has reason to expect that they will feed on the Scriptures, which will enable them to develop spiritually.

2. The pastor has a right to expect that a critical spirit will be kept in abeyance. Paul prayed on behalf of the Philippians that "your love may abound still more and more in knowledge and all discernment" (Phil. 1:9). From this it may be said that if there is to be judgment or criticism of fellow-members in the church, it should be done in love and with a constructive purpose. Unfortunately some believers are too quick in judging the motives of others. Often these snap judgments are wrong and cause serious emotional injury.

Need it be said that there ought to be fair judgment with respect to the pastor? The present writer once heard of a church member who carried with him a notebook in which he kept a list of the mistakes of his pastor. Of course there is always room for helpful, constructive criticism. But there is no room for faultfinding, censorious, heartless criticism. They belittle the one guilty of them, injure the one toward whom they are directed, and hurt the testimony of the church; for to a large extent the pastor represents the congregation in the community.

One wonders how many slanderous criticisms, how much gossip and injurious talk would actually be expressed, if love controlled the heart. Yet this is the ideal the apostle set before believers.

3. The pastor has a right to expect approval on the part of his congregation of all that relates to sound doctrine. Paul prayed that believers might "approve the things that are excellent" (Phil. 1:10), that is, to be able to discern what is best. The verb rendered "approve" is δοκιμάζω, which was used of assaying or testing

metals to determine whether the ore was good or worthless. And so members of the church ought to be able to distinguish readily between such things as salvation and rewards, law and grace, the church and the kingdom; and Israel, the Gentiles, and the church of God. As Unger has written "Failure to distinguish themes that differ is one of the most prolific sources of the doctrinal jumble that parades under the aegis of the church of Christ."[2]

4. The pastor has a right to expect sincerity in the life of his members. Paul prayed that believers may be "sincere and blameless until the day of Christ" (Phil. 1:10*b*). The word "sincere" (εἰλικρινεῖς) comes from two Greek words which taken together mean "to judge by sunlight," as when a jar is held up to the light to see if it has any cracks or flaws. The verb has the idea of being pure and unsullied, free from offense. Sincerity is the opposite of hypocrisy, affectation, deceitfulness, dishonesty. Christians are expected to be separate from all spiritual uncleanness. They are to be radiant examples of the faith, to be fully separated to the things of God.

The sincerity of one's profession will be manifest by a consistent daily walk with God and a constant interest in and support of the things of God. Such a person will indeed reckon himself or herself dead to sin and alive to God. Others will sense that he or she has experienced God's transforming power. The pastor has a right to expect sincerity and commitment on the part of his membership, including faithful attendance at church.

5. The pastor has a right to expect that his members will apply the truth to their daily living. Paul desired that Christians be "filled with the fruit of righteousness" (Phil. 1:11). The imputed righteousness of the believer ought to be expressed in righteous living before the world. This is the principal thing for which a pastor labors. He rejoices every time he sees Christian graces exemplified in his members. His heart is saddened when he sees failure at this point. God has supplied the means whereby His children can have victory in their lives and He expects no less than this from them.

Thus the pastor expects from his congregation much more than can be expected from those of the world who do not know Christ. He looks for the fruit of "love, joy, peace, patience, kindness, goodness, faithfulness, gentleness, self-control" (Gal. 5:22–23). When a pastor sees these qualities in his people, he rejoices and takes courage, for he knows the Word of God is having its effect and believers are growing in the knowledge and likeness of the Lord Jesus Christ.

These expectations on the part of congregations and pastors are reasonable and biblical. Their realization will make the church the dynamic witness the Lord intended it to be.

CHAPTER 10

The Credibility of the Preacher

Donald R. Sunukjian

In 1947 three groups of college students listened to the same recorded speech—a 15-minute address advocating compulsory health insurance for all Americans. The first group was told that the speech was by Eugene Dennis, Secretary-General of the Communist Party of America. The second audience was told that the voice belonged to Dr. Thomas Parran, Surgeon General of the United States. Those in the third group were told that the speech was given by an anonymous Northwestern University sophomore.

Before hearing the speech, each student marked a ballot indicating whether he thought health insurance should be compulsory in the United States (Yes, No, or Undecided). After listening to the recording, each student then marked his after-speech opinion as compared with his original opinion (i.e., More Sure, Less Sure, Change to Yes, Change to No, Change to Undecided, No Change).

The results showed that the speech by "Dr. Parran" caused more people to change, and to change to a greater degree, than did either of the other two speeches.[1] Since all groups had heard the same recording, the differing results had to be due to the varying credibilities of the speakers. The difference in effectiveness was not due to *what* was said, but to *who* said it.

This early study was one of the first statistical demonstrations of the power of ethos in communication.[2]

The Definition of Ethos

The term *ethos* comes from classical rhetoric and refers to the perceived credibility of the speaker. A preacher's ethos is the opinion his listeners have of him as a person. If their opinion of him is high, he will have high ethos, or great credibility, with them. This means they will be inclined to believe whatever he says. On the other hand if their opinion of him is low, his ethos or credibility will be poor, and they will "turn him off" even before he speaks.

It should be noted that ethos is a perceived quality, not an actual one. It is not what the speaker is, but what the listener thinks him to be. Just as beauty is in the eye of the beholder, so ethos is in the mind of the listener.

Since credibility, therefore, depends on the hearer's perception and affects whether he will respond to the message, it would be helpful to know the factors that contribute to the listener's opinion of the speaker. If preachers know what determines their listeners' impressions of them, they can work with this knowledge for God's good.

The Dimensions of Ethos

Researchers have isolated two separate dimensions of ethos.[3] The first dimension is *competency*. If a listener feels that the speaker is competent—intelligent, alert, accurate, qualified—he will assign him high credibility and will be inclined to respond to his message. On the other hand if the listener concludes that the speaker is muddleheaded, uninformed, lethargic, and inept, he will judge him as incompetent and tend to discard his words.

The second dimension of ethos is *character*. If a listener has a high view of the speaker's character, seeing him as a man who is without guile and growing in godliness, he is more apt to be affected by his words. If, however, he feels that the speaker is self-centered, manipulative, or deceitful, he will be less likely to accept his message.

These two dimensions operate independently in any given preaching situation. A speaker can be high in one and low in the other, thus mixing his potential impact. But to the extent that he can communicate both competency and character, he will increase his effectiveness as a speaker. How then does a preacher communicate competency and character?

COMMUNICATING COMPETENCY

Experimenters have determined that speakers communicate competency and gain credibility by means of an attractive appearance, a fluent delivery, an organized message, and an evident awareness of human events.

Personal appearance. Mills and Aronson discovered that an attractive speaker will more successfully influence the views of an audience than an unattractive one.[4] They arranged for a young woman to be in the audience of several college classes. As each class began, the instructor explained that he was conducting a study of how students feel about the relative values of a broad liberal-arts education versus a specialized career-oriented program. He wanted them to answer a questionnaire on this topic, but felt that the results would be much more valid if they could have a chance to think about the questions beforehand. Therefore in order to familiarize them with the questionnaire he asked for a volunteer to respond publicly to the questions first.

In each of the classes the young woman "volunteered" and was "chosen" by the instructor. For some of the classes she had been made to look extremely attractive. Her clothes were fashionable, her hair was stylish, her makeup was becoming. For other classes, she had been made to look unattractive. She wore ugly, ill-fitting clothes, her hair was messy, makeup was conspicuously absent, the trace of a mustache was on her upper lip, and her complexion was oily and unwholesome looking.

In responding to the questionnaire in front of the group, the woman gave previously prepared answers which showed an extreme preference for a general liberal-arts education. In all class situations, both attractive and unattractive, she gave identical responses to the questions. When she had completed her answers, the questionnaires were distributed to the rest of the students. Each student's response was then compared to his answers given two months earlier to an opinion survey on this and other topics. The results of the experiment showed that when the communicator was attractive she was more effective in influencing the audience toward her view.

Someone might counter that clothes and grooming are not real indicators of competency. Logically this objection is true, but psychologically the listener's mind makes a connection between the two. Contemporary "Dress for Success" books and articles are premised on this subconscious judgment. Preachers, therefore, need to be concerned about their appearance.

Perhaps the spirit of Paul—"I have become all things to all men so that by all possible means I might save some" (1 Cor, 9:22, NIV)—might include having clothes that are clean, tasteful, and moderately in fashion. Such simple things as shined shoes, pressed pants, clean nails, combed hair, and pleasant breath might also help convey to others that God's man is capable to minister.

This same attractiveness should characterize church materials and programs. Letters should be produced on a good typewriter or printer and be free from error, bulletins and brochures should be aligned on both margins and printed with offset quality, overhead transparencies and other visuals should be graphic and clear, slide presentations and films should unfold without hitch. All these will communicate an aura of excellence because a perception of competence comes from appearance.

Delivery. Competency is also communicated by means of a fluent delivery. The more sure a speaker is of his words, the more competent he will strike his audience. But if he gropes for words ("For *uh* the benefit of our children we ought to *uh* . . ."), his credibility will go down.

Miller and Hewgill played an identical message to five groups.[5] The only difference was the number of nonfluencies (*uh's*) occurring within each message. One group heard a message containing no nonfluencies, which was 1,054 words in length and approximately seven minutes and 15 seconds in duration. The other four groups heard the same speech, the only difference being the frequency with which the speaker groped for words. These frequencies were 25, 50, 75, and 100, or one groping for words (*uh*) every 42, 21, 14, and 10.5 seconds respectively.

	Number of nonfluences				
	0	25	50	75	100
Mean Competency Ratings	22.8	18.9	15.9	16.3	15.6

Immediately after hearing the message, each listener rated the anonymous speaker as to his perceived competency. As the following chart indicates, the mean ratings on a scale of 4 to 28 (28 being the highest competency score possible) were fairly consistent. The scores reveal that the greater the fluency, the greater the perception of competency[6]

The encouragement to preachers is obvious. They must know what they are to say and be able to say it without groping or stumbling. They must have the sermon "under their belts," This may require writing the message in full, or practicing before a mirror, or listening to themselves on tape. However it is achieved, the words must flow smoothly, for that is what helps the listener to say, "He knows what he's talking about."

Organization. A third way to gain credibility is to be clear and organized in one's preaching. Sharp and McClung found that the attitude of an audience significantly changes toward a speaker who delivers a disorganized speech.[7] They prepared two speeches. One was judged by a panel of experts to be well organized. The other was identical in content, but was constructed by randomizing the sentences within the introduction, body, and conclusion. As measured by pretests and posttests, the listeners "exposed to a disorganized speech thought less of the speaker after his talk than before he spoke."[8]

Church audiences also grow in their respect for a preacher whose sermons are clearly structured. Their esteem and openness heighten as their mind acknowledges, "He's easy to follow," or "I understand what he's trying to say." This is in contrast to that bewilderment or occasional stupor that masks the realization, "I have no idea what he's talking about."

Since the latter complaint will seldom be voiced loud enough for the preacher to make midcourse correction, he must prepare against it in the study. Every outline should be honed to a singular focus and an orderly flow. There should be unity to the message as a whole and observable progression from point to point. Subpoints must be logically subordinate to main points. Transitions must stand out to the ear of the listener. "Restatement"[9] should occur in previews, reviews, and whenever a new point emerges. All these will bring a clarity that commends the preacher and that opens a channel for impact.

Human events. Listeners respect a speaker who is aware of what they are aware of. They have confidence in a man who knows the same things they know, whose wide-ranging interests reveal a familiarity with their world of news, jobs, stresses, and personal situations.

"Opinion leadership" research has demonstrated that certain people exercise more influence in communicative situations than others. Characteristically, these opinion leaders tend to be great consumers of the mass media: "They listen more, read more, and view more [instructional] television than their followers."[10] They also tend to interact more: "They ask for information and they give information. . . . There is a constant interactive process going on."[11] As a result, they are more knowledgeable concerning world and national affairs, social and ethical issues, economic trends, business practices, scientific discoveries, and individual hobbies.

The man of God should be a voracious assimilator of

knowledge. He should subscribe to a local newspaper and to national magazines, both secular and Christian. He should understand the local teachers' strike, the rippling effect of government policies, and the arguments for and against various debatable issues. Above all, in his daily contacts he should be inquisitive, always learning from people about their jobs, schools, families, skills, stresses, and decisions. Then, as this wide-ranging familiarity with human life shows in his preaching, the hearer will perceive that he is competent to bring the eternal Word to a modern world.

COMMUNICATING CHARACTER

The second dimension of ethos is character. Listeners respond more readily to a speaker they like and can trust. Even more important than the perception of competency is the conviction that the speaker is a man of admirable personal qualities and that he has the hearers' best interests at heart.[12] Centuries ago Aristotle wrote that a man's own character is perhaps his most persuasive power.

> We believe good men more fully and more readily than others. This is true generally whatever the question is, and absolutely true where exact certainty is impossible and opinions are divided. . . . It is not true, as some writers assume in their treatises on rhetoric, that the personal goodness revealed by the speaker contributes nothing to his power of persuasion; on the contrary his character may almost be called the most effective means of persuasion he possesses.[13]

The listener's evaluation of character falls into two categories— what he thinks of the speaker, and what he thinks the speaker thinks of him. Stated in other words, a preacher's ethos is high and his potential for effectiveness is great when the listener can make the twofold statement, "I like him, and he likes me."

"I like him." The importance of developing admirable personal qualities and of having these qualities apparent to the listener was demonstrated in an experiment involving four audiences. A fifteen-minute talk was prepared on the assets and liabilities of the American political system. The speech itself was couched in sufficiently temperate terms so that if read it would create no strong bias for or against the American system. Four professional actors were enlisted to deliver the speech, two male and two female, all of average physical build and personal appearance. One male and one female were asked to simulate socially obnoxious

and unfriendly traits during delivery. The other male and female were instructed to win over their audiences if possible with charm and goodwill. After each speaker had addressed his group the listeners were asked to indicate agreement or disagreement with the talk as a whole on small cards. The results of the 100 listeners were as follows:

Listeners	Admirable Speakers		Obnoxious Speakers	
	Male	Female	Male	Female
Agreeing with	25	17	7	4
Disagreeing with	5	3	23	16

The conclusion is simple but profound: Listeners tend to agree with a speaker they like and disagree with one they do not like.[14]

The application to preachers is, of course, as inexhaustible as the forms of godliness. To the extent they commend themselves to others—whether by elder qualities (1 Tim. 3; Titus 1), the Spirit's fruit (Gal. 5:22–23), or their worthy walk (Eph. 4–6)—to that extent they woo others to God's truth. As others see what manner of men they are, those people become imitators of the messengers and the Lord (1 Thess. 1:5–6). As they find the preachers' Christlikeness attractive, they find the message compelling. As they like the preacher, they like what he says.

This likeableness is communicated in a thousand ways: how they treat their wife and children; how they handle their money; whether they are stable in temperament and self-disciplined in eating; whether they avoid one-sided views and premature judgments; whether they are teachable and rebukeable and in the process of growing .

Most of all, a preacher gains others' favor as they note the absence of pride. As this first and greatest sin abates, the mind of Christ takes hold in the communicator, and grace and truth are beheld once again. To find a preacher who is not building his own reputation, who is not miffed if another part of the service is more meaningful than his sermon, and who freely pushes others to occupy the spotlight, is to find a man who is liked and listened to.

"He likes me." When a listener feels a speaker loves him, he is ready to accept almost anything the speaker says.

When a listener says to himself, "I feel safe with this speaker; I do not doubt his motives; I do not believe he would knowingly harm me or lead me wrong; I believe he means me well; he can be trusted because of his kind intention toward me"—then that listener has given that speaker great access to his heart.

How does a preacher convey that he has his listeners' best interests at heart? What can he do to cause the listener to say, "He likes me"?

One of the main things he can do is *smile*! A preacher's facial expression is the single most important factor in whether his hearers will feel liked or not. Listeners judge from a speaker's face far more than from his words or even his tone of voice as to whether he is favorably disposed toward them or not. Two studies have documented first the value of "tone of voice" over "content of words," and then second, the overwhelming value of "facial expression" over both of these.

In the first study Mehrabian and Wiener chose nine words to be played to college students.[15] Three of the words conveyed positive content—"honey," "thanks," and "dear." Three conveyed neutral content—"maybe," "really," and "oh." Three conveyed negative content—"don't," "brute," and "terrible." Each of the nine words was read in three tones of voice—positive, neutral, and negative. The reader was instructed to say the words, irrespective of contents, in such a way as to convey (a) an attitude of liking, high evaluation, or preference; (b) a neutral attitude, that is, neither liking nor disliking; and (c) an attitude of disliking, low evaluation, or lack of preference. All possible combinations of three contents and three tones were recorded on tape, and a random order of the combinations was then played to each student individually. The students were told to imagine each of the words as being said by the speaker to another person, and to judge the degree of the speaker's positive versus negative attitude toward the addressee.

Some of the students were instructed to take both aspects of the word into consideration—content and tone. Others were told to make their judgment only on the content of the words and to ignore the tone of voice. Still others were instructed to use only the tone and to ignore the content-meaning of the words. On a scale of +3 to –3, the results were as follows:

Inferred Attitude of Speaker

Instructions	Content	Tone		
		Negative	Neutral	Positive
Use content only	Negative	-1.33	-1.00	-0.67
	Neutral	-0.47	-0.17	0.35
	Positive	1.03	1.30	1.70
Use tone only	Negative	-2.47	-0.03	1.40
	Neutral	-2.07	-0.67	1.73
	Positive	-1.37	0.17	1.63
Use tone and content	Negative	-1.77	-0.30	1.21
	Neutral	-1.67	-0.40	1.10
	Positive	-0.87	0.40	1.10

These results show that when the students consciously focused on either the content or the tone, their judgments reflected the positive or negative force of that single aspect. But when the students were left to respond to the total communication, the tone of voice had a disproportionately greater effect on their judgment. They inferred the speaker's attitude from his tone of voice, even when the content of his words pointed in the opposite direction.

In the second study, Mehrabian and Ferris instructed three female speakers to vary their tone of voice while saying the neutral word "maybe," so as to communicate like, neutrality, and dislike toward an imagined addressee.[16] In addition, photographs were taken of three female models as they attempted to use facial expressions to communicate like, neutrality, and dislike toward another person. All possible combinations of positive, neutral, and negative tones of voice and facial expressions were then presented to individual students. Each student was shown photographs of different facial expressions and at the same time heard recordings of the word "maybe" spoken in different tones of voice. He was told to imagine that the person he was seeing and hearing (A) was looking at and speaking to another person (B). For each presentation the student was to indicate on a scale of +3 to −3 what he thought A's attitude was toward B. The following table expresses the results:

Inferred Attitude of Speaker

	Facial Expression		
Tone of Voice	Positive	Neutral	Negative
Positive	2.45	1.31	-0.91
Neutral	1.33	0.50	-1.62
Negative	0.20	-1.07	-2.47

These results indicate that listeners are more affected by a speaker's facial expression than they are by his tone of voice when judging his attitude toward them. What they see on his face tells them even more than what they hear, whether he likes them or not.

Putting the two studies together, Mehrabian and Ferris suggest that a listener's decision as to whether he is liked or disliked will be influenced seven percent by the speaker's content, 38 percent by his tone of voice, and 55 percent by his facial expression.[17]

A preacher's smile, therefore, more than any other single thing, says to his people, "I love you." As he stands by a door, or walks through the halls, or strolls across the grounds, his warm glance, his cheery wave, his hearty laugh all convey his enjoyment of God's people. As he stands to preach, his pause to embrace the audience with a smile says to them, "I'm glad to be here, I'm glad you're here, I like you, and I have a good word from God for us."

When a preacher's smile is followed by loving tones and gracious words, he completes the message of his favor toward his listeners. His preaching does not scold or berate or assume the continuous failure of God's people, but rather woos and encourages and commends their growth. The motivations of guilt and fear are balanced by reasonings that are attractive and by visualizations of God's full pleasure. No unwholesome talk comes out of his mouth, but only what is helpful for building others up (Eph. 4:29). A bruised reed he does not break, and a smoldering wick he does not snuff out (Isa. 42:3). And what was said of his Lord is said of him—he is full of grace as well as truth (John 1:14).

Conclusion

Competency and character—these determine the preacher's credibility. His competency is suggested by his appearance, delivery, clarity, and awareness of human events. But the perception of his character depends on the work of God in his life. And in the end, it is this work that will make all the difference in his effectiveness. "How good we are as preachers depends—not altogether, but (make no mistake!) primarily—on how good we are as men."[18]

CHAPTER 11

A Paradigm for Preaching

Timothy S. Warren

The challenge of Christian ministry is to proclaim God's changeless eternal truth while applying it to ever-changing temporal situations. This demand is especially acute in the realm of homiletics. The biblical preacher must recognize and represent the timeless truth of God's Word and then relate that truth to his audience.

That the world is changing stimulated the writers of *Megatrends 2000*, for example, to describe the "large social, economic, political, and technological changes" that "influence us . . . between seven and ten years, or longer."[1] Sociology of religion, more specifically, has identified a shift in religious attitudes and behavior in recent decades. Changing postures toward law and formal education, transitioning from an agricultural to an industrial to an informational economy and work ethic, and media permeation have left North Americans feeling disconnected from God, themselves, and others.[2] Unable, or perhaps unwilling, to understand and respond, preachers have failed the challenge, capitulating to culture and offering mere fragments of meaning, personhood, and fraternity.

> Rather than saying to culture, "This is what religion is," [the churches] have been much more inclined to say to culture, "What do you want religion to be?" Rather than presenting religion as a system of meaning that insists on informing all of one's life, the [churches] have broken it down and offered it as a wide variety of belief practice, program, and service items.[3]

Many are preaching to independent, insignificant, and isolated listeners[4] in search of transcendence, significance, and community.[5]

> Here then are the three major quests in which many people are engaged today. Though they probably would not articulate them in this way, it may be said that looking for transcendence, they are trying to find God; looking for significance, they are trying to find themselves; looking for community, they are trying to find their neighbor. For this is humankind's universal search—for God, for one's neighbor, and for oneself.[6]

At each point of disconnection, society has lost contact with authority and relevancy. Contemporary legal theory, no longer based on universals, has resulted in a relativistic pluralism that replaces right and wrong with "rights."[7] Advances in industrialization and information, which demand increasing technological specialization rather than philosophical deliberation, have led to a decrease in individual creativity and responsibility for the final product.[8] Materialistic consumerism, devoted to personal well-being and security, has perpetuated the false doctrine of egalitarianism in which egotistic individuality has replaced sympathetic relations.[9] Henry laments, "The self has displaced the soul, values have replaced right and wrong, openness and autonomy have eroded authority. In short, modern man has become 'spiritually detumescent.'"[10]

The Preaching Challenge

The challenge is clear. Preachers must address the demands for authority and relevancy.[11] Bibby concluded that "when religion becomes . . . wedded to culture, it finds that its authority is . . . eroded." Then he added, "But if there are elements of religion that transcend culture, ideas that claim to have more than only a cultural source, then religion . . . should find itself . . . 'contradicting the times.'"[12] This authority must eventuate, however, in relevance, for the "old *content* [authority] may need to be translated if it is to be understood, and . . . old *forms* [relevance] may need to be torn down in order for the old and valued product to be transmitted with success."[13] Addressing authority and relevance in the three spheres of human quest renders a value-added result that fragmented preaching never achieves.

> When religion doesn't stop with God but reaffirms the potential of individuals, and further is concerned about interpersonal ties both proximate and global, it has the possibility of having a measure of influence over how lives are lived. When religion is presented as something that is intended to address all of life, it at least has the potential to influence some aspects of life. When reduced to consumer-oriented fragments, however, it predictably has a significant influence on the values and concerns of relatively few.[14]

The goal, then, is to demonstrate in preaching both the authority and the relevance of God's Word to listeners' search for God, themselves, and others.

THE QUESTION OF AUTHORITY

If people are listening for messages that carry elements of authority to guide their lives, where will they find such authority? What in the preaching event is authoritative? Is it the preacher himself? No. It is the Scriptures that confer authority.

> Since the prophets proclaimed *God's* word, their preaching was authoritative. This relationship suggests that the authority of the prophets did not reside, ultimately, in their person, their calling, or their office; rather, their authority was founded in the word of God they proclaimed. So it is with preachers today: they have a word from the Lord, but only if they speak the Lord's word. The only norm we have today for judging whether preachers speak the word of the Lord is the Bible.[15]

Robinson has warned that

> the man in the pulpit faces the pressing temptation to deliver some message other than that of the Scriptures—a political system (either right-wing or left-wing), a theory of economics, a new religious philosophy, old religious slogans, a trend in psychology. . . . Yet when a preacher fails to preach the Scriptures, he abandons his authority. He confronts his hearers no longer with a word from God but only with another word from men.[16]

God is the source of truth; He has spoken in the written Word, man's only sure authority. Preaching must clearly reflect commitment to divine authority. All true preaching must be biblically based, biblically sourced. And listeners must have some certainty that the message is biblically testable (Acts 17:11). "When we have extracted . . . from the text instead of imposing . . . on it, we may speak with more confidence that the word we share . . . has an authority which is not our own, but is borrowed from the text."[17]

Further, Ross correctly observes that every part of the sermon must be grounded in the text.

> Too many so-called expositors simply make the one central idea the substance of their message. The narrative may be read or retold, but the sermon is essentially their central expository idea—it is explained, illustrated, and applied without further recourse to the text. This approach is not valid exegetical exposition. In exegetical exposition, the *substance* of the exposition must be clearly derived from the text so that the central idea unfolds in the analysis of the passage and so that all parts of the passage may be interpreted to show their contribution to the theological idea.[18]

Exposition must find its substance in the biblical text.[19] Ross further identifies a failure specifically with regard to application made by many preachers. Though his focus is on narrative exposition, the critique carries validity in the preaching of any biblical genre.

> Frequently today in the preaching of Old Testament narrative, the would-be expositor creatively embellishes the narrative in an attempt to make it interesting or relevant, filling in the details and circumstances that the biblical writer left out. Such an expositor frequently draws applications from the material just added to the text. The resulting sermon may be biblical or reflect a biblical philosophy of life, but it did not come from the text being used.[20]

The problem is not in the effort to make relevant, 20th-century application, but in the failure to follow a method that guards the accuracy and authority of the text. Preaching must never exclude relevancy simply because some preachers use a flawed method.

It is at this point that Ross appears unconvinced of the challenge of homiletics. When he argues, "It should be a relatively simple matter to move from the exegetically derived theological statement to the application,"[21] he underestimates, or at least understates, the demands of relevance. Cultural analysis of one's audience and legitimate persuasion are not relatively simple. As Smart argued, as far back as 1970,

> the predicament of the preacher has been created to a large extent by the hiatus between the biblical and the practical departments in our theological seminaries. . . . the biblical departments in seminary rightly make the student labor with care to discern what the text meant when it was first written or spoken. But frequently the assumption is made that, without any further research or assistance or extension of his methodology, he can move from the original meaning to the contemporary meaning, as though there were no serious problems in making that transition.[22]

Showing how the truth of Scripture is relevant to the lives of listeners is the major unaddressed requirement in preaching.

THE QUESTION OF RELEVANCY

God's authoritative Word must be presented in ways relevant to the hearers in their own context. "The . . . ultimate goal in communication has always been to present the supracultural message of the gospel in culturally relevant terms."[23] Preachers must ask, "What about this audience demands a different presentation than any other audience?" They must give more attention to audience analysis[24] and adaptations[25] in order to discover the varying strategies for communicating timeless truth to audiences with distinctive characteristics. Contemporary listeners demand a message that is significant. "Will this truth work?" "How will it work?" These questions must be answered.[26] So preachers must be committed not only to the text, but also to their audience and its specific needs.

Though the call for application is legitimate,[27] how to move to application without sacrificing authority is the question.[28] If the preacher turns to application too early in the process, he risks allowing the audience to influence his exegesis and/or theology, of allowing significance to determine meaning. Phillips Brooks, in his 1877 *Yale Lectures on Preaching* (reprinted in 1989 as *The Joy of Preaching* by Kregel Publications), warned students of this applicational hazard.

> The student preparing to be a preacher cannot learn truth as the mere student of theology for its own sake might do. He always feels it reaching out through him to the people to whom he is some day to carry it. He cannot get rid of this consciousness. It influences all his understanding. We can see that it must have its dangers. It will threaten the impartiality with which he will seek truth. It will tempt him to prefer those forms of truth which most easily lend themselves to didactic uses, rather than those which bring evidence of being most simply and purely true. That is the danger of all preachers. Against that danger the man meaning to be a preacher must be on his guard, but he cannot avoid the danger by sacrificing the habit out of which the danger springs.[29]

How does the preacher prepare and preach with the audience in mind, yet without allowing the audience to influence either the exegetical or the theological process? How does one guard the truth of the message? The answer rests in distinguishing between the separate but related steps of sermon preparation. They are exegesis followed by theology, followed by homiletics. These essential components, processes, or skills must be identified and delimited. Preachers ought never feel pressured into an either/or choice between authority and relevance. If they have a method that allows for both, and they must, then that method can relieve them of the dilemma.

Toward a Homiletical Method

Stott identified the exclusivism that polarizes authority and relevance as "one of the greatest tragedies of our time."[30] He observed that "on the one hand, conservatives are biblical but not contemporary, while on the other liberals and radicals are contemporary but not biblical."[31]

Brooks perceived the problem a century ago. He defined preaching in a way that combines its two necessary elements. "Preaching is the communication of truth by man to men," and just as the apostles were "able to take God's truth in perfectly on one side and send it out perfectly on the other side of their transparent natures," so also the preacher transmits truth "by the opening of his life on both sides, toward the truth of God and toward the needs of man."[32] Arguing that the truth of Scripture never changes, but is the "fixed and stable element" of preaching, Brooks added that this truth must become "related to each special age. It is brought to it through the men of the age. If a preacher is not a man of his age, in sympathy with its spirit, his preaching fails."[33]

Perhaps, for conservatives, the challenge of bringing these two elements together has been complicated by seminary training.[34] Many seminary students learn to do exegesis in the Epistles and learn to preach the Epistles. The Epistles, of course, are especially theological and homiletical in their nature.[35] They do not challenge the preacher to wrestle with the process that takes one through the exegetical, then through the theological, and finally through the homiletical processes. Paul already did all that, and students learn to preach Paul's homiletically developed message. What process he went through to gel his "sermon" is not stated. A paradigm is needed that describes and prescribes a homiletical method that sufficiently attends to both the changeless text (especially in handling nonepistolary genres) and the ever-changing audience.

Recent studies in hermeneutics have helped clarify the issue.[36] Phenomenologists introduced the problem of horizons, pointing out some of the barriers, or supposed barriers, to interpretation as a result of horizon or vision limitations. Having wrestled with the distance between the past and the present, Thiselton concluded,

> "The hermeneutical goal is that of a steady progress towards a fusion of horizons. But this is to be achieved in such a way that the particularity of each horizon is fully taken into account and respected. This means both respecting the rights of the text and allowing it to speak."[37]

How to accomplish this fusion of horizons, especially for the preacher who goes beyond mere interpretation, is not made clear.

In 1982, Stott described this dilemma for preachers. He posed the problem of the two worlds, the world of the ancient text and the world of the immediate audience.

> It is because preaching is not exposition only but communication, not just the exegesis of a text but the conveying of a God-given message to living people who need to hear it, that I am going to develop a different

metaphor to illustrate the essential nature of preaching . . . that of bridge-building.

We should be praying that God will raise up a new generation of Christian communicators who are determined to bridge the chasm; who struggle to relate God's unchanging Word to our ever-changing world; who refuse to sacrifice truth to relevance or relevance to truth; but who resolve instead in equal measure to be faithful to Scripture and pertinent to today.[38]

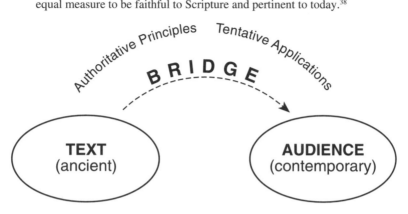

Stott's bridge-building metaphor is more satisfying than the fusion metaphor, which seems to merge the two worlds rather than connect them. Still, he does not describe how this connection is to take place. Stott's conclusion that "the principal features of a preaching ministry which is conceived as an activity of bridge-building between the revealed Word and the contemporary world" are being "authoritative in expounding biblical principles, but tentative in applying them"[39] leaves too much to imagination.

Listening to others preach and trying to learn how to preach, homiletics students may have been led to believe that some kind of "magic" happens when, having carefully gleaned the exegetical meaning of the text, the preacher blinks his eyes and "Behold!" a relevant message appears. The process that enabled preachers to bridge that gap with authority and relevancy has not been delineated.[40] And too often the "blinks" have brought forth ineffective results. One homiletician has written, "As professional skills go, sermon construction ranks among the most inexact."[41] Perhaps a new preaching paradigm, a kind of blueprint for bridge builders, will enable sermon preparers to understand the preaching process in greater detail and isolate the variety of skills necessary for both authoritative and relevant preaching.[42]

A New Paradigm

Although preaching does seek to bridge between the ancient text (expressing authority because of its absoluteness)[43] and the modern audience (demanding tentativeness because of its relativity),[44] the process is more complex than that, as Stott suggests. Rather than a uniform bridge spanning from text to audience, the more detailed paradigm suggested in this chapter shows a full preaching process consisting of four distinct sections connecting four separate points along the way.

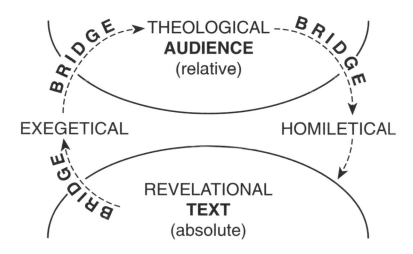

The diagram above reveals the four sections required of authoritative, relevant preaching. Beginning with Scripture, which is God-given and therefore absolute and authoritative,[45] the first step moves the preacher out of the world of the absolute expression of God's truth, into the world of changing expressions[46] of that truth, and toward the product of the exegetical process. This exegetical process begins to bridge the gap between the world of the text and the world of the audience. The exegetical product is a statement of the text's meaning in terms of structure, proposition, and purpose. The next section consists of the theological process, which moves the preacher from the exegetical to the theological product. The theological product is the statement of universal theological principles the preacher has discovered in the text through the exegetical and the theological processes. The third section goes from the theological to the homiletical product. This is the sermon delivered to the listeners. The final section in the entire preaching process involves not only the preacher but also the listeners, whose lives demonstrate change for having heard and responded to the sermon. The process is not completed until God's people think and act differently for having heard the Word expounded. This is the revelational process, for its goal is to manifest or reveal God's truth by living it out.[47] Though this final bridging process moves back toward the absolute, one must be careful to expect not perfection but an approximation of Christ-likeness that points to the absolute perfection.[48]

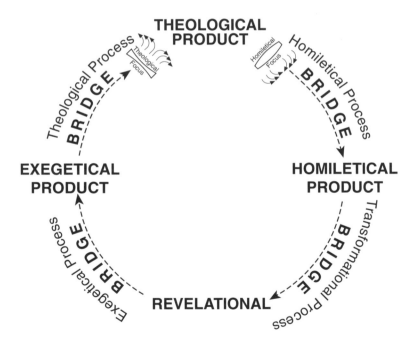

For the method to be helpful, each section must be distinguished and correctly valued. There must be no merging of sections and no eliminating of sections. If, for example, a preacher allows his knowledge of the audience to enter into the exegetical process, he may read them into the text and discover a 20th-century meaning rather than a first-century meaning. Also if he skips the theological process, for example, he risks applying a temporal or limited principle such as requiring observance of the Sabbath.

EXEGESIS

The move from text to the first product of the preaching process, the exegetical, demands the process of exegesis. This process follows the grammatical, syntactical, historical-contextual, literary-rhetorical, literal approach to understanding the meaning of the text.[49] The exegetical bridging spiral represents the retroductive apprehension[50] of whole and part, beginning with a heuristic guess as to the meaning of the passage and culminating in a validated claim. The exegete thereby discovers the exegetical supporting material, structure, proposition,[51] and purpose of the text studied. The interplay between the Holy Spirit and the human spirit makes the process spiritual as well as objective/subjective.[53]

The exegete's theology and audience must have been bracketed out[54] of the exegetical process so that their influence will not interfere with discerning the meaning of the text in its own context. As Greidanus implies, exegesis must be completed before starting theological labor, and that must be completed before homiletical inquiries commence. "*Once* the theme of that text has been formulated in its literary context, [*then*] that theme should be traced through the Scriptures for confirmation. . . . *With that information*, it should be projected onto the horizon of the contemporary audience."[55] It is also essential that the exegete constantly test his exegetical discoveries against available evidence. "An ungrounded belief is easily swayed and abandoned, even though it might be correct. Only when we have provided warrant for our beliefs can we avoid changing our minds irrationally or believing irresponsibly."[56] Exegetical judgments must demonstrate both reasonableness and rationalness.[57]

The result of the exegetical process is the exegetical product. The significant textual details will be recorded, structure laid out, proposition articulated, and purpose expressed. These four products will be surrounded and supported by reasonable and rational arguments of a grammatical-syntactical, historical-contextual, literary-rhetorical, literal nature.

THEOLOGY

Once the exegetical conclusions have been sufficiently identified, the preacher begins the theological process. Based on, but going beyond the exegetical,[58] the (now) theologian seeks to identify the biblical theology of the passage. He "is concerned with the reason why something was written as well as with the content of what was written. [He] not only examines the product but investigates the procedures and presuppositions that went into the writing of the Scriptures."[59] His concern is not yet with the final meaning of the teachings of the entire Bible (systematic theology) nor with the relevance of that meaning for today, contemporary application. These elements of the entire process will be bracketed out for the moment. His goal is to identify what the writer of the text in question regarded as truth from his particular historical/theological perspective.

> Every Biblical text has within it some facet of theology expressed in such a way as to be part and parcel of the fabric of its contents. While that theology cannot be torn from that text, it, nevertheless, often has roots which were laid down *antecedent* to that text.
> The only correction that we know for past and present abuses that have taken place in the name of doing theological exegesis is to carefully restrict the process to (1) examination of explicit affirmations found in the text being exegeted and (2) comparisons with similar (sometimes rudimentary) affirmations found in passages that have *preceded* in time the passage under study.
> . . . in our summaries we should point out [later theological] developments for the sake of updating and putting everything in its fullest context. However, in no case must that *later* teaching be used exegetically (or in any other way) to unpack the meaning or to enhance the usability of the individual text which is the object of our study.[60]

Like the exegetical, the theological process is retroductive rather than deductive or inductive. The theologian does not labor to prove that something must be, or that it actually is, but rather that it may be.[61] He seeks to present the Spirit-intended theology that "fits the facts" expressed in the text.[62] Thus the theological spiral represents not only the retroductive apprehension of whole and part, but also the interplay of the Holy Spirit and the human spirit.

At the end of the theological section is the theological focus. This lens represents systematic theology, "the correlation with the theology of the book and with the Bible as a whole."[63] After the biblical theology has been discovered, but before the theological product is articulated, the preacher must run his biblical theological conclusions through the lens of systematic theology in order to account for the theological truth of the passage in light of the progress of revelation.[64] The truth expressed within the confines of the particular text by its author in his context must be opened up to reflect the complete revelation of God in His Word. "Each human author of Scripture had a particular audience for whom he wrote. But the scope of his intention, supplemented by unconscious implication, has meaning much beyond the original referent."[65] The sacrificial system of the Old Testament, for example, does not express God's fully developed expression of redemption as found in Hebrews. The truth "must be broadened from the particular instance . . . which is one example of the outworking of the theological truth, to the general theological principle it conveys."[66]

The theological product will be a theological proposition and structure that "should express the timeless theological truth that the passage teaches, in a way that would be applicable to the original situation as well as to the contemporary corresponding situations."[67]

> Far from imposing any tradition of a later theology (no matter how biblical and how excellent it is) on an earlier text, this method respects the integrity of the original revelation of God to the writer. Yet it also legitimately enriches the same text by its emphasis on the accumulating, ramifying, and informing theology.
>
> If this informing theology was what made the text timeless and full of abiding values for the people in that day . . . then could not this same diachronic accumulation of theology provide the same heart of the message for all peoples in all times? Yes, for even in the text's historical particularity, it also carried in its very bosom an enduring plan of the everlasting God.
>
> We believe that this informing theology provides the interpreter with the key to all the emphases, application, appeals, and offers of hope or warning of judgment which must be made if the text is to mean anything to our day and age.[68]

The proposition, therefore, will be stated in terms of theology rather than history. As a result the preacher will be articulating universal truth that answers the question, What does this passage tell about God, creation, and the relationship between the two? It is crucial that the theological product be clearly and sufficiently linked to the original passage, for "once the expositor demonstrates that the message is from the text, then the exposition [theology] will carry the authority it must have to be effective" in ensuing preaching.[69] Theology then is the "hermeneutical arch that reaches from the text to the contemporary sermon."[70]

HOMILETICS

The third process is the homiletical, leading to the sermon as it is delivered. The first element of this section is the homiletical focus. Whereas the theological lens opens up the particular biblical theology so that it may be expressed in universal terms, the homiletical lens closes down the scope to concentrate homiletical efforts on the specific preaching audience.[71] This step distinguishes what will be different from one audience to another, from one culture to another.

Hesselgrave and Rommen suggest a seven-dimension lens that enables the preacher to analyze his distinct audience. These dimensions include world views (ways of viewing the world), cognitive processes (ways of thinking), linguistic forms (ways of expressing ideas), behavioral patterns (ways of acting), communication media (ways of channeling the message), social structures (ways of interacting), and motivational sources (ways of deciding).[72]

While both exegesis and theology remain stable (one meaning), homiletics varies according to the differing audiences (many applications). The homiletical focus therefore is a sociological tool that identifies the demographic particularities and philosophical preferences of the audience. Affirming that Christian communication must be both authentic and effective, Hesselgrave concludes,

> Authenticity is primarily a matter of interpreting the text in such a way as to arrive, as closely as possible, at the intent of the author through the application of sound hermeneutical principles. Through this process interpretation biases occasioned by the interpreter's own culture can be gradually overcome and, in that sense, the message can be decontextualized. Effectiveness is primarily a matter of contextualizing or shaping the gospel message to make it meaningful and compelling to the respondents in their cultural and existential situation.[73]

The next task in the homiletical process is to ask and answer developmental questions in light of the previously analyzed audience. Robinson has identified and discussed the role of developmental questions.[74] These questions have long been the key to developing the major proposition of oral communication,[75] for they enable the preacher to determine what aspect(s) of the theological proposition will need to be explained to the audience, what aspect(s) of the theological proposition will need to be proved to them, and what aspect(s) of the theological proposition will need to be applied to them. Developmental questions also suggest which rhetorical strategies—biblical, logical, ethical, or emotional[76]—will provide sufficient explanation, validation, and application of the universal theological principle for a specific audience.

It is essential to understand that developmental questions must be reserved for use only after the theological proposition has been clearly identified. This is not to say that the developmental questions have no value, for instance, in coming to grips with the exegesis or theology of a passage as the preacher prepares his message. The questions asked in light of the original (biblical) audience and the universal audience may aid in the discovery of meaning. However, the developmental questions asked in light of the theological proposition and the immediate audience are not only most fruitful but also necessary.[77]

Once again, the homiletical bridging spiral represents a retroductive process[78] and the interplay between the Holy Spirit and the preacher's human spirit. Kaiser warns,

> Even when we have faithfully discharged our full range of duties as exegetes and when we have also pressed on to apply that exegesis by principlizing the text paragraph by paragraph into timeless propositions which call for an immediate response from our listeners, we still need the Holy Spirit to carry that word home to the mind and hearts of our hearers if that word is ever going to change men's lives.[79]

The homiletical product is the sermon with its own particular purpose, proposition, structure, and support material. Though the purpose of the sermon may be different from the purpose of the text (e.g., lovingly to limit one's Christian liberty in attendance of the movie theater as compared to the Corinthians' lovingly limiting their liberty in meat-eating), the purpose of the sermon will not violate the purpose of the text, for "whenever preachers depart from the purpose and the intent of a biblical portion, to that extent they lose their authority to preach."[80] The specific homiletical purpose therefore will reflect both the text and the immediate audience. The sermon proposition will also take the text into account as it seeks to state the eternal truth, expressed in the text, in terms of the contemporary listeners. Rather than excluding exegetical and theological conclusions, the homiletical process and product take into account the results of previous study.

The homiletical structure will, on the other hand, reflect the specific rhetorical strategies of the preacher in light of his immediate audience rather than merely duplicate the author's strategic outline for the original audience.[81] Support material will be chosen with a goal of meeting the needs of the audience. Since varying listeners require varying levels of information, validation, and application, the support material necessary to meet these requirements will change as the audience and/or subject matter changes. The entire homiletical product will be surrounded and supported by reasonable and rational arguments of a biblical, logical, ethical, and/or emotional nature.

The final portion of the preaching process is transformational and revelational. It is here that the preacher himself and the listeners exhibit changed lives for having heard the Word preached. The goal of expository preaching is, after all, to see lives change.[82] Attitudes and behaviors will stop, start, or perhaps continue as those exposed to truth work to bring their lives into conformity with the truth. The goal is justification for the unbeliever and sanctification for the believer. The maturation process reflects the interplay between the Holy Spirit and the human spirit as the individual seeks to approximate the absolute perfection of Christ as revealed in Scripture. To the extent that listeners' changed lives more accurately reveal the character of the Lord Jesus, preaching may be said to fulfill its purpose.

This then is the preaching process. The gap between the ancient text and the modern audience is bridged by the exegetical, the theological, the homiletical, and the revelational processes. Four distinct processes, demanding a variety of skills, enable the preacher to meet the transcendence, significance, and community needs of the ever-changing world with the authority and relevance of the changeless Word of God.

Guarding the Integrity of Application

A final major question requires an answer. How is the authority of relevance preserved throughout this expositional process? In other words what gives authority to the application(s) the preacher makes when it is not identical with the biblical application? What guarantee is there that the transcultural theological principle will not be misapplied by an overzealous preacher? For example "one may not simply draw a historical equation mark between God's revelation in the Old Testament and God's message for today."[83]

Though there are no guarantees, a couple of applicational safeguards may prove helpful. A faithful adherence to the purpose and the audience of the text must be maintained as well as a knowledge of the contemporary need. "Preaching is *truth applied. . . .* the truth of God revealed in Scripture came in an applied form and should be reapplied to the same sort of people for the same purposes for which it was originally given."[84] In the figure below purpose arches over the theological and homiletical processes. Audience arches under both processes. Both purpose and audience serve like guardrails on a bridge to protect the authority of the sermon's application.

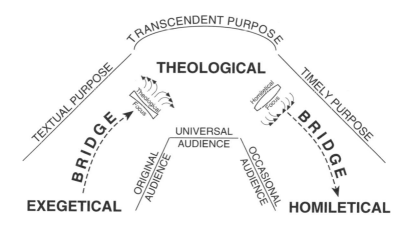

The purpose that arches over the theological process, limiting the theological reasoning, is the textual purpose. Neither biblical theology nor systematic theology should move outside the original author's intended purpose.[85] This purpose will have been discovered in the text[86] during the exegetical process. The purpose arching over the theological product is the transcendent purpose, which encompasses the full range of biblical intent,[87] transcending the constraints of specific contexts whether exegetical or homiletical. The purpose that arches over the homiletical process, limiting the homiletical reasoning, is timely purpose. The timely purpose demarcates a congruent, yet relevant, expression of the intent of the text. Though every legitimate application must be in accord with the transcendent purpose as expressed in the text, Richard has argued that every biblical expression allows for meaning that is also relevant to innumerable specific situations.

> This field of meaning is on three levels: *statement, implication,* and *extrapolation.* All three levels are founded in the text. . . . The command "Thou shalt not commit adultery" is a *statement.* The sanctity of marriage is an *implication* drawn from the statement. By *extrapolation* one sees the condemnation of all sexual sins, as substantiated by the rest of Scripture.[88]

Thus the timely purpose may be different from but not contrary to the original text. It may not be the same, but it will be congruent, as seen in Paul's application of Deuteronomy 25:4 in 1 Corinthians 9:8–12. There Paul applied Moses' command, "You shall not muzzle an ox while he is threshing," to supporting ministers of the gospel financially. The purpose guardrail indicates that "while an author can willingly state more than he is consciously aware of, he cannot willfully imply something contrary to his statement."[89]

The audience that arches under the theological process, confining the scope of the biblical theological deliberations, is the textual audience. Biblical theology considers the theology of the text in light of the original audience with its knowledge of God's dealings with His creation.[90] The audience that bounds the theological focus, the theological product, and the homiletical focus is the universal audience. "Universal audience" means believing, informed students of the entire written revelation of God— everyone with the knowledge and objectivity to identify those timeless truths, transcultural principles, and theological absolutes that are universally authoritative and relevant. The audience that arches under the homiletical process, confining the scope of immediate application, is the "occasional audience," the listeners the preacher is addressing directly.

Consideration of the audience-reference and the audience-trait[91] enables the preacher to identify applications that are not only consistent with the theological product, but also mutually relevant to both the textual and occasional audiences. Audience-reference identifies the recipients of the original autograph (the nation of Israel with its king, priests, and people, for example), and searches for the correspondence between them and the contemporary audience. Audience-trait identifies the various characteristics of those original readers/hearers (evil kings, evil priests, and abused people, for example), and discovers similarities or dissimilarities between their attributes and those of the immediate audience. "When the elements in both the biblical and the contemporary situations match, the abstracted principle may be reapplied."[92]

When the preacher labors within the guardrails of purpose and audience, limiting the theological principle and the application(s) to the perimeters of textual statement and listener needs, one may be sure of advancing toward valid application in the sermon.

The Immediate Challenge

The reader who, having evaluated the paradigm presented in this chapter, accepts its basic claim may ask how practical the method may prove in light of his present skill levels. For some, applying the paradigm will require only a small step, for others, a great leap. For some, the method may enhance next week's sermon, for others, next year's. How might they begin to incorporate the model into their reality? The immediate challenge includes at least four demands: exegetical skills will be broadened, basic theological skills will be developed, basic homiletical skills will be acquired, and all three skills will be integrated into the expositional process.

BROADER EXEGETICAL SKILLS

Preaching the whole counsel of God demands broad exegetical skills. Along with expertise in exegeting epistolary and poetic literature, expository preachers bear the responsibility of becoming proficient in exegeting narrative, legal, wisdom, prophetic, and apocalyptic literature as well. A sound strategy for properly handling all of God's authoritative Word provides a necessary legitimacy to the claim of authority, for one must possess the capacity to understand the Old Testament properly in order to understand the New properly, for example. Only when the exegete is able to interpret the entire biblical literature is he able to interpret Scripture in light of Scripture.

For those who lack exegetical training or expertise, continuing education is a must. Whether through a self-study program of reading or a formal course at a college seminary, the preacher's exegetical skills must be broadened to include all biblical genres.

BASIC THEOLOGICAL SKILLS

Preaching that lacks solid theological footing also lacks authority. Students of preaching must become students of theology as well, developing skill in doing theology. Adopting a system of theology may provide an essential starting point, but preachers must also learn how to do theology, both biblical and systematic. To move from the contextualized exegetical meaning, dealing with a multitude of specifics, to the single universal statement of truth is a skill that is never learned or seldom demonstrated by many preachers. The road from text to truth is especially necessary once one moves out of the Epistles.

The basic skills of studying theology—the theology of the book, the theology of a pericope within that book, and systematic theology—cannot be ignored. The risks of misrepresenting and misapplying the text are great for the preacher who ignores or misunderstands the theological message of the particular text. Working to avoid the tendency to spiritualize, especially in the narrative and prophetic passages, the faithful preacher will commit to an informal or formal means of training in basic theological skills.

BASIC HOMILETICAL SKILLS

Whereas the major demand of developing exegetical and theological skills relates to the preacher's authority, the major issue of developing homiletical skills relates to his relevance. Too many so-called sermons fail, not for lack of exegesis or even theology, but for lack of significance. Listeners have little interest in the subject and no clue as to how the message relates to their immediate living.

Preachers must learn how to exegete their audience as well as the text. Too little attention has been devoted to the development of this skill. Though most preachers have received some training in exegetical and theological skills in their college or seminary training, few of the fundamental skills of sociology and communication have been learned and developed. Until preachers can be relevant as well as authoritative, their sermons will fall short of the goal.

Speaking so that people listen and respond is an essential skill that committed preachers acquire. Helpful courses in public speaking are offered at many colleges and universities. Opportunities for informal instruction exist as well, providing training and encouraging effective speaking.

INTEGRATION OF SKILLS

Finally, the effective preacher must learn to integrate all these skills in sermon preparation and delivery. Even if exegetical, theological, and homiletical expertise was not fully integrated throughout one's seminary training, being faithful to one's calling demands a full and balanced integration of all the necessary skills for preaching. To eliminate one, or even to slight one of these skills, places the authority and relevance of his sermons in jeopardy. To integrate all three skills into the preaching process is the immediate challenge of all who would be faithful preachers of the Scriptures.

CHAPTER 12

Is the Pulpit a Factor in Church Growth?

Earl V. Comfort

One could easily get the impression from church growth experts that the pulpit plays little or no part in church growth. A survey of books and articles on church growth communicates strongly that the pulpit is passé. For instance, *The Pastors Church Growth Handbook*, a compilation of suggestions for those involved in church growth, mentions nothing about the place of the pulpit. Ken Parker, one of the contributors, lists "seven characteristics of a growing church" and completely ignores the pulpit ministry.[1] Robert Schuller talks about "three characteristics of a successful pastor," and not once does he mention the role of an effective communicator.[2] Charles Mylander writes about "how to build morale in your church," but does not mention the pulpit.[3]

Donald McGavran's book, *Understanding Church Growth*, is the most comprehensive study ever published on church growth. But he makes little mention of the pulpit ministry. When it is mentioned, however, it is done so in a deprecating manner.

> Research should make a sharp distinction between reproducible patterns of growth and those which cannot be duplicated. Some of the most striking church growth is the work of extraordinarily gifted men—geniuses. We rejoice in these men, but do not expect to find many Dwight L. Moodys or Henry Ward Beechers in our congregation. . . . for church growth which is dependent on exceptional men one thanks God; but realizes He probably will not grant us that kind of growth. Research should look for *reproducible patterns of growth* possible to ordinary congregations, ordinary pastors, and ordinary missionaries.[4]

Arn, a collaborator with McGavran on church growth, wrote:

> *Unfortunately*, many churches in choosing a pastor place greatest priority on the man's ability to preach. Certainly congregations are entitled to prepared and well-delivered messages. Yet, sermon delivery represents a very small portion of the pastor's total work week. Indications are that

the sermon, by itself, is a relatively minor factor in the growth of the church. How then should its pastor spend his time to have the greatest effect in church growth?[5]

And yet when church growth situations are examined in this country one cannot overlook the fact that at the heart of growth is an effective pulpit ministry. Many churches experiencing church growth are pastored by men who emphasize effective communication. Smith, heavily involved in the body-life ministry of a large church, wrote about the relationship of preaching to other church functions.

> Total Christian education should be our goal. As one of my colleagues says, It's like a big burner: the expository pulpit ministry is the *center of the burner*, and the complementary efforts with their greater participation possibilities form the outer rings of the burner. . . . Let's light up the big burner, not to make things hot for everyone, but to warm up the saints and condition the atmosphere. . . . In order to do this we must get back to the kind of expository teaching that is dedicated to lifting up and presenting the true sense of the text so that God can reach our wills through our minds.[6]

A combination of factors is needed for a church to experience healthy spiritual and numerical growth; and one of those elements ought to be biblical preaching. Robinson also spoke of the need for a corrective to the overemphasis of many church-growth philosophers. After stressing the need for an effective pulpit ministry, someone said that not every pastor could preach effectively. Robinson responded in this way:

> In most churches, if the pastor is an effective communicator and articulates to the congregation what the church is to be about, one of two things will happen. One, they will get rid of him—they will find that his preaching doesn't match what they want. Or, two, he will surround himself with people who share his vision and they will move forward with him. There are pastors who cannot preach, but I think that a preacher who cannot preach is like a clock that doesn't run. It is called a clock, but it isn't functioning. A preacher who can't preach has a tremendous disadvantage in most of our Protestant churches. The man who can preach has the tremendous advantage of being able to stand before his congregation and articulate to them what they ought to be about and where they ought to be going. Before long he'll be surrounded with people who share his vision. The better a communicator he is, the stronger his position will be.[7]

To deemphasize the effective proclamation of the Word of God is to do a grave disservice to the Scriptures and to the people in today's congregations.

The Jacksonville Chapel, pastored by this writer, is a suburban church situated in north New Jersey. According to the standards set up by church-growth leaders, this church is growing. In 10 years, attendance increased from 300 to 1,200. Its church leaders recently decided to plan additional facilities to serve this growing congregation. Preliminary to this decision, the leaders agreed to seek to ascertain which factors had contributed to its numerical growth. In this way, it was believed that those factors could continue to be emphasized in following years. A brief questionnaire was included in the bulletin one Sunday morning. Of the approximately 1,000 youth and adults that Sunday, 900 filled in the questionnaire. The questionnaire was concerned with two issues: What had first attracted these people to the Chapel? What had caused them to remain? (see Table 1, p. 136)

The results to the first question correspond very closely to the order of the importance of those items as researched over the years by church-growth authorities. Most people said they were attracted to the Chapel by their friends or relatives. The second question sought to discover those factors that caused the people in the congregation to continue coming to the Chapel. The respondents could rate the degree of importance of eight factors, using a scale from 1 (not very important) to 5 (very important). By far, the aggregate total for sermons showed that this was the most significant factor in growth. It exceeded the second highest factor by almost 900 cumulative points. The church leaders concluded from this evidence that they should never sacrifice the Chapel's pulpit ministry for anything else.

But what factors contribute to an effective pulpit ministry? To find an answer to this question, a second survey was conducted. This one was directed to the 120 members received into the church over the previous two years. Eighty-five questionnaires were returned (a 70% response). This questionnaire included several factors on a scale of 1 (poor) to 5 (excellent). Even though all categories received a score of between 4 and 5, the highest point total was given to the biblical content of the messages. (see Table 2, pp. 137-138)

From these two surveys, then, two conclusions were drawn: (a) The pulpit is a decisive factor in church growth. (b) The pulpit, in order to be effective, must have seven qualities. True, not all pastors can be Spurgeons or Moodys, but all can seek to improve.

1. Preaching must be *biblical*. Sermons must not merely make general references to the Bible; they must expound the Bible.
2. Preaching must be *understandable*. Every effort should be taken to communicate the Word of God effectively. Transparencies, outlines, charts, and other media can be used to "bring home" Bible truth.
3. It must be *"warm."* Lloyd-Jones wrote. "To love to preach is one thing; to love those to whom you preach is quite another."[8]
4. It must be *positive*. People should leave a church service with a positive attitude toward God. A young teenager who became a Christian shared with this writer why she was first attracted to the Chapel. She said after her first visit, "I think God likes me."
5. It must be *practical*. Preaching should provide meaningful answers to life and its problems. "It is always our business to be contemporary; our object is to deal with the living people who are in front of us and listening to us."[9] Robinson observed, "A preacher, therefore, should forget about speaking to the ages and speak to his day."[10]
6. It must be *exemplary*. Pastors must live out what they preach. The biblical truth which the expositor shares must first be applied by the Holy Spirit "to the personality and experience of the preacher and then through him to his hearers."[11]
7. It must be *exciting*. Lloyd-Jones wrote that "a dull preacher is a contradiction in terms; if he is dull he is not a preacher."[12]

These characteristics of an effective pulpit do not come by accident. They require work—hard, difficult labor. Perhaps that is one reason other methods of church growth are such an attractive substitute. Preaching God's truth requires sacrifice, study, and effort. "All its diamonds do not lie exposed on the surface to be picked like flowers. Its richness is mined only through hard, intellectual and spiritual spade work."[13]

If effective biblical preaching, along with other factors, is provided for congregations, they will grow both spiritually and numerically.

Table 1

Results of Congregational Survey

A. What are the two most important factors that first caused
   you to come to the Chapel?

	Aggregate of Responses	Rank
Friend or neighbor told me	533	1
Other	347	2
Family told me	280	3
Drove by and was curious	74	4
Child is attending Sunday school	62	5
Newspaper ad	16	6
Child is attending weekday clubs	14	7
Listing in the Yellow Pages	5	8
Recommended at Bible bookstore	4	9

B. How important are these factors in causing you to
   continue coming?

	Aggregate of Responses on 5-point scale	Rank
Sermons	4,072	1
Friendliness	3,201	2
Music/choir	2,700	3
Personal friends here	2,653	4
Sunday school program	2,475	5
Body-life emphasis	2,152	6
Youth/College and Career	2,031	7
Visit by a Chapel representative	1,528	8

Table 2

Survey of New Members

A. How would you rate the pulpit ministry (sermons) of
Jacksonville Chapel?

	1	2	3	4	5
(1=Poor; 5=Excellent)					
Instructive (I learn)	—	—	—	—	—
Interesting (Not boring)	—	—	—	—	—
Humorous (I laugh)	—	—	—	—	—
Warm (I feel comfortable)	—	—	—	—	—
Biblical (Bible-based)	—	—	—	—	—
Logical (I follow the thinking)	—	—	—	—	—
Positive (I feel better)	—	—	—	—	—
Illustrative (I understand)	—	—	—	—	—

B. How would you rate the "delivery" of the sermons?

Mobility (movement)	—	—	—	—	—
Voice modulation (fluctuation)	—	—	—	—	—
Eye contact	—	—	—	—	—
Gestures	—	—	—	—	—
Clarity (easy to hear)	—	—	—	—	—

C. How would you rate the aids used in the sermons?
  1. The Printed Outline

Helps me follow the sermon	—	—	—	—	—
Fill-ins are helpful	—	—	—	—	—
Helps in later study	—	—	—	—	—

  2. The Projected Overheads

Aid in understanding	—	—	—	—	—
Well-designed	—	—	—	—	—
Attractive	—	—	—	—	—
Help me remember	—	—	—	—	—
Hold my attention	—	—	—	—	—
Help me understand the Scriptures	—	—	—	—	—

  3. I would like to see the use of
  visual aids continue   _____ Yes _____ No
  4. I would like to see the use of visual aids
  _____ decreased _____ increased _____ remain the same

Table 2, cont.

D. How would you compare the pulpit ministry of Jacksonville
    Chapel with your previous church experience?

	Worse	Same	Better
Instructive	—	—	—
Interesting	—	—	—
Humorous	—	—	—
Warm	—	—	—
Biblical	—	—	—
Logical	—	—	—
Positive	—	—	—
Illustrative	—	—	—
Visual aids	—	—	—

E. What suggestions would you make to improve the pulpit
    ministry of Jacksonville Chapel?

CHAPTER 13

The Biblical Concept of Elder

Ed Glasscock

The term "elder" is familiar to most Christians, but it is also misunderstood by many. To some, the elder is the pastor of a church; to others, he is one of many pastors; or to still others, he is one of a board of elders who serve with a pastor. The one constant idea in all these is that he is a leader of the church.

Such a concept, however, is not sufficient. Several factors unfold the meaning of "elder"—lexical definition, historical use of the term, and the context in which it appears. Above all, it is critical to divorce oneself from contemporary concepts of the church and to keep in mind the Jewish context in which the term "elder" was used. Often overlooked, this Jewish heritage gives a significant dimension to the meaning of "elder." The word has a lexical meaning determined by its cultural and historical setting. Paul's idea of what an elder was is critical to a proper understanding and function of that office in the church.

Definition of Terms

The Greek word for elder (πρεσβύτερος) refers to age ("an individual persona older of two . . . in contrast to the younger generation οἱ πρεσβύτεροι, *the older ones*") or an office ("elder, presbyter") among both Jews and Christians.[1] Πρεσβύτερος is a comparative form of πρέσβυς, which Liddell and Scott define primarily as "old man."[2] There is no doubt that the basic meaning of the word concerns "age." Yet this is often overlooked today when men are appointed to the office of elder or pastor. The sense of "age" is even more emphasized by the comparative form.

Bornkamm notes that the comparative sense could fade but that the word would still "simply mean 'old,' 'the old.'"[3] Perhaps people take its root meaning for granted, but when Paul told Titus to appoint elders in every city (Titus 1:5), he obviously knew the implication of age and assumed the men appointed were of sufficient age to be called older, that is, older men in the congregation.

NEW TESTAMENT CONSIDERATIONS

What exactly constituted an "older" man is open to debate, but obviously it was in contrast to a young man. Bauer, Arndt, and Gingrich offer the suggestion of 50 to 56 years of age.[4] However, an example from the Qumran community sets the age of 30 as the minimum required to serve as an elder in the community.[5] Since Qumran's background and roots are thoroughly Jewish and its existence was close to the apostolic period, it is a reliable example of what that culture viewed as the minimum age for leadership.

There is another reason for assuming a minimum age of 30. When Christ was only 12 years old, His knowledge and wisdom shocked and confounded the teachers in the temple (Luke 2:46–47). But having superior knowledge was not the only requirement for Christ's work. He returned to Nazareth with His parents to wait an additional 18 years, during which time He "kept increasing in wisdom and stature" (Luke 2:52). The word for stature, ἡλικία, most naturally means age (cf. NASB marginal note). Bauer, Arndt, and Gingrich define ἡλικία as "age, time of life" or "age generally" and suggest that in Luke 2:52 the word means He was "increasing in years."[6] Luke wrote that "when He began His ministry, Jesus Himself was about thirty years of age" (Luke 3:23). It is likely that His age was given not simply as a matter of historical trivia but because this was the accepted age for beginning a leadership or teaching role. Robertson points out that this was the age when Levites entered full service.[8] Tenney gives further support for this 30-year limit, pointing out that due to the age requirement of the Sanhedrin, if Paul literally cast a vote for the death of Christians, he would have been at least 30 years of age.[9]

Thus there seems to be ample evidence that an acceptable leader or teacher must be at least 30 years of age. The idea is that one needs not only training but also experience and maturity. To lead, advise, and instruct other people requires an understanding based on wisdom and humility, and age seems to provide these. The experiences of time are great teachers and help put into perspective what one knows theoretically. If the Lord waited until He was about 30 years of age, thus gaining wisdom by what He experienced and enabling Him to meet human needs more effectively (Heb. 4:15–16; 5:8–9), then how much more do potential Christian leaders need to wait until they have years of maturity before they start directing the lives of others. It is safe therefore to assume that 30 would be the minimum age for one to be called an elder.

OLD TESTAMENT CONSIDERATIONS

Though it is superfluous to state that Paul and the other apostles were Jews—a point Paul was ready to bring to the attention of his Gentile readers (Phil. 3:5)—this fact is significant in determining the meaning of the word "elder." Cultural understanding of scriptural vocabulary is an important key for properly interpreting apostolic instructions. The difference between what Paul meant by πρεσβύτερος and what many American churches mean by "elder" is significant. It might be compared to what the word "freedom" means to an American in contrast to what it means to a citizen of Russia or China. Jewish apostles spoke in words that held a certain meaning for them, and the student of Scripture must understand that meaning. The apostles were brought up with the Old Testament and Judaism. They read of the elders in the Old Testament and saw them in the temple, synagogues, and marketplaces. They had been taught to respect the "tradition of the elders" (Matt. 15:2).

The Hebrew word for "elder" is almost identical in meaning to its New Testament counterpart. As a verb, זָקֵן means "to be or become old," or as a predicate adjective it simply means "old."[10] Also, like "elder" in the New Testament, it can refer to an office— sometimes the leaders of a village, a tribe, or even the nation itself.[11] Lewis defines זָקֵן as "aged, ancient, ancient man, elder, senator, eldest, old, old man, old woman."[12] Thus in the Septuagint זָקֵן is translated by πρεσβύτης or πρεσβύτερος .

Besides the lexical meaning there is a further connection between Paul's word "elder" and the Old Testament word. The office of elder in Israel was established before the Exodus. After the Exodus, God had Moses select 70 from among all the elders and He gave them His Spirit, even as He had to Moses, so that they might share the burden of leadership with him (Num. 11:16–25). Thus elder in Israel became a spiritual office as well as being the traditional position of honor that it was among most ancient Near Eastern cultures. (Scripture refers to elders in Egypt, Moab, and Edom, as well as in Israel.)

The Old Testament word זָקֵן, then, has many ideas. It, of

course, designated one who was no longer a young man (Ps. 37:25), but it also signified a "fully accredited adult in the national assembly."[13] It also referred to a leadership group both locally and nationally—"from the older men there are then chosen the narrower colleges of elders which represent the tribe, city, locality, or people."[14] Throughout the Old Testament they functioned as judges in civil as well as religious matters. They advised kings, counseled people in their towns, and at times were associated with the high priest. In the New Testament they were found (primarily in opposition to Christ) identified along with the priests, scribes, and the high priest (e.g., Matt. 16:21; 26:3).

Therefore to Paul or any other Jew, an official elder was not just an older man. He was also a leader, an adviser who judged and counseled. Elders did not function individually, as did the prophets, but were always seen as a college or council. They were recognized as "the wisest and most experienced men."[15] Ideally an elder was to have proven himself to be wise (far more than just intellectually trained) and spiritually gifted. This concept of elder shaped the vocabulary of Paul and the other New Testament writers.

SUMMARY

In many churches today men are placed into positions of pastor or elder based on education, personality, or professional achievements. However, the Bible does not consider any of these. In the Scriptures an elder was an older, mature adult who was recognized for his wisdom and experience. He was to be looked up to for advice and guidance. His character, not his achievements, was important.

Age 30 seems to have been accepted as the time when men had experience and maturity necessary to be responsible leaders. However, this is not automatic; therefore the Scriptures give further instructions that not every man was an elder in the official sense. They were selected from the older men based on their wisdom (common-sense application of the truth) and experience. A most important qualification emphasized in the New Testament is the evidence of the Holy Spirit in the life of the man.

New Testament Office of Elder

The word "elder" was used in most cultures of the ancient Near East. And Greek and Roman societies used πρεσβύτερος as a title for village officials.[16] But the apostles, who were chosen by God to structure the church, a spiritual organization, and who were Jewish, would have had in mind the concept of elder leadership presented in Numbers 11 rather than secular, pagan ideas.

Discussing specific spiritual, moral, and ethical qualifications in 1 Timothy 3 and Titus 1 helped prevent Gentile churches from misunderstanding the spiritual nature of the work—a problem that could easily have arisen from their culture in contrast to the Jewish apostolic culture.

JEWISH ORIGIN

Failure to recognize the Jewish nature of the New Testament references to "elder" may create misunderstandings. The New Testament elder appears in the early church without any explanation (Acts 11:30). This is in contrast to the explanation of the appointment of those who would serve the church as deacons (Acts 6). One reason for this lack of introduction is that the elder was the common officer of guidance and leadership. The apostles probably appointed elders in the church soon after Pentecost. Plummer also sees this natural step of organization. "They had inherited from Judaism the ordinances of the Jewish Church. To administer these, there was the Sanhedrin. . . . Congregations which consisted chiefly of Jewish Christians had 'elders' analogous to 'elders' among the Jews."[17]

This point clarifies the origin of the office and perhaps explains why qualifications were not given until Paul wrote to Timothy and Titus, who were appointing and training elders in Gentile churches. Gentiles did not have the same understanding of the office because in their society it was a secular post filled by greedy and untrustworthy men. By contrast, New Testament elders were godly men who were to take *spiritual* responsibility for their congregations (Acts 20:28). The elders in the Jerusalem church knew their role in God's program in the church (Acts 15). They worked along with the apostles and James to settle the dispute over circumcision. Calvin pointed out that not all the aged Jewish Christians were elders, but only "those who did excel in doctrine and judgment and those who, according to their office, were competent judges in this matter."[18]

THE GENTILE CHURCH

As the church spread into the Gentile world, a need arose for explaining God's program and methods. The new Gentile converts were unaccustomed to the spiritual truths of God's Word, and a whole body of Christian literature (Paul's epistles) was written to acclimate them to their new Jewish-oriented faith.

Leadership was clearly one of the key areas where they had to learn principles. Christ had warned His disciples of the difference: "You know that the rulers of the Gentiles lord it over them, and their great men exercise authority over them. It is not so among you" (Matt. 20:25–26). Brought up under the Roman governmental system, it was difficult for Gentiles to abandon their idea that leaders should "lord it" over others. But the apostles' example and Paul's clear instructions helped move the Gentiles toward the spiritual character of leadership God intended. The change from a Jewish church to a predominantly Gentile church was a gradual process. At first the Jerusalem church (with elders, apostles, and James) was giving directives to Gentile believers (Acts 16:4).

The Gentile church soon began to take on the design and order of the Jerusalem church. Paul and Barnabas appointed elders in every new church (Acts 14:23). As Hort observed, "Paul and Barnabas follow the precedent of Jerusalem by appointing elders in Jewish fashion (elders being indeed an institution of Jewish communities of the Dispersion as well as of Judaea), and with this simple organization they entrusted the young Ecclesiae to the Lord's care, to pursue an independent life."[19]

In Paul's letter to the Philippians, he addressed both bishops (ἐπισκόποις)[20] and deacons, showing a structure similar to that in Jerusalem (Phil. 1:1). In Acts 20:17, 28 Paul reminded the Ephesian church elders of their responsibilities as spiritual leaders.

QUALIFICATIONS

As stated earlier, elders appeared in the church without any formal introduction, instruction on how they were to be selected, or qualifications being stated. There are two reasons for this: (a) since the church was Jewish, it was already familiar with the idea of elders and their qualifications; (b) elders were presumably appointed by either apostles, prophets, or teachers instead of selected by congregations (Acts 14:21–23; Titus 1:5). Carrington agrees with this observation. "We are not told how the local ministers had been appointed in Ephesus, but we see that they were appointed in Crete by apostolic men. There is no sign that congregations could elect their ministers."[21]

As the church changed from a Jewish to a Gentile majority, the need for an explanation of the office and its spiritual qualifications became necessary. Thus Paul wrote to two of his trusted coworkers, stating the qualifications for elders. The list of qualifications was probably not so much for the benefit of Timothy and Titus as it was for subsequent generations.

The two lists of qualifications (1 Tim. 3:1–7; Titus 1:5–9) give at least 22 qualifications. These may be grouped into four categories: personal character, public testimony, family, and ministry. Some of these naturally overlap, that is, any family failure will affect one's ministry or personal qualifications. These qualifications and their meanings are as follows:

PERSONAL QUALIFICATIONS:

1. "Temperate"—avoiding extremes
2. "Prudent"—showing good judgment, common sense
3. "Not addicted to wine"—not abusing wine
4. "Not pugnacious"—not having a violent temper
5. "Gentle" (in contrast to pugnacious)—being patient or considerate
6. "Uncontentious"—being peaceful in nature
7. "Free from the love of money"—not being greedy for personal gain
8. "Not a novice"—having been saved long enough to develop spiritual maturity and wisdom
9. "Not self-willed"—not trying to get one's way, looking out only for oneself
10. "Not quick-tempered"—not being easily angered
11. "Loving what is good"—being loyal to moral and ethical values
12. "Just"—being fair and honest
13. "Devout"—being devoted to God in worship
14. "Self-controlled"—being able to control oneself under adverse or tempting circumstances

PUBLIC QUALIFICATIONS:

1. "Above reproach"—having no questionable conduct that would bring accusations
2. "Hospitable"—being receptive and open to people
3. "Good reputation with those outside"—having a morally and ethically upright testimony with the unsaved

FAMILY QUALIFICATIONS:

1. "Husband of one wife"—literally, being "a one-woman type of man," that is, not a flirtatious man but one who is content with his wife[22]
2. "Manages his own household well"—being a spiritual leader of his family
3. "Children under control with dignity"—having children who obey respectfully
4. "Children who believe, not accused of dissipation"—having children who display faith (possibly "faithfulness"), who are not living recklessly, who are not rebellious to their fathers

MINISTRY QUALIFICATIONS:

1. "Able to teach"—having ability to instruct in doctrine (possibly "teachable")
2. "Holding fast the word of truth"—being firm in doctrine and not compromising Scripture
3. "Exhort with sound doctrine"—encouraging believers by means of correct doctrine
4. "Refute those who contradict"—standing against and stopping false teaching

These qualifications clearly emphasize the character of the person rather than his educational achievements. In summary the characteristics indicate that an elder is to be unselfish, of good reputation, a good family leader, and able to handle Scripture. These qualities are essential in godly leadership.

A man may desire to be an elder (1 Tim. 3:1), but in addition he must meet these qualifications. The fact that these are requirements, not ideals toward which an elder might hope to strive, is indicated by the words "must be" in 1 Timothy 3:2. The word "must" (δεῖ) means "it is necessary"; it denotes "compulsion of any kind."[23] Obviously to meet these requirements a man would need to be of sufficient age to have manifested these characteristics in his life. Thus from among the πρεσβύτεροι (older men of the congregation) those who desire the office of ἐπίσκοπος (overseer) are to be examined according to these qualifications. Those who are approved are then to be appointed to their work in the local church. It has been a tragic error in church history to assume that these qualifications are optional or that they can be replaced with academic degrees.

Functions of Elders in the Church

As stated earlier, the Old Testament elders were always seen as a council; they were not mentioned as having authority individually. This same pattern is followed in the New Testament. In every instance where elders are mentioned in connection with the church, there are plural elders in a singular church (e.g., James 5:14, τοὺς πρεσβυτέρους τῆς ἐκκλησίας; Acts 14:23, κατ' ἐκκλησίαν πρεσβυτέρους).[24] This fact establishes the apostolic pattern of plural leadership for individual churches and also strongly implies that the authority and function of elders were restricted to a particular local church. This latter point can be seen in Acts 20:17, 28: "And from Miletus he sent to Ephesus and called to him the elders of the church. . . . 'Be on guard for yourselves and for all the flock, among which the Holy Spirit has made you overseers, to shepherd the church of God which He purchased with His own blood.'" The words "among which" (ἐν ᾧ) refer to the flock in Ephesus.

This writer believes a distinction is to be made between the office of elder and that of pastor-teacher (or perhaps better simply "teacher"). Their functions and responsibilities, however, are similar and they share certain duties. Thus the suggested organizational structure of a New Testament church is teacher, elders, deacons. This is similar, though not identical, to the Sanhedrin, in which there were ruling elders and also a president.[25] This similarity should not be pressed too far, but it does reflect that the early church was familiar with a separately identified leader who worked along with other men.

Elders are to be shepherds and guardians of the flock. Their function covers a broad range from ruling to ministering to the sick. In the New Testament they are seen ruling with the apostles (Acts 15:2, 4, 6, 22) and the letter from the Jerusalem church deciding the issue of circumcision is recorded as a decree of the apostles and elders (16:4). It seems that the elders were responsible for the relief funds sent to Jerusalem (11:29–30) and were the official delegation (along with James) to receive Paul's report of his missionary journeys. Some key areas of responsibility may be enumerated.

Ruling. Elders judged in matters of faith and practice (Acts 15:1–6). Fisher explains, "The early episcopacy, where it existed, as we see from the Epistles of Ignatius, was valued as a means of preventing division and preserving order."[26] Also "elders who rule well" were to be recognized by the assembly (1 Tim. 5:17). The elders should guide the church through controversy and normal growth problems by offering sound biblical judgment. The congregation is to obey those who rule them, because the rulers must give account for their souls (Heb. 13:17). Thus the elders are responsible for taking an active part in judging matters that affect the lives of the flock. They must decide for the good of the congregation in matters of doctrine, personal conflicts, and moral and ethical dilemmas, as well as direct the overall plans and programs of the church.

Caring. Paul told the Ephesian elders to guard their own lives, that is, to protect their testimonies and moral conduct, and to care for (ποιμαίω) the flock among whom they were placed by the Holy Spirit (Acts 20:28). The sick of a church were to call on the elders of that church for ministry, both physical and spiritual (James 5:14). The purpose in summoning the elders is to involve them as spiritual leaders in the physical needs of the flock. They are to deal with any potential sin and pray with the sick. Peter exhorted the elders to shepherd (feed, protect, and lead) the flock (1 Peter 5:1–3), which also shows personal involvement and concern. Polycarp, a disciple of John, exhorted the elders in Philippi, "The presbyters also must be compassionate, merciful towards all men, turning back the sheep that are gone astray, visiting all the infirm."[27] Thus elders are to be compassionate, being involved with the flock personally.

Instructing. Some elders had special responsibility for preaching or teaching (1 Tim. 5:17). All elders are to be "able to teach" (διδακτικόν, 3:2), which probably refers to instructing individuals in doctrine, but 5:17 seems to imply a more formal type of public exhortation not expected of all the elders. A strong statement related to this function of the elders is found in Titus 1:9–11. Paul expected them to "hold fast" the Word of truth, that is, defend the truth, not compromising the Scriptures. This involves exhorting believers through sound doctrinal teaching or counseling, as well as refuting error. This last challenge is often ignored by present-day church leaders. Paul warned that those who teach error are to be silenced (Titus 1:11), and this responsibility falls on the council of elders. They are to protect the flock, as well as to rule, feed, and care for them.

Conclusion

Elders are a body of godly men, selected from among the mature Christian men of a local assembly of believers. They must be willing to accept the responsibility, being aware that the Holy Spirit has made them overseers of the flock (Acts 20:28). Each elder must meet the qualifications of 1 Timothy 3:1–7 and Titus 1:5–9. His decisions, actions, and example must always be for the welfare of the people and not for his own selfish ends. He must be willing to cooperate with the pastor-teacher and other elders, not being self-willed (Titus 1:7). An elder must be a serious, honest student of God's Word, able and willing to instruct, reprove, encourage, and protect God's people.

The elders as a group must function in unity, offering the assembly single-minded leadership. They must actively watch over and guide the flock, making sure that heresy, immorality, divisions, or neglect are not creeping into the assembly. Above all, they must make sure that they themselves meet the biblical qualifications and are setting the proper example of commitment and purity for the rest of the church.

The church is to recognize their immense responsibilities and give them proper respect for the work they do (1 Thess. 5:12–13). Accusations against an elder must have adequate support before they are accepted. This will help protect them from unjust slander (1 Tim. 5:19).

Elders are to be carefully selected and ordained to their work only after they have demonstrated the spiritual qualities as given in the Word of God. Then they are to serve the Lord diligently and voluntarily—not as lords over the people, but as examples to them (1 Peter 5:1–3). The elder must be one who will put the well-being of the flock above his own personal desires and opinions. His authority never extends beyond the Word of God and he is to work as a member of a team, not as an independent ruler.

Scripture does not offer instructions as to the procedure of electing elders, but general guidelines suggest that they are appointed to their sacred post (Acts 14:21–23) and cannot be self-appointed.

The honorable work of the elder should be taught with strict biblical instruction. Godly men in the assembly should be sought out and trained for this high service to Christ. Elders should never be degraded to political figureheads, but should seek to protect the flock and honor the Lord. This plurality of godly leadership is the pattern God has always honored (cf. Num. 11:16–25) and will continue to honor.

CHAPTER 14

Behind the Word *Deacon*: A New Testament Study

D. Edmond Hiebert

The English word *deacon* is a loan word coming through the Latin (*diaconus*) from the Greek word διάχονος.[1] The basic meaning of the term is a "servant." When a person refers to someone appointed as a "deacon" in a local church, the concept of a servant is united with that of office. The term "deacon" thus denotes an office involving the basic duty of rendering service to others. A deacon then is one who is placed in an official position for a ministry of service to benefit others.

The Greeks, with their strong sense of personal freedom, held a rather low view of servants. They did not exalt the servant's position, but they did have a keen understanding of various aspects involved in the servant concept. They developed a remarkable variety of terms to express different aspects of it.[2] These terms naturally shade into each other and frequently it is not necessary to seek to bring out the different shades of meaning involved. But each term can be used to convey its own distinct emphasis.

Perhaps the most common was the word δοῦλος, "a slave, a bond servant." As the opposite of a man who is "free," this term carries the thought of one who belongs wholly to his master and is obligated to do his master's will. The early church found it a fitting term to express the spiritual reality that a believer belongs wholly to his heavenly Lord and consequently must obey Him in total submission.

The term οἰκέτης was often used as the practical equivalent of the word δοῦλος (cf. 1 Peter 2:18), but it is more specific and denotes "a house slave." It portrays a closer and more intimate relationship between servant and master than δοῦλος (cf. Rom. 14:4).

Two kindred terms, μίσθιος and μισθωτός, both rendered "hired servant," embody the picture of one working for pay.

These self-centered terms are not used in the New Testament in connection with its "servant" teaching. Jesus used the latter term of the inferior "hireling" as contrasted to the "good shepherd" (John 10:12–13).

Another term is θεράπων, denoting a willing servant who serves out of respect and concern for others; it carries a note of tenderness. As a technical term it was used to denote one who rendered a service of healing (cf. the English word "therapy").

The word παῖς, which means "child," was at times used of a person who was a slave (Luke 7:7); so used, the term expressed the affectionate attitude of the master toward his servant. This term is used of Christ as the Son and Servant of God.

The noun λατρεύς[3] originally meant one who worked for pay, rather than out of compulsion as a slave; hence he was a hired servant. But in the Septuagint and the New Testament the cognate verb (λατρεύω) is always used of religious service, either to the true God or to false gods in heathenism.[4] It thus expresses the thought of service to God in worship (Rom. 1:9; Heb. 9:9; 10:2).

The word λειτουργός denotes a public servant, one who discharges a public service on behalf of the people or the state. The term was used of the priests ministering in the temple. In Romans 13:6 Paul used it of pagan governmental officials, while in Philippians 2:25 he used it of the ministry of Epaphroditus to him on behalf of the Philippian church. Since this noun implies officers of rank and dignity, it is not used in the New Testament of the Christian ministry and its functions.[5]

Another noun conveying the servant theme is ὑπηρέτης (originally denoting an under-rower in a war galley ship). It denotes one who works under the direction of another as his superior. It is the word used in the Gospels of the officers of the Jews, acting under the direction of the high priest, who arrested Jesus in the garden. The term implies the position of a "staff officer"[6] (cf. Acts 13:5). In John 18:36 Jesus used the term of His own disciples, implying their dignity. In 1 Corinthians 4:1 Paul used this term in referring to a Christian minister in the widest sense.

The noun διάκονος refers to a servant in relationship to his activity, one who renders a service to another for the benefit of the one being served. Unlike the word for slave (δοῦλος) διάκονος implies the thought of voluntary service. It is used of the "servants" at the wedding in Cana (John 2:5, 7, 9). They were individuals who had voluntarily assumed this activity out of good will for the bride and groom. Among these various Greek words this one has the nearest approximation to the concept of a love-prompted service. Thus basically the word "deacon" denotes one who voluntarily serves others, prompted by a loving desire to benefit those served.

The derivation of this word διάκονος is not certain. It has been held that the term is a compound of the preposition διά, meaning "through," and the noun κόνις, "dust,"[7] so that the term denotes one who hurries through the dust to carry out his service. But this suggested derivation is not generally accepted today.[8] More probably the verbal root was διήκω, "to reach from one place to another,"[9] akin to the verb διώκω, "to hasten after, to pursue."[10] Then the root idea is one who reaches out with diligence and persistence to render a service on behalf of others. This would imply that the deacon reaches out to render love-prompted service to others energetically and persistently.

The term behind the word "deacon" appears in three forms in the New Testament. The verb διακονέω occurs 37 times, with various renderings for it in English,[11] generally, "to minister to" or "to serve." The noun διακονία denotes the concept of the service being rendered; it occurs 33 times, with various renderings in English such as "ministry," "ministering," "service," "serving," or "doing service." The personal noun διάκονος occurs 30 times. It is usually translated "servant" or "minister," though three times it is rendered "deacon." Together, these three Greek terms, all coming from the same root and having the same basic meaning, occur 100 times in the Greek New Testament. All these occurrences provide material for a study of the concept underlying the word "deacon" in the New Testament. As indicated in the renderings above, the noun διάκονος is used in an official as well as a nonofficial sense.

Deacon As an Official Term

In three verses the noun διάκονος is a technical term and is rendered "deacon."

PHILIPPIANS 1:1

In addressing his letter to "all the saints in Christ Jesus who are in Philippi," Paul added the unique expression "including the overseers and deacons." This is the first certain occurrence of διάκονος as a term of office in the New Testament. Mention of only these two offices in the salutation of the epistle implies that they were the only two officially established offices in the Philippian church. Though they constitute two distinct offices, they are closely related; Paul named both with one preposition. The order gives precedence to the overseers. Both terms are in the plural; neither office was confined to a single individual. The plurals leave undetermined how many overseers and deacons the Philippian church had. That, of course, would depend on the size and needs of the local church.

The term "overseers" (or "bishops," KJV) points to the basic duty of this office. The meaning of "deacons" simply points to a service function. No further hints of the respective duties of these two offices are given in this epistle. The order and basic meanings of the two terms suggest that the deacons somehow assisted the overseers in their ministries.

1 TIMOTHY 3:8, 12

In 1 Timothy 3:8 and 12 the word διάκονος also clearly has a technical force to denote a specific office. In this chapter Paul discussed the qualifications of two church officers, the "overseers" and the "deacons." The overseer is again placed first (3:1–7), but the discussion of the "deacons" follows in close connection (3:8–13). In verse 8 Paul listed the personal qualifications of deacons, in verse 9 their spiritual qualifications, and in verse 12 their domestic qualifications. Whether verse 11 refers to the wives of the deacons or to deaconesses has been much debated; possibly it means the latter.[12]

In 1 Timothy 3:10 Paul mentioned the testing of persons for appointment to the office of deacon. The meaning is not that they should be given a trial appointment as deacon, but rather that the church should constantly be examining and testing the members of the congregation, so that whenever the need for selecting deacons arises, they will know which members are qualified for appointment.

In this significant chapter on church leaders Paul gave some clear intimations concerning the function of the overseers (cf. vv. 2, 5), but he said nothing about the duties of deacons. Apparently Paul did not associate certain fixed duties with the office. The context suggests that the deacons served as assistants to the overseers. It may be suggested that "they were the church's relieving officers."[13] In view of the designated qualifications, they would be men who shared with the overseers a concern for the total needs of the congregation, and under the guidance of the overseers they aided in relieving those varied needs as they were able.

Doubtful Usages of the Word Group

In a few passages where the terms in this word group are used it is not clear whether an official position is involved.

ACTS 6:1–6

Many scholars accept the view that the origin of the office of deacon is described in Acts 6:1–6. The passage relates the story of seven members of the Jerusalem church who were appointed by the apostles to minister to material needs of the widows and the poor in the church. The personal noun διάκονος ("deacon") does not occur, but the related noun διακονία occurs twice. In verse 1 that word refers to "the daily ministration" (KJV) or "the daily serving" (NASB) of the needed food to the widows, but in verse 4 the word refers to "the ministry of the Word," the apostles' preaching. This double usage indicates that the concept of "deacon service" is not limited to material things. The cognate verb διακονέω (v. 2) relates to serving tables; the apostles indicated that it was not fitting that they should curtail their primary work of preaching to "serve tables." So they suggested that seven qualified men be appointed to take over this duty, which apparently up to then the apostles had taken care of. A relieving office was being established. But the seven who were appointed are nowhere called deacons.

While unquestionably Stephen faithfully performed his assigned task of serving tables, he did not regard himself as limited to such a material ministry. He also carried on an effective spiritual witness, as Acts 6:8–7:60 makes clear.

ROMANS 16:1

In Romans 16:1 the noun διάκονος (which may be either masculine or feminine gender) is applied to Phoebe, "who is a servant of the church which is at Cenchrea" (NASB). Again it is not certain whether the term is used here as a general designation of Phoebe's voluntary ministries to others or is intended as an official term, calling her a deaconess of the Cenchrean church. "Of the church" (not "in the church") may indicate that her ministries were not mere private efforts but were performed under the authorization and approval of the church. Dodd asserts, "We may assume that whatever the 'deacons' were at Philippi, that Phoebe was at Cenchreae."[14] Verse 2 makes clear that Phoebe was amply qualified for such an appointed service. The view that Phoebe held the office of deaconess in the church at Cenchrea seems the most plausible.[15] If so, then this is the first occurrence of the official meaning of the term in the New Testament.

1 TIMOTHY 3:13

The English rendering, "They that have used the office of a deacon well" (KJV; cf. "served well as deacons," NASB), limits the reference to the office of the deacon. The original is simply an articular participle and may accurately be rendered, "Those who have served well." Since this clause has no limiting object, it seems best to hold that the verbal form here is used to include the acceptable service of both overseers and deacons. It forms a suitable conclusion to the discussion in verses 1–13. The verb elsewhere is not restricted to the office of the deacon. The stress is on the action rather than the office.

Nonofficial Usages of the Word Group

In the vast majority of the New Testament occurrences of this word group, a nonofficial usage is clear. These occurrences give a fuller understanding of the concept that lies behind the term "deacon." A variety of usages appears.

WAITERS OF TABLES

The original sense of the verb διακονέω, "to wait at tables," is clear in Luke 17:8. Jesus spoke of a slave owner ordering his slave, returning from work in the field, to gird himself "and serve me until I have eaten and drunk." This is also the meaning in Acts 6:2. It is also the obvious meaning of the noun διάκονος in John 2:5, 9. This basic meaning of the cognate noun διακονία is evident in Luke 10:40 which uses it of Martha in whose home Jesus was a guest. While Mary sat at Jesus' feet, Martha was "cumbered about much serving" (KJV). She was greatly concerned about getting an appropriate meal ready for Jesus; she was engaged in "deacon service" on behalf of Jesus personally. Peter's mother-in-law, healed by Jesus, rendered a similar service in the privacy of her home (Matt. 8:15). These terms were often used of the domestic services of women. Also angels rendered such a service to Jesus at the end of His wilderness temptation (Matt. 4:11). They were rendering "deacon service" to Him in supplying His physical needs after 40 days of fasting.

RENDERING SERVICE TO ANOTHER

Often the scope of the service was broader than table service and denoted service generally for the benefit of another. Jesus used the noun διάκονοι to denote the personal servants of a great king (Matt. 22:1–14). In the first part of the parable (vv. 3–4, 6, 8, 10) Jesus used the ordinary word for slaves (δοῦλοι), but later He changed to the word διάκονοι, to denote those servants who stood in a close relationship to the king and served him personally in any desired capacity.

Jesus used these terms to depict the relationship of believers to Him: "If any one serve (διακονῇ) Me, let him follow Me; and where I am, there shall My servant (διάκονος) also be" (John 12:26). In this more general sense believers today are challenged to render "deacon service" to Christ Himself. Jesus added the encouraging assurance that such service will have its reward: "If any one serves Me, the Father will honor him" (John 12:26c). Such a love-prompted service to Him will express itself in service to others. Jesus taught that He would recognize such service as done unto Him (Matt. 25:40–45).

Jesus taught that believers must voluntarily serve other believers, motivated and inspired by His own example of service (Matt. 20:26–28; Mark 10:45). The terms thus came to denote loving service to brothers and neighbors, which is to be the distinguishing mark of Christ's followers. Jesus taught His disciples that instead of lording it over others, they must be willing to serve others (Matt. 20:25–26). Such service was the way to greatness among them, "Whoever wishes to become great among you shall be your servant" (διάκονος; Matt. 20:26). Those who aspire to be leaders must voluntarily stoop to serve.

Paul used the noun διακονία of the voluntary ministry that Stephanus and his family were rendering to the Corinthian church (1 Cor. 16:15). It involved a voluntary use of strength and possessions for the benefit of others, thus furthering the fellowship of the church. And in Hebrews 1:14 this term is used of the angels who are "sent out to render service (εἰς διακονίαν) for the sake of those who will inherit salvation." This pictures angels divinely sent to render "deacon service" to the saints. This service involves protecting believers and furthering their well-being. Thus these terms for service are often used in a general sense to denote any kind of service rendered for the benefit of others.

A MONETARY MINISTRY

This family of words is also used of serving others through monetary means. When Jesus was preaching in the cities of Galilee, He was accompanied by certain women whom He had healed, who "were helping to support them out of their own means" (Luke 8:3, NIV). Out of love and gratitude they used their money to supply the material needs of Jesus and His disciples. They formed the first "Ladies Peripatetic Missionary Society" in that they used their material means to further missionary goals.

Paul used these terms in connection with the collection being raised for the poor saints at Jerusalem (2 Cor. 8–9). In these chapters Paul did not use the word "money"; instead he used terms that characterized the collection as a spiritual service. By means of "this ministry to the saints" (2 Cor. 9:1) the local churches reached out to believers elsewhere as a ministry in building up the whole body of Christ (Eph. 4:12; cf. Acts 11:29; 12:29).

Dealing with money matters is commonly accepted as a phase of the work of church deacons. But when deacons deal with money, it should not be viewed simply in terms of cold cash; the money entrusted to them must be viewed as a means to minister to others for spiritual ends. When the Gentile believers sacrificially raised money for the Jewish believers in Jerusalem (2 Cor. 8:1–5), they were rendering "deacon service" toward them. They desired the total welfare of their fellow believers in Judea. Thus all believers have the opportunity to render "deacon service" to others through their material means.

GOVERNMENTAL OFFICIAL

The term διάκονος is also used in the New Testament to denote governmental officials. Paul, speaking of the secular ruler, wrote, "for he is a minister [διάκονος] of God to thee for good" (Rom. 13:4). This designation is repeated in the latter part of the verse. Human government is God's beneficent arrangement for human welfare. It was established to further God's moral order by punishing the evil and promoting the good.

SERVANTS OF A SPIRITUAL POWER

Διάκονος is often used figuratively in the New Testament of one who is the servant of a mighty spiritual power. This power may be either good or bad.

Paul used the noun διάκονος of false teachers who are the servants of Satan (2 Cor. 11:15). Paul commented that it was no surprise that men should be the deceptive servants of Satan since Satan likewise transforms himself into an angel of light.

But in most instances the word denotes a good power, the God whom believers serve. Paul referred to his coworkers as διάκονοι of God. Paul said Epaphras was "a faithful servant of Christ" (Col. 1:7). The apostle also used this noun to describe Tychicus (Eph. 6:21; Col. 4:7), and he used the verbal form in referring to Timothy and Erastus (Acts 19:22) and Onesiphorus (2 Tim. 1:16–18).

Paul also used διάκονος of himself to describe his position as furthering the cause of God. He used the term to describe his relation to the gospel and its message of hope (Col. 1:23) and of his relationship to the church (Col. 1:25). As commissioned by Christ, he performed a deacon service in voluntarily furthering the interest of both. His God-given ministry (διακονία) was among the Gentiles (Acts 21:19; 1 Tim. 1:12). Paul described his God-given work as a "ministry of reconciliation" (2 Cor. 5:18), a service that aimed at bringing men into spiritual reconciliation with God through the gospel.

Paul sent Archippus a special message: "Take heed to the ministry [διακονία] which you have received in the Lord, that you may fulfill it" (Col. 4:17). It was a delegated ministry and in thought the usage approaches the concept of the office of the deacon. But the context suggests rather that he had been chosen for pastoral service to replace Epaphras, their minister, while he was with Paul at Rome.[16] The ministry Archippus was to perform was pastoral in function, but as a voluntary service for the spiritual benefit of the church it had the character of deacon service.

Being used of God to convey His message to others is another phase of such a ministry. Peter referred to this ministry by the Old Testament prophets when they made known to New Testament believers the sufferings and glory of the Messiah (1 Peter 1:12).

To be the channels of making known to others the revealed message of God is a ministry in which deacons can freely share but it is not limited to the office of the deacon.

CHRIST AS SERVANT

Paul used the word διάκονος of Christ Himself: "Christ has become a servant to the circumcision on behalf of the truth of God" (Rom. 15:8). And Jesus said of Himself, "For even the Son of Man did not come to be served, but to serve (διακονῆσαι), and to give His life a ransom for many" (Mark 10:45; Matt. 20:26). In the Upper Room, Jesus, the uncontested superior of His disciples, washed their feet (John 13:1–17) as a lesson of love-prompted service. Though the one being served is the accepted superior, He pointed them to "the actuality: I am among you as a servant. . . . He is instituting in fact a new pattern of human relationships" through His personal example.[17] And "this summons to service becomes binding because behind it stands the sacrifice of Jesus, who came 'not to be served but to serve, and to give his life as a ransom for many'" (Mark 10:45).[18] In His earthly ministry Jesus Himself was the "Deacon" par excellence. He set the example not only for deacons but also for all believers.

Jesus said, "If any one serves Me, let him follow Me; and where I am, there shall My servant also be" (John 12:26). When Jesus uttered those words He was facing the cross. He knew that for His incarnate ministry to be spiritually fruitful He must die (John 12:24). That imperative lies on all His followers: "Where I am, there shall my servant also be." Believers too must be willing to die to self, if they are to be His fruitful servants.

Conclusion

The nontechnical usages of this word group extend beyond the narrow limits implied in the English word "deacon," which designates an ecclesiastical office. These Greek words provide a spiritually rich concept of service. For a true understanding of the biblical import of the term ''deacon'' this high concept of "deacon service" must be retained.

The basic concept underlying the word "deacon" is that of a voluntary, love-prompted service for the benefit of others. It is a service that desires the true welfare of those ministered to. "Deacon service" may well involve prosaic, material "table service," but it should go beyond such service and seek to further the highest spiritual welfare of others.

The work of the deacon, related to the local church and to the whole cause of Christ, must be spiritually motivated and be Christ-centered. It finds its motivation and encouragement in the self-sacrificing example and call of Christ. "The diakonos is always one who serves on Christ's behalf and continues Christ's service for the outer and inner man; he is concerned with the salvation of men."[19] It is a demanding and consuming service, but it has Christ's sure promise of reward: "If any one serves Me, the Father will honor him" (John 12:26).

CHAPTER 15

Reexamining Biblical Worship

Kenneth O. Gangel

Worship in evangelical churches today is too often a congregational adaptation of good old American pragmatism: people do what they like and they like what they do. Worship experience has become a means to an end as hymns, Scripture reading, and prayer serve as "preliminary activities" leading up to the focal point of worship, the preaching of God's Word. Without diminishing the importance of exposition, it is possible that one man's comments about the Bible may be no more important than the worship pattern, no more truth-serving than singing God's Word or listening to it read in its purest, uninterrupted form.

Biblical worship is often corrupted by boredom, lack of purpose, and nonparticipational behavior which leads the congregation to go through the motions without genuine heart involvement. The opposite extreme offers little more than secular entertainment with a religious veneer, a packaged plastic program so perfect and professional that even the most sincere worshiper can scarcely break through its shrink-wrapped design to get his hands on true worship.

What Is Worship?

Webber defines worship as "a meeting between God and His people" and calls for renewal of worship based on the Scriptures and the history of the church.[1] He suggests that evangelicals actually suffer from an illness of which the failure to worship is a symptom. He warns that "the remedy consists of repentance, a *metanoia*, a turning away from all shallow and uninformed approaches to worship."[2]

Many people think the Gospel of John focuses on evangelism, the message that "whosoever will may come." But in his presentation of Jesus Christ the Son of God, John is concerned that people recognize His deity and bow before Him in worship. A

161

blind beggar came to faith in the Savior after his sightless eyes saw light for the first time. Within hours he fell before the One who created sight "and he worshiped Him" (9:38).

In the Lord's encounter with the woman of Samaria (John 4) John mentioned "worship," "worshiped," or "worshipers" 10 times (out of its 13 occurrences in his Gospel). The 10 usages appear within five verses (4:20–24), dramatically demonstrating the difference between religion and Christianity. The Samaritan woman was deeply religious and knew precisely the appropriate place of worship which in her view was Mount Gerizim. The Lord Jesus shoved aside the discussion of both place and time. Religion may emphasize man's struggle to find God but the message of John's Gospel identifies how God has revealed Himself to man. It is not a matter of worshipers seeking for a hidden God but of a self-revealed God actively seeking the right kind of worshiper.

God is Spirit and His worshipers must worship Him "in spirit and truth" (John 4:23). The word "spirit" refers not to the Holy Spirit but to the spirit of the worshiper. One's posture in worship (kneeling, standing, bowing) is not the important thing. God is concerned with attitude before act; and wrong attitudes produce wrong acts.

To worship "in truth" means to be concerned for honesty before God and man. It also suggests that believers be biblical in their worship.

Small wonder that Paul affirmed, "God highly exalted Him, and bestowed on Him the name which is above every name, that at the name of Jesus every knee should bow, of those who are in heaven, and on earth, and under the earth, and that every tongue should confess that Jesus Christ is Lord, to the glory of God the Father" (Phil. 2:9–11). To the confused woman by the well the Lord offered the only voluntary declaration of messiahship in the entire New Testament "I who speak to you am He" (John 4:26).

What then is worship? Worship is *affirmation*. In worship a believer acknowledges that God's revelation of Himself in Jesus Christ demands response. The self-revealed God awaits the reaction of His creation and that response is a duty for God's redeemed people, not some kind of emotion that sweeps over them in a certain hour on a certain day. In true worship believers affirm that they are His people and that He is their God. Worship looks above.

Worship is also *conservation*. The corporate worship of the people of God preserves and transmits the faith. They identify themselves with the people of God of all times and places. The Word and the words used to communicate the faith are a foundation to conserving and transmitting God's truth.

Worship is also *edification*. The worshiper gains increasing understanding of God's Person and truth because proper worship teaches theology. In this sense biblical worship serves both the vertical and horizontal dimensions, though the latter should not be placed ahead of or even on a level with the former.

Worship is *celebration*. Believers celebrate their union with the Creator of the universe and with the Father of His people. They celebrate His marvelous works. They celebrate the birth, life, death, resurrection, and coming reign of the victorious Savior. And they invite others to join them in their homage.

> All people that on earth do dwell,
> Sing to the Lord with cheerful voice
> Him serve with fear, His praise forth tell,
> Come ye before Him and rejoice.
>
> For why? The Lord our God is good,
> His mercy is forever sure;
> His truth at all times firmly stood,
> And shall from age to age endure.
>
> —William Kethe, "All People That on Earth Do Dwell"

Worship As Celebration

Celebration and joy are appropriate faith responses to God's work in His world. In ancient times Israel's leaders called the people to a festal mentality at times of worship. "Then Nehemiah the governor, Ezra the priest and scribe, and the Levites who were instructing the people said to them all, 'This day is sacred to the Lord your God. Do not mourn or weep.' For all the people had been weeping as they listened to the words of the Law. Nehemiah said, 'Go and enjoy choice food and sweet drinks, and send some to those who have nothing prepared. This day is sacred to our Lord. Do not grieve, for the joy of the Lord is your strength'" (Neh. 8:9–10, NIV).

How much more do New Covenant believers have reason to respond to God's grace as they are "speaking to one another in psalms and hymns and spiritual songs" (Eph. 5:19). They rejoice in God's people as well as in God Himself, for their life together in the community of believers is cause for celebration. Not only this, but they also rejoice in their expectation of the Lord's return and the establishment of His kingdom on earth. True worship concentrates all one's physical, emotional, and spiritual faculties on a corporate self-giving to God in response to His love and in praise of His glory.

Often in the history of doctrine, worship has been viewed as the process of trying to give something to Someone who has everything. Thomas Aquinas, for example, concluded that worship is not for God's sake at all but for the sake of believers. Calvin responded that proper adoration of God is the prime purpose of Christianity.[3]

So dominant is the reality of grace, however, that believers find it extremely difficult to separate what God is from what God does. The question becomes, What can one give to Someone who gives everything? God's gifts provide an occasion to celebrate the Giver, and worship stimulates spiritual reaction. As Gilkey put it, "Worship is a response to the presence of God, our reaction to the appearance of the holy."[4]

When worship takes the form of response to a giving God, it honors grace by affirming that the heavenly Father has taken the initiative. The ultimate gift, of course, was the Cross. One's response to Calvary adorns the worship of the New Testament, causing it to stand in contrast to the cultic worship of first-century Mediterranean paganism. Christian worship was "decultified." Rather than secret rites practiced in darkened, scented cathedrals, worship is a normal, natural, and lifelike part of everyday behavior.

At certain times during the week Christians gather for collective praise. As Flynn put it in a book title, "Together we celebrate."[5] This corporate response of celebration does three things for the church:

1. It acknowledges God's supremacy by affirming who He is and what He has done. It agrees with God, honors Him, and says yes to His Word.
2. It rehearses God's goodness by affiliating with His great plan for the world in natural, personal, and special revelation (Ps. 100).
3. It proclaims God's truth by accenting that His message

is more than just "gospel"; it is the total scope of truth which always has its source in God (Ps. 93).

Clement of Alexandria described worship as celebration: "all our life is a festival: being persuaded that God is everywhere present on all sides, we praise Him as we till the ground, we sing hymns as we sow the seed, we feel His inspiration in all we do."

I sing th'almighty pow'r of God
That made the mountains rise,
That spread the flowing seas abroad
And built the lofty skies.
I sing the wisdom that ordained
The sun to rule the day;
The moon shines full at His command
And all the stars obey.

I sing the goodness of the Lord
That filled the earth with food;
He formed the creatures with His word
And then pronounced them good.
Lord, how Thy wonders are displayed
Where e'er I turn my eye,
If I survey the ground I tread
Or gaze upon the sky!

There's not a plant or flow'r below
But makes Thy glories known;
And clouds arise and tempests blow
By order from Thy throne;
While all that borrows life from Thee
Is ever in Thy care,
And everywhere that man can be,
Thou, God, art present there.

—Isaac Watts, "I Sing the Mighty Power of God"

Practicing God's Presence

"There is no life," wrote T. S. Eliot in his poem "The Rock," "that is not in community, and no community not lived in praise of God." In ancient Israel the act of assembling focused on collectivity, the people of God in congregation. To be sure, there was a focus on place (tabernacle or temple). Sacred shrines and pious personnel are not essential ingredients of biblical worship, but the gathering of God's people, congregated in His presence, began at Mount Sinai where the assembling involved the actual formulation of a nation (Deut. 9:10, 14).

Many New Testament words express the act of gathering and reflect the sense of community so strategic in Paul's teachings. But none is more descriptive than the familiar word ἐκκλησία. Used more than 100 times by New Testament writers, it speaks of people who are gathered out of the world.

Modern-day individualism has diminished and diluted the communal emphasis in Scripture. Piety has become compartmentalized, relegated to a private personal pocket of life. The result is a religious consumerism that describes worship as "attending the church of your choice." Western culture drowns in humanistic religion with its focus on "getting something out of the service."

Biblical worship, on the other hand, sees the Shepherd gathering the sheep, the Father gathering the children. The relational unity that God's people have with Him is, by its very strength, an antidote to individual loneliness (Ps. 106:47; Isa. 11:12; John 11:52; Eph. 1:7–10).

When Christians gather for worship they practice God's presence by affirming His plan in their lives and in the entire world (Col. 1:15–20). People gather in groups for all kinds of reasons—fellowship, hospitality, fun, and even mutual service—but none other than worship exalts the glory of the Triune God.

Many Christians have come to think of "orthodoxy" as correct doctrine when, as a matter of fact, a more specific use of the word would be "right worship." As the disciples gathered with Jesus in informal ways and places, they certainly were taught correct doctrine. But their communion with the Master stressed a relationship they were to cultivate rather than merely a volume of truth they were to learn. It is probably not incorrect to say that worship is "theantric," or in other words, man and God coming together in a unique relationship designed and sustained by the Holy Spirit.

Practicing God's presence emphasizes the spirit of worship, not its forms. The church is an inn, not a fort. The gathered body is itself, even apart from its teaching and preaching, an act of evangelism, a symbol, a demonstration to an unbelieving world that the good news has been communicated and has been received (Acts 2:42–47).

> We gather together to ask the Lord's blessing;
> He chastens and hastens His will to make known;
> The wicked oppressing now cease from distressing,
> Sing praises to His name: He forgets not His own.
>
> —Netherlands folk hymn, "We Gather Together"

How Important Is the Day?

Ignatius of Antioch, heir to the apostolic traditions, wrote, "Those who had walked in ancient practices attained unto newness of hope, no longer observing Sabbaths but fashioning their lives after the Lord's day, on which our life also arose through Him."

Yet the Sabbath is grounded deeply in Old Testament history. Rooted in creation, its observance hallowed time (Gen. 2:2–3). Rooted in the Mosaic Covenant, its honor served as a reminder of God's creative work (Exod. 20:8–11), a reminder of the Exodus (Deut. 5:12–15), and as a sign between Israel and God (Exod. 31:13, 17). The Sabbath was to be hallowed by Israel (Lev. 23:3; Isa. 58:13–14).

But the Sabbath was made for man, not man for the Sabbath. Jesus often ministered on that great day much to the horror of the Pharisees (Mark 2:27–28; John 5:17). That the early Christians were Jews makes their transition all the more remarkable. Keeping one day out of seven, they changed the emphasis from the seventh to the first day (John 20:1, 19, 26; Acts 20:7; 1 Cor. 16:2). By the end of the first century the first day had become known as "the Lord's day" (Rev 1:10). The Resurrection had brought assembly and rest under its first-day authority.

Justin Martyr, who lived and wrote approximately A.D. 100–165, had opportunity to note how several generations of Christians understood the observance of Sunday. He concluded, "We all hold this common gathering on Sunday since it is the first day on which God transforming darkness and matter made the universe, and Jesus Christ our Savior rose from the dead on the same day."[6]

First-day worship has always been characterized by newness, freedom, joy, and the recognition of the day as one of God's great gifts. How tragic that through the years Christians have freighted it with the baggage of duty, guilt, and sadness.

Christians hold a sacred vow of the past with its glorious reminders of Creation, Incarnation, Crucifixion, and Resurrection. Believers treasure the precious hours of the present governed by the living Lord and indwelt by His vibrant Spirit. But essentially they are future-oriented since the first day looks at what is ahead as surely as the last day looked at what was behind.

The New Testament teaching regarding the church repeatedly affirms its function as a body and as a family. The images affirm the need for assembling together, for neither bodies nor families can work in a disjointed form. The church thrives, therefore, when it is together, always in spirit, often in literal physical form. The day of gathering is a reminder of the believers' interdependence. In the late 20th century the Lord's followers need to heed again the words of the Apostle Peter: "The end of all things is at hand; therefore, be of sound judgment and sober spirit for the purpose of prayer. Above all, keep fervent in your love for one another. . . . Be hospitable to one another without complaint. As each one has received a special gift, employ it in serving one another as good stewards of the manifold grace of God. Whoever speaks, let him speak, as it were, the utterances of God; whoever serves, let him do so as by the strength which God supplies; so that in all things God may be glorified through Jesus Christ, to whom belongs the glory and dominion forever and ever Amen" (1 Peter 4:7–11).

> O day of rest and gladness,
> O day of joy and light,
> O balm of care and sadness,
> Most beautiful, most bright;
> On these the high and lowly,
> Through ages joined in tune,
> Sing "Holy, holy, holy,"
> To the great God triune.
>
> Today on weary nations
> The heav'nly manna falls;
> To holy convocations
> The silver trumpet calls,
> Where gospel light is glowing
> With pure and radiant beams,
> And living water flowing
> With soul refreshing streams.

New graces ever gaining
From this our day of rest,
We reach the rest remaining
To spirits of the blest;
To Holy Ghost be praises,
To Father and to Son;
The Church her voice upraises
To Thee, blest, Three in One.

—Christopher Wordsworth,
"O Day of Rest and Gladness"

In Remembrance of Me

In the Passover feast, devout Jews remind themselves of who they are and whose they are. And though the Lord's Supper is no more a Christian Passover than Sunday is a Christian Sabbath, the worship life of the church is bound up with eating and drinking. Indeed, spiritual hunger and thirst rest at the foundation of the life in Christ (Ps. 23:5). Meals are shared both in family and church. Animals grab a morsel and slink off to chew it alone. But believers fellowship together at food, both physical and spiritual. The English word "Lord" comes from the Old English words for "loaf" (*hlāf*) and "keeper" (*weard*);[7] He is the "Keeper of the bread," the One to whom believers look to be fed. Promises of future gatherings for feasting abound in New Testament teaching (Matt. 8:11; Rev. 19:9).

New Testament believers ate together with regularity, sharing their homes with one another. But one meal stands out in the New Testament as "the Lord's Supper," the communion of modern Christian worship (1 Cor 11:23–25). How much like the early church do Christians today celebrate this ordinance? Why does the New Testament describe so little form, leading to such wide divergence of practice among God's people? When and how did the love feast and the Lord's Supper become divided? Did the early believers observe a fellowship feast as part of their worship?

Communion is the *Lord's* Supper. The focus is on Him and therefore celebration and affirmation become proclamation (1 Cor. 11:26). Any hint of duty or requirement rather than joy and freedom detracts from the reality of the worship experience.

The New Testament suggests that this meal sanctifies all others. Every communion meal offers an occasion for worship, an acknowledgment that believers are guests in God's world and that He is the host. All worship gatherings of believers do not observe ordinances, nor are all the gatherings the sharing of a bounteous physical feast. But in reality, all such gatherings recognize hunger and thirst, a desire to come to the table of the Lord and be refreshed from His hand with song, prayer, Scripture, and other elements of the worship "meal."

As a fellowship feast the Lord's Supper emphasizes what the Lord's people have in common ("communion"). The elements may be distributed in varying forms, but the emphasis on one loaf, one cup, and eating in unison focuses the celebration of the whole church without regard to denominational or even congregational boundaries. Deep historical significance underlies the celebration of the communion. It is a traditional thanksgiving to God, a form of prayer. The remembrance brings the reality of the Cross down to one's daily existence; believers' partaking of the elements of worship acknowledges a giving of themselves to God in response to what He gave and continues to give.

> Here, O my Lord, I see Thee face to face;
> Here would I touch and handle things unseen,
> Here grasp with firmer hand th'eternal grace,
> And all my weariness upon Thee lean.
>
> This is the hour of banquet and of song,
> This is the heavenly table spread for me,
> Here, let me feast and feasting still prolong
> The brief bright hour of fellowship with Thee.
>
> Feast after feast thus comes and passes by,
> Yet passing points to the glad feast above,
> Giving sweet foretaste of the festal joy
> The Lamb's great bridal feast of bliss and love.
>
> —Horatius Bonar, "Here, O My Lord,
> I See Thee Face to Face"

Worship as Service

Germans say it well with their word *Gottesdienst*, commonly used for worship but literally meaning "service of God." Central to a New Testament understanding of service is the word διακονέω, from which comes the English word "deacon." It denotes more an act of service than the state of servitude (Luke 22:27; 1 Peter 1:12;

Heb. 6:10). Common acts of self-abasement are translated in New Testament theology to acts of service for each other. As Jesus put it to the disciples on the night of His crucifixion, the true host takes the role of a waiter (Luke 22:24–27).

In a world of pagan religions full of temples and shrines Paul told Christians that they are God's building (1 Cor 3:9). Christian service purposes to build up the building and thereby build up the body and family. Is it fair to say that Paul does not emphasize worship as service to God, service to self, or service to a neighbor, but rather service to the entire body of Christ? Perhaps the unity of ministry cannot be so divided.

Worship as service describes people allowing God to work through them in order to create a spiritual community. Worship as service involves the understanding and application of spiritual gifts and their role in the body of Christ (Rom. 12:6–8). The unity, diversity, and mutuality of the church abound when worshipers serve and servants worship. The worship affirmation in Romans 11:33–36 is followed by the appeal in 12:1 for "reasonable service" or "logical liturgy" ("spiritual worship"). The apostle then describes the unity of Christ's body ("each member belongs to all the others," 12:5, NIV), details some of the spiritual gifts by which this worship-service is carried out, and discusses the whole lifestyle of the church active in worship and service.

The practical application of all this activates the involvement of the entire congregation in worship. Was Paul scolding the Corinthians when he wrote, "When you assemble, each one has a psalm, has a teaching, has a revelation, has a tongue, has an interpretation. Let all things be done for edification" (1 Cor 14:26)? Or did he simply suggest that this kind of mutual sharing had taken on a dimension of disorder at Corinth and needed to be brought back into proper perspective and practice? The diversity of participation in New Testament worship can be easily defended. Worship was not one actor being watched by a multitude of spectators. Focus was not fixed; leadership was not single.

> Holy God, we praise Thy name;
> Lord of all, we bow before thee;
> All on earth Thy scepter claim,
> All in heav'n above adore Thee.
> Infinite Thy vast domain,
> Everlasting is Thy reign.

Lo! the apostolic train
Join Thy sacred name to hallow;
Prophets swell the glad refrain,
And the white-robed martyrs follow;
And from morn to set of sun,
Through the Church the song goes on.

Holy Father, Holy Son,
Holy Spirit, Three we name Thee;
While in essence only One,
Undivided God we claim Thee,
And adoring bend the knee,
While we sing our praise to Thee.

—Attributed to Ignace Franz,
"Holy God, We Praise Thy Name"

Marks of True Worship

True worship must be offered to God alone in deep appreciation of His majesty and rulership in the world and in believers' lives. The worshiper engages God on a spiritual rather than physical level and the worship experience, private or public, must be *dominated by God's Spirit.*

An attitude of settled dependence on the Holy Spirit leads to cleansing, readiness, and a cultivation of the proper mind and heart attitude for worship. Worship becomes then a *total response* in which spiritual. emotional, and physical factors tune together to draw attention to the heavenly Father.

The biblical worshiper sees himself as Paul described him in Ephesians 1, the recipient of a vast undeserved bounty of spiritual riches provided entirely by the grace of God. He worships *in the truth* regarding the Triune Godhead and particularly Jesus Christ the atoning Son. The preaching of the Word of God does not conflict with the solitude of quiet meditation for both have their distinctive roles in the total worship experience. As God's people worship, they focus their attention on the worthiness (worth-ship) of God. Consequently song and other forms of praise flow almost spontaneously from God's adoring, joyful people.

Certainly one of the marks of true worship is *confession of sin.* In the Old Testament the priests washed their hands before entering the tabernacle; an emphasis on cleansing dominates the Old and New Testaments alike. Too often the freedom of many churches generates a happy fellowship that makes the worship room sound like a busy airport before services are officially begun. Can they not learn to use the prelude time for personal preparation for true worship? Corporate worship particularly is an activity of the gathered body taught in the church during its formal meetings.

May the Lord give believers the wisdom and courage to purge themselves of clock-watching, spectatorism, cheap shoddiness, and self-centered emotionalism as they carry out their attempts at worship in harmony with the New testament.

> Immortal, invisible, God only wise,
> In light inaccessible hid from our eyes.
> Most blessed, most glorious, the Ancient of Days,
> Almighty victorious, Thy great name we praise.
>
> Unresting, unhasting, and silent as light,
> Nor wanting, nor wasting, thou rulest in might;
> Thy justice like mountains high soaring above
> Thy clouds, which are mountains of goodness and love.
>
> To all, life Thou givest, to both great and small.
> In all life Thou livest, the true life of all.
> We blossom and flourish as leaves on the tree.
> And wither and perish—but naught changeth Thee.
>
> Great Father of glory, pure Father of light,
> Thine angels adore Thee, all veiling their sight;
> All praise we would render; O help us to see
> 'Tis only the splendor of light hideth Thee!
>
> —Walter C. Smith, "Immortal, Invisible"

Designing Creative Worship Experiences

Perhaps creative worship will take a nudge toward progress if Christians begin to realize that worship does not consist merely of Bible study or any other single activity. Certainly prayer will be involved, as will *praise*; but a third word beginning with that letter clamors for more attention —*participation.*

The involvement of the people of God in the worship of God when they come to the house of God is a primary maxim on which all other plans for creative worship must rest. Too much time may be spent in the preparation of the sermon and too little time in preparation of the rest of worship. Some pastors want to rush through all the "preliminaries" to get to the "really important" aspect of the service, the preaching.

Innovations in worship must be carefully planned and the very element of variety itself can be a mark of creativity in worship. At a small church where this writer served for several years, no two Sunday services are exactly alike. The order of service changes, people who are involved in participation and what they do in the service often changes, and the congregation has learned to expect a different approach to worship each time they meet.

Of course change simply for the sake of change is not desirable. The concern expressed here is for an upgrading of the quality of worship experience in the church. Here are a few specific examples of the kinds of things that can be done to bring about creative change in corporate worship. They might not work for all churches.

1. Read the Scriptures in unison or antiphonally, or perhaps from various versions so that people who have brought the King James Version all stand and read a portion of the text of the week, people who have the NASB do likewise, the NIV the same, and so forth.
2. At different points in the service introduce helpful liturgical items such as leader-people response, original liturgies written by creative people in the church, and participational response of various kinds.
3. Introduce creedal recitation, on occasion using the Apostles' Creed or perhaps even the Nicene Creed.
4. The sermon could be delivered in sections divided by its major points and punctuated by hymns, other music, or congregational responses of various kinds.
5. A sermon reaction panel consisting of elders, young couples, or teenagers can interact with the pastor for 5 or 10 minutes after the sermon.
6. If the church is not too large, a roving microphone can be handled by one of the ushers as people are allowed to ask questions about the sermon.
7. On occasion the familiar prelude and postlude can be replaced with meditative silence.
8. Vary the Scriptures and comments used in the communion service. First Corinthians 11 is fine but it is not necessarily the only passage in the Bible that speaks of communion in the Lord's Supper.

9. Use the bulletin creatively to include sermon outlines, interpretive verses, different names for the activities of worship, and for the printing of congregational response in whatever form it is used.
10. Take time to teach people how to worship. Explain the different things being done and why they are done. Worship must become meaningful.

All this, of course, must begin on an individual basis. People bring to corporate worship the attitudes and readiness (or lack of it) which set the standard not only for what they give and receive in a public service but how they influence family members and friends over a long period of time. May God's people never forget that the focus of worship is not themselves but their heavenly Father and His glorious Son, the Savior.

> Thine is the glory risen, conqu'ring Son;
> Endless is the vict'ry Thou o'er death hast won.
> Angels in bright raiment rolled the stone away,
> Kept the folded graveclothes where Thy body lay.
>
> Lo! Jesus meets us, risen, from the tomb;
> Lovingly He greets us, scatters fear and gloom;
> Let His church with gladness hymns of triumph sing,
> For her Lord now liveth; death hath lost its sting.
>
> No more we doubt Thee, glorious Prince of Life!
> Life is naught without Thee; aid us in our strife;
> Make us more than conqu'rors, through Thy deathless love;
> Bring us safe through Jordan to Thy home above.
>
> — Edmund L. Budry, "Thine is the Glory,
> Risen, Conquering Son"

CHAPTER 16

The Place of the Small Church in Today's World

Kenneth O. Gangel

S ixty percent of all Protestant churches in the United States and Canada have fewer than 200 members each. Two-thirds of those average less than 120 in a Sunday morning worship service. And at least one half of all Protestant congregations in North America can be labeled "small."[1]

Furthermore the population shift over the past decade actually favors the viability of small churches. According to research reported by the United Methodist Church, the towns and countrysides of this nation added people nearly twice as fast as did the cities from 1970 to 1980, a trend which is expected to continue. The last time nonurban counties outgrew urban ones was more than 160 years ago.

Meanwhile, religious leaders at all points on the theological compass are rethinking the super-church craze of the 1970s. Speaking of the largest Protestant denomination in the world, Danielsen writes, "We praise the Lord for large churches, but the fact of the matter is that churches with over 1,000 in membership make up about 11 percent of the churches in the Southern Baptist Convention. Churches with membership under 300 make up 61.3 percent of the churches in the Southern Baptist Convention."[2] In the United Methodist Church congregations with fewer than 200 members represent 64 percent of all the congregations, and in that mainline denomination, 10 percent of the churches have an average attendance of under 20 at the morning worship service, 26 percent average fewer than 35, and 57 percent maintain all average attendance of fewer than 75.[3]

But what is "small" when that tag is applied to churches? Researcher Schaller identifies a figure of 175 worshipers on Sunday morning as an ideal.[4] Allowing for a flexibility factor of 25 either way from that mean, one might say that a church of 150 or fewer worshipers on Sunday morning (or at its principal weekly service) is small. Of course this is a relative designation since before the days of urbanization, industrialization, and centralization, that size would have been considered more than ample. When viewed against the backdrop of the current infatuation with size, "150" and "small" seem synonymous.

> History is on the side of the small church. Bigness is the new kid on the block. Historically, Protestant denominations in the United States have been comparatively small. At the time of the Civil War, the size of the average Protestant church was less than 100 members. A few large churches were in the center of the city, or at the center of the ethnic community. By the turn of the century, the average congregation still had [fewer] than one hundred fifty members.[5]

But Schaller makes an important point when he says that the number of people in attendance is not the issue. He suggests that an entirely different mentality, a distinctive outlook in the small church makes it something other than a scaled-down version of larger congregations in its town or denomination.

> To switch analogies, the congregation averaging less than 35 or 40 at worship can be represented by an acorn squash, the church averaging 125 at worship can be depicted by a pumpkin, the congregation averaging 200 at worship might be portrayed by a horse, and the huge church averaging 500 or 600 or more at worship can be symbolized by a fifteen-room house. They are not simply different size specimens from the same genus or species. They are almost as different from one another as a village is unlike a large central city. It is impossible to produce a pumpkin pie by combining three acorn squashes.[6]

As formerly the pastor of a small church (under 100), this writer wonders what other metaphors Schaller might have chosen to describe the church of 3,000, 5,000, or 10,000!

Several years ago Paul Madsen authored a book entitled *The Small Church: Valid, Vital, and Victorious* (Valley Forge, PA: Judson, 1975). Without furrowing the same ground farmed so well by Madsen in that book, the viability of this vast block of "small" churches may again be reviewed.

Is the Small Church Really Valid?

The question, of course, is moot since 60 percent of the churches on the North American continent will not thereby fold up their bulletins and fade away. Perhaps "viability" is a better word than "valid." Is it viable or even wise for these denominations or local congregations to sustain a ministry that probably does not have the strong possibility of growing to 175 or more within the foreseeable future? After all, more than 50,000 churches in the United States are closed and that specter certainly must haunt a congregation with declining attendance and membership roles in double digits. Yet some distinctive strengths of the small church may not rest in those areas generally advanced by church growth studies and literature. These are areas of extreme importance, however, and may well be closer to the heart of biblical concern than topping last year's attendance records or beating the church across the town in an annual Sunday school contest.

STRENGTHS OF THE SMALL CHURCH

One strength of the small church is its *relational emphasis*. All churches are or should be macrocosms of the family microcosm. Pushed to its ultimate concern, the family finds its parallel in the universal church, the heavenly Father, the bridegroom metaphor, and the relationship of believers as spiritual children. Large churches find it necessary to design small-group experiences to capture a relational emphasis that comes naturally in the small church not only by virtue of size but also by perspective. In the large church people are identified and recognized by virtue of office (e.g., "That woman over there is our pianist") while in a small church almost everyone is known by his or her name, and, it may be added, usually the first name. Stated in sociological terms, the small-church congregation experiences a sense of "primary group" rather than "secondary group." Of course there are many primary groups in a large church but the congregation as a whole functions as a secondary group. As Ray points out, this is a need-meeting arrangement.

> The primary or family group meets three needs people have. First, it gives identity. People have a name and a responsibility. They are recognized when they are there and missed when they are not. Second, it gives people security. They belong and have a voice. They expect the church to be dependable. As one of our members said, "If you need a favor, you don't feel hesitant to ask because you know someone will be happy to help." Third, it is what Dudley means by the "caring cell." People do care about one another.[7]

A second strength of the small church is its *decentralized focus*. To be sure, small churches led by autocratic pastors may not appear to be decentralized. But autocracy carries with it a bureaucratic climbing impulse that tends to catapult most leaders into larger churches as soon as they can seize an opportunity for upward mobility. Small churches may not be punctual or visibly efficient but they get the job done. Their organizational style tends to be much looser, more informal, more democratic; and it allows for decisions to be made by consensus with a special concern for families and individuals. A planning manual designed for use by churches affiliated with the United Church of Christ promotes an organizational style called "provolution." The emphasis is on looking ahead and using the group's energy to design strategies for the future rather than a problem-solving orientation that is much more existential. Provolution focuses on available group resources and the importance of emphasizing strengths.[8]

It is fascinating to note that this decentralized style, which the small church tends to develop without a great deal of thought, is in line with the wave of the future. Chapter five of John Naisbitt's bestseller *Megatrends* (New York: Warner, 1982) emphasizes how late 20th-century society is moving from centralization to decentralization. All this produces in the small church a stronger sense of ownership, loyalty, and faithfulness—and that is a distinct strength.

A third strength of the small church is its *resilient persistence*. D. Campbell Wyckoff's line about the Sunday school being as "American as crabgrass" can be applied to the small church. It survives disaster after disaster, flies in the face of demographic trends, comes almost to the verge of extinction not once but numerous times, and yet lives on. In the late summer of 1983 this writer was privileged to visit the "homecoming" festivities of the first church he pastored, beginning in 1957. The similarities were mind-boggling. It was almost as though nothing had changed— the building, the grounds, many of the people, the size of the congregation, its outlook, its problems, and its blessings. The congregation, under 50 a quarter of a century ago, is still a congregation under 50. Church growth specialists would have predicted its demise decades ago. Yet the church was founded in 1824. Schaller gives eight reasons for the toughness of the small church: (1) The fact that it is not a branch office. (2) The fact that it reinforces community. (3) The fact that subsidies increase vulnerability. (4) The socialization factor. (5) The importance of shared experiences. (6) The centrality of worship. (7) The role of the laity. (8) The focal point for loyalty.[9]

When a church's emphasis is on shared experience rather than multitudinous functions; when preaching is central and life-related; when lay leadership is vital; and when Sunday worship is central in its life, that church is "tough."

Weaknesses of the Small Church

The small church also has numerous weaknesses, one of which is *inadequate resources*. This helps explain why small churches are small. According to Madsen five factors persist: an inadequate program, an inadequate field (limited population to draw on), inadequate evangelism, inadequate vision, and inadequate personalities.[10] Inadequacies of the small church are amplified by constant comparison with other large and prosperous congregations nearby. The upright piano does not sound so good after one hears the pipe organ at First Presbyterian; the ladies trio pales by comparison with the 60-voice choir at Faith Baptist; and the struggling, overworked pastor seems at an unfair advantage when stacked up against a 12-member multiple staff team over at Calvary Bible. This is less a problem for the rural church than the urban or suburban church since the points of comparison are magnified in the latter two situations.

One of the resources often found to be inadequate is money. Willimon and Wilson claim that "finances are a perennial problem. The small congregation tends to spend a large proportion of its income (often between one-half and two-thirds) for pastoral services. Even then, it generally shares the pastor with one or more other churches, or employs a part-time minister who also holds a secular job."[11]

A second weakness may be called an *exclusionary atmosphere*. Schaller makes a distinction between the fellowship circle and the membership circle. He refers to the dividing line as a wall that protects the insiders from the outsiders. Hansell expands the concept to include three concentric circles inside a square (see the chart on page 181). Everything inside the square is membership but "acceptance" does not occur till a parishioner makes it into circle B (this is parallel with Schaller's membership circle). Point C on the Hansel diagram is comparable to Schaller's fellowship circle but Hansell adds point D to describe the area where the real power of the church resides.[12] This model does not fit every church. However, the fact that levels of acceptance do exist within the local church emphasizes the exclusionary atmosphere that can come because of long-term leadership dominance by certain membership families.

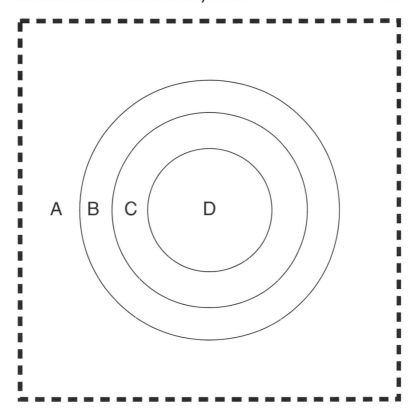

Levels of Acceptance in the Small Church

Another weakness of the small church is *pastoral discouragement.* In many small churches the pastor is the outsider, a fact often headlined by the common phrase, "We've seen pastors come and go here." Pastoral tenure is generally very short in North American churches—a fact that complicates ministry in a small church, especially when mixed with inadequate resources and the control of a few strong families in an exclusionary atmosphere. Sometimes discouragement comes simply from inappropriate comparison. Besides being difficult and unnecessary for a small rural church to be transformed into a large church, it is probably unwise. *The key issue is meeting needs through the Word of God, not a sense of self-actualization through successful involvement in the numbers game.*

Then, too, few things are private in a small community. Everyone knows the pastor's family, his finances, and his faults. Some men find this transparency difficult to handle and therefore view the small church only as a stepping stone to a "stronger ministry." Inadequate congregational identity may lead to inadequate ministerial identity, an uncertain road to discouragement. Pastors of small churches should memorize and frequently recite 1 Corinthians 1:26–30.

> Brothers, think of what you were when you were called. Not many of you were wise by human standards; not many were influential; not many were of noble birth. But God chose the foolish things of the world to shame the wise; God chose the weak things of the world to shame the strong. He chose the lowly things of this world and the despised things— and the things that are not—to nullify the things that are, so that no one may boast before him. It is because of him that you are in Christ Jesus, who has become for us wisdom from God—that is, our righteousness, holiness and redemption.

Can the Small Church Be Vital?

In the light of what has already been written this question is rhetorical, but it requires reaffirmation. Yes, the small church can be vital.

THE SMALL CHURCH CAN BE VITAL IN ITS WORSHIP

Willimon and Wilson state that "there may be small churches without a building, without an educational program, without a budget, and without formal organizational structure, but there are no small churches without preaching and worship."[13] Of course, not all small churches are carrying on satisfactory worship programs but that does not detract from the fact that worship is central in the life and experience of every church. Danielsen identifies "four adjectives that describe effective worship in the small church": important, indigenous, innovative, and inclusive.[14] The list speaks for itself and serves as a reminder that the enhancement of worship experience is probably a need in most congregations of any size.

THE SMALL CHURCH CAN BE VITAL IN ITS PREACHING

Willimon and Wilson emphasize that a preacher, perhaps especially in the small church, is to be a "servant of the Word." They correctly emphasize the significance of variety and relevance in small church preaching and warn that the quality of preaching in the small church must never be judged by showmanship and the size of the crowd.

> Preachers on television and in immense city churches may be great rhetoricians; occasionally, they may be great expositors of the Word. But they will never be great servants of the Word, because they lack the pastoral, day-to-day encounters with the total life of God's people, which is a prerequisite for faithfulness to the Word. . . . In the small church, where the preacher, known by the congregation, stands before a congregation known by the preacher, and where it is apparent that this is a family, gathering before the riches of their Book, and that the word that is spoken is understood to be the contemporary family's word, great preaching begins.[15]

In order to be vital, the small church must emphasize lay leadership. Few small churches will be multi-staff ministries. Few will have the advantage of high educational levels in the congregation or the involvement of already trained and experienced leadership. The pastor therefore becomes an enabler in contrast to the managerial role of the multi-staff team leader. Such a skilled facilitator, working within the relational patterns of the small church, can cultivate magnificent vines in the vineyard of the Lord if he is willing to labor there for the time it takes to produce the fruit. Of the many reasons why such fruit does not regularly grow in the small church, two are paramount: (1) It takes much patience and humility to stay with a small church for that many years. (2) Seminaries may not have trained pastors to be enablers.

THE SMALL CHURCH CAN BE VITAL IN ITS EDUCATION

In the small church the pastor is his own minister of education and therefore becomes the key person in the nurturing program. He is responsible for interpreting the educational ministry, organizing its various facets, and providing inspirational leadership to Sunday school teachers, youth sponsors, visitors, teachers of home Bible classes, and all the work in the educational framework. The enabling relationship is once again most obvious. However, a wise pastor will soon gather around him a small but effective Christian education committee. As disciples these committee members can absorb his enthusiasm for the educational ministry and learn the process of directing and facilitating the work of others.

The genius of successful Christian education ministries in small churches is adaptation, the clarification of what community needs are and how the church proposes to meet them. Carolyn Brown is on the right track when she says:

> The point is not to do everything, but to select those forms of Christian education that fit your church, and to do them very well. In doing this, I expect you will find yourselves capable of providing your members with opportunities to grow in their faith that will prove interesting, exciting, and more effective than you ever dreamed possible.[16]

Willimon and Wilson also speak of the educational value of the regular events of church life. "Never forget that pastors are educating each time they lead worship. In fact, for the small church, worship may be (as it always should have been for the church) the primary educational event. Pastors must take care when they lead worship that they teach the things they really mean to teach!"[17]

The qualities that make up effective education—relational emphasis, verification of needs and objectives, affirmation of the importance of each student as an individual member of the whole, and ownership of programs by the people who lead them—are components which come more easily to the small church than to the large.

THE SMALL CHURCH CAN BE VITAL IN ITS
    CONGREGATIONAL LIFE

Though the large church may often and loudly say it is people-oriented, it tends to be centered on programs. But the personality of the small church emerges from the collective experiences and relationships of its members.

> The larger congregation knows who it is because of what it does, and it must keep on doing, in order to reassure its existence. The small church has identity because of the experiences that it brings from the past. Its primary satisfactions are in the relationships among people who share experiences in faith. They find identity in their character, not in their activities.[18]

A church without vast buildings and programs virtually is forced to say to visitors and potential members, "We are who we are, the people of God in this place." The emphasis in such churches can thus be on their uniqueness and distinctives rather than on likeness to other congregations.

THE SMALL CHURCH CAN BE VITAL IN ITS EVANGELISM

Two false ideas must be eliminated if the small church is to be vital in evangelism. One is the social role, so often played in rural areas, in which the church serves as a *transmitter of culture*. This is less a problem for evangelical congregations, of course, but there is still that nagging link with the past that detracts from the mission of the present. A second dangerous notion is *survival orientation*. Most small churches are far from Maslow's "self-actualization" need level. Shedding a survival mentality does not mean doubling or tripling in size; rather it is a focus on what God wants to do with a given congregation in a given place at a given time. When these two false concepts are removed, small churches can give themselves more actively to the winning of souls.

Is the Small Church Really Victorious?

Leaders in small church congregations are more likely to be victorious, in the proper spiritual and biblical understanding of that word, if they have taken their eyes off of society's values and placed thcm on eternity's values. Ray calls for Christians to be delivered from "sizism."

> Permeating our consciousness is an assumption that smaller is lesser and bigger is better. In the world of the church, it is the churches with the biggest Sunday School, the biggest mission budget, the biggest membership, the biggest fleet of busses, or the biggest building that get the biggest press and prizes.[19]

A new orientation of perspective, priorities, and power is needed.

TOWARD A NEW PERSPECTIVE

A major step in developing a victorious perspective is to understand what Schaller means when he says "the small church is different." Of course, small churches can be defined and described statistically, geographically, economically, sociologically, and theologically. But they must also be understood psychologically, particularly with respect to the issue of self-esteem and mission orientation. A small church should ask itself these questions: "Is there a positive enthusiasm about the ministry of our church? Do we experience a healthy cooperation between pastor and lay leadership? Do our ministers generally exceed a tenure of two or three years? Are we able to articulate our goals and move objectively toward our goals? Are we regularly considering new ministries to reach different groups of people, perhaps those who have been neglected by other churches in the community? Have we broken down the walls between membership and fellowship and mastered the task of assimilating new members?" Positive answers must be given to these and other questions to keep the perspective of the small church genuinely victorious.

TOWARD NEW PRIORITIES

A small church cannot do everything it would like to do. Among its various and noble goals, therefore, it must identify specific priorities and work toward those aspects of ministry. The endemic strengths of the small church ought to lead to some understanding of priorities. The essentiality of worship, for example, leads to a strong emphasis on the Sunday morning worship service. The relational nature of the congregation might lead to a strengthening of fellowship groups or body-life emphasis in connection with one of the regular services.

Schaller identifies the priority concerns of small-church members as "money, morale, members, and ministerial leadership."[20] These are priorities expressed in the most general terms. Each congregation must identify for itself what emphases it will adopt in the ministry to which God has called it.

TOWARD NEW POWER

Here it is important to distinguish between sociological and spiritual values. Some of the thrust of these paragraphs has dealt with cultural and sociological factors since the church is both organization and organism. Indeed many of the advantages of the small church are sociological in nature and dare not be minimized, though they are not found in the more preferable theological domain. Power for ministry, however, comes not from patterns of makeup but rather from the Word and the Spirit. The pastor of a small church dare not "endure" its temporary difficulties on his way to a larger more significant ministry. It is imperative that he serve the Word and the people as though he will minister in that church for several decades. Like Titus on Crete or Timothy in Ephesus, he is a servant sent by God to be His representative to a specific part of the universal body of Christ.

What lies ahead for the small church? The demographics are most encouraging.

> From 1820 to the mid-1960s (with the exception of a five-year period in the 1930s during the Great Depression), the basic population migration in the United States has been from rural to urban areas. A long term reversal of this pattern began during the mid- to late 1960s. The dominant

migration pattern in the United States (and in most parts of Canada) today is from urban to rural communities.[21]

The demographic trend, when coupled with what Yankelovich has called the "search for self-fulfillment in a world turned upside down," leads Schaller to conclude that

> the next fifteen years will find thousands of small congregations accomplishing what they always knew they could not do. Some will open a Christian day school. Others will remodel their buildings to accommodate the physically handicapped. Thousands will relocate and construct new meeting houses in order to accommodate newcomers from urban areas.[22]

It appears Madsen was correct—the small church can be valid, vital, and victorious. Its impact, far surpassing the size of a certain congregation or even the collective strength of all small churches, represents one of the great evidences of the faithfulness of God to His people. And the history of small churches in the past augurs a positive expectation for the future. Though each one is small, together they have great potential for spiritual impact. Willimon and Wilson describe the reaction of American troops to the German army's surprise attack at the Battle of the Bulge in December 1944.

> No one of these little road junction stands could have had a profound effect on the German drive. But hundreds of them, impromptu little battles at nameless bridges and at unknown crossroads, had an effect of slowing enormously the German impetus. . . . these little diehard "one man stands" alone in the snow and fog without communications, would prove enormously effective out of all proportion to their size.[23]

So it is with the small church in today's world.

CHAPTER 17

Women in Ministry: An Exegetical Study of 1 Timothy 2:11–15

Ann L. Bowman

Since the beginning of the church on Pentecost, believers have met together for worship, fellowship, prayer, teaching, and the Lord's Supper. Both men and women have participated in these times of corporate worship. In 1 Timothy 2:11–15 Paul wrote instructions on the role of women in the worship assembly to Timothy, his apostolic representative to the church in Ephesus.

This is a difficult passage, containing unusual vocabulary (αὐθεντέω, ἡσυχία), awkward grammar (the link between vv. 14 and 15), references to the Old Testament (Gen. 2 and 3) whose New Testament usage needs to be determined in 1 Timothy 2:13–14, significant theological issues (e.g., the use of σώζω), and a flow of thought that is not so clear as it may seem at first glance. Over the centuries scores of solutions have been offered for the various problems.

Since this is only one of many passages in the New Testament whose meanings are disputed, it is helpful to ask why some passages are so difficult to interpret. A major reason lies in the occasional nature of the Epistles.

The Occasional Nature of the Epistles

The New Testament epistles are called "occasional documents" because they were occasioned by a special circumstance on the part of either the author or, more commonly, the recipient. The circumstance might be a doctrine or a practice in need of correction, or it might be a misunderstanding in need of clarification. Thus the selection of theological issues and the extent to which they were discussed was shaped by the circumstances that occasioned a particular epistle.

Three results of the epistles' occasional nature are noteworthy.

First, while an epistle answers a problem situation, the exact nature of the problem may not be fully reported. Second, the lack of a thorough discussion of a theological issue may limit the modern-day interpreter's understanding of a passage or doctrine. Third, the epistles were answering questions occasioned by their own circumstances, not those of a later century.[1]

These three results are well illustrated in Paul's first letter to Timothy and particularly in his instructions concerning women in the worship assembly. First, the historical situation in the Ephesian church that evoked Paul's instructions in 1 Timothy 2:11–15 is not entirely clear. Historical reconstructions generally fall into three categories. Some commentators suggest that the basic problem was one of women seeking improperly to assert authority over men in the worship assembly.[2] Other commentators suggest that some women in the church were teaching heresy and that Paul sought to prevent them from using the worship assembly for that purpose.[3] Still other interpreters suggest that Paul's prohibitions were given because women were doctrinally untaught and were thus more susceptible to false teaching.[4]

Second, in this passage Paul did not give a complete discussion of the role of women in the worship assembly. In fact nowhere did he comprehensively discuss the teaching role of women either in the worship assembly or in the larger ministry of the church. Other passages do touch briefly on their participation in the worship assembly (e.g., 1 Cor. 11:5; 14:26). But even if these and other passages are carefully integrated, the picture of how women served in the assembly and elsewhere is far from complete. Many similar unresolved issues exist, such as Paul's assertion that believers will judge both the world and angels (6:2–3), the exact method of baptism, and how certain spiritual gifts were exercised (e.g., word of wisdom and word of knowledge, 12:8), to name a few. In such issues the modern-day interpreter must be content with some limits on his or her knowledge.

Third, Paul was answering a question concerning the conduct of women in the worship assembly as it was known in the first century. He was not answering questions that are raised today, such as whom a woman should teach in Sunday school or in a parachurch training class, for these are situations that did not exist in the first century. While one possibly may draw applicable principles from this passage, the passage does not speak to these current issues directly.

The Context of 1 Timothy 2:11–15

THE PURPOSE OF 1 TIMOTHY

False teachers had arisen in Ephesus since Paul's last visit there (1 Tim. 1:3–11; 4:1–5; cf. Acts 20:17–38). Quite possibly they were from within the church and may have included recognized elders (Acts 20:29–30).[5] Paul was eager to refute them (1 Tim. 1:3–11; 6:3–10) and to defend against further attacks through the teaching of correct doctrine (4:6, 13–16; 6:2, 17–18), through promoting godly living of both leaders (3:1–13; 5:17–25; 6:11–16) and laity (5:1–16; 6:1–2, 17–19), and through ensuring correct church practice (2:1–15; 3:1–13).

Stated formally, Paul instructed Timothy to refute false teachers, to teach the truth of the gospel, to ensure proper conduct in the worship assembly, to select qualified church leaders, and to promote godly behavior and motives on the part of both leaders and laity so that Timothy might fully carry out his responsibilities as apostolic representative to the church in Ephesus.

PROBLEMS IN THE EPHESIAN WORSHIP ASSEMBLY

Public prayer for all. Certain problems had arisen in the worship assembly, and Paul addressed four of them in chapter 2. He began by explaining the necessity of offering public prayers for all individuals, especially those in positions of governmental authority, so that the church might have a peaceful life (2:1–2). Such prayer has intrinsic excellence and is acceptable before God, who desires all persons to be saved (vv. 3–4) and has made salvation available through Christ's saving work on the cross (vv. 5–7).

Men with cleansed consciences. Next Paul instructed the men in each of the home churches in Ephesus to pray with a cleansed conscience, free from the stain of interpersonal conflicts (v. 8). Though it was not uncommon for believers to pray with raised hands,[6] Paul's focus was not on the physical act but on the heart attitude. "Holy hands" serves as a figure of speech representing a cleansed conscience.[7] In particular, cleansing was especially needed from a quarrelsome spirit ("without wrath and dissension"). Throughout the Pastoral Epistles, Paul gave admonitions against contentiousness to overseers/elders (1 Tim. 3:3; Titus 1:7), men generally (1 Tim. 2:8), deacons (3:8), Timothy (2 Tim. 2:24), and believers in general (Titus 3:2). Paul's exhortation to the men in 1 Timothy 2:8 would indicate that a quarrelsome spirit was a sin the men of Ephesus must take special care to avoid.

Women dressed appropriately. In 1 Timothy 2:9–10 Paul addressed a third issue needing correction in the Ephesian worship assemblies, namely, women's adornment. He exhorted the women to adorn themselves both with modest apparel (v. 9a) and with a modest attitude (v. 9b). By contrast, they should not adorn themselves with ostentatious attire (v. 9c) but, as women who profess godliness, they should adorn themselves with good deeds worthy of eschatological reward (v. 10).

Two reasons for Paul's directive are possible. First, some women may have been dressing in a showy, possibly sensual manner that, while congruent with their former, pagan lifestyle, was totally inappropriate for the church of God.[8] Second, and more probable, some women may have been dressing in a way that reflected their superior social status.[9] The Ephesian church included some who were wealthy (1 Tim. 6:17–19), but the majority would certainly have been from lower socioeconomic strata and such ostentatious attire could have been a barrier to their sharing in the life of the church (cf. 1 Cor. 11:20–21). Whichever reason is correct, Paul made it clear that a woman's outward adornment is not the primary issue in God's eyes. Instead, He is interested in a godly attitude that issues forth in good works worthy of heavenly reward.

The Exegesis of 1 Timothy 2:11–15

Paul then turned to a fourth area that concerned him as the Ephesians met together for worship. He desired the women to learn with an attitude of quiet submissiveness rather than to be involved improperly in teaching and leading the men in the assembly.

VERSE 11

Addressed to women generally. The group of individuals under discussion here is women generally; that is, this directive is not limited to wives. Three factors make this clear. First, in the preceding verses (2:8–10) Paul directed men (ἄνδρας) to pray and women (γυναῖκας) to adorn themselves properly. Since it is unlikely that these instructions are limited to husbands and wives, it is unlikely that verses 11–15 are limited to wives. Second, in this context Paul was viewing men and women as part of a worshiping community, not as family members (as he did, e.g., in Eph. 5:22–33).[10] Third, had Paul been speaking of the husband-wife relationship, a definite article or possessive pronoun before ἀνδρός in verse 12 might have been expected (as in Eph. 5:22–25, 28–29, 31, 33).[11]

Directive to learn. Paul directed the women in the worship assembly to learn (μανθάνω). This verb is used seven times in the Pastorals; in this verse it carries the connotation of learning through instruction (2 Tim. 3:7, 14; John 7:15; 1 Cor. 14:31).[12] Paul assumed that women both could and would learn. Since Paul later noted that the Ephesian false teachers had gained influence over some of the women (e.g., 2 Tim. 3:6–7), it seems he knew it was important that they be well grounded in the Scriptures.

Manner of learning. The manner in which women were to learn is twofold. First, they should learn "in quietness" (ἐν ἡσυχία). The word ἡσυχία and its related forms occur only 11 times in the New Testament. The meaning of ἡσυχία ranges from "silence" (Acts 22:2) to "rest, quietness" (1 Tim. 2:2; 2 Thess. 3:12).[13] The translation "quietness" is best here, since it would have been normal for women to speak in the worship assembly (1 Cor. 11:5; 14:26).[14] The next phrase, "in all submissiveness," seems to underscore the idea that Paul's emphasis in this passage is on the attitude of heart that is to accompany learning.

Second, Paul directed the women to learn "in all submissiveness" (ἐν πάσῃ ὑποταγῆς). Clark explains that "subordination extends beyond obedience to commands to also include respectfulness and receptiveness to direction."[15] The question then arises concerning to what or to whom a woman is to be submissive. There are at least three possibilities. First, it may mean that a woman is to be submissive to her husband. While this truth is taught elsewhere (Eph. 5:22; Col. 3:18; Titus 2:5), such a meaning is unlikely here, where the focus is on men and women as worshipers. Second, Paul may have meant that a woman is to be submissive to the church elders.[16] Since false teachers were leading believers astray, submission to church elders may have been part of Paul's solution to that problem. A third possibility, closely related to the second, is that women are to submit themselves to sound doctrine.[17] Either of the last two views provides an adequate explanation. A combination of these two views is also possible: women were to submit themselves only to those elders who taught sound doctrine.

Summary. Women in the worship assembly are to receive instruction with an attitude of quiet receptivity and submissiveness. The emphasis here seems to be not so much on literal silence as on an inner attitude in which the spirit is at rest in submitting to the teaching (and the teachers) in the assembly.

VERSE 12

By means of an example of contrasting behavior, Paul reinforced his call for women to receive instruction in quietness. They were neither to teach nor to have authority over a man in the worship assembly. The initial "but" (δέ, untranslated in NIV) shows that the following situation contrasts with what precedes it.

Meaning of οὐκ ἐπιτρέπω. Paul continued his instruction by stating, "I do not permit" (οὐκ ἐπιτρέπω). Some writers suggest that Paul used this term to express a personal preference.[18] Other interpreters argue that the statement is to be considered binding on the church.[19] The latter view is preferable for two reasons. The first reason concerns the use of ἐπιτρέπω in 1 Corinthians 14:34. There Paul stated that—in the situation envisioned in that verse—women were not permitted to speak; and in verse 37 he underscored the importance of this injunction by saying, "The things which I write to you are the Lord's commandment" (a reference to 1 Cor. 14:26–36, which includes his directive in v. 34).[20] Second, Paul was most probably using his own personal authority to back up the prohibition of 1 Timothy 2:12 in the same way he did elsewhere. In 1 Corinthians 11:16, for example, he used his personal authority as the basis for reaffirming an approved practice that was common throughout first-century churches.

Paul wrote that women should not be involved in two aspects of the public worship assembly: They are neither "to teach or exercise authority over a man." In this much-disputed statement several points need to be clarified.

Meaning of ης διδάσκειν. One issue concerns the meaning of the term "to teach" (διδάσκειν). The verb διδάσκω and its cognates are the most common terms for teaching in the New Testament. The word refers almost exclusively to public instruction or teaching of groups.[21] In the New Testament a teacher is one who systematically teaches or expounds the Word of God and who gives instruction in the Old Testament and apostolic teaching (1 Cor. 4:17; 2 Tim. 2:2).[22] The spiritual gift of teaching enables individuals to grasp revelation that already has been given and to communicate this truth effectively to others. In addition there is a strong applicational aspect to the ministry of teachers as they demonstrate to their hearers the implications of God's inspired Word for daily living (cf. Matt. 28:19–20).[23]

Meaning of αὐθεντεῖν. The term αὐθεντεῖν is variously translated as "to have, exercise, or usurp authority." It is used only here in the New Testament and is rare in extant Greek literature. While scholars continue to debate its meaning, three points are relevant to the present discussion. First, the rarity of the verb and its cognates, especially before and during the New Testament period, make it difficult to reach an absolutely certain conclusion on its New Testament meaning.[24] Second, it seems significant that Paul used this less common term rather than the more common terms ἐξουσία ("authority") and ἐξουσιάζω ("to have authority"). The choice of the term αὐθεντεῖν would indicate that he had a special nuance of meaning in mind.[25] Third, the sense of "have or exercise authority"[26] and the sense of "domineer or usurp authority"[27] both seem to be possible meanings for αὐθεντεῖν during the New Testament period.

The meaning "to exercise authority" may be preferable, since the six clear usages of the word cited by Knight consistently support this meaning. He demonstrates that this is a legitimate meaning for the word when the New Testament was written.[28]

One command or two. Another issue involves the nature of the grammatical construction in which the two infinitives are joined by οὐδέ ("or"). Was Paul giving one prohibition or two? If one, the two infinitives form a hendiadys whose meaning would be either "to teach authoritatively"[29] or "to teach a man in a domineering way"[30] (depending on the meaning assigned to αὐθεντεῖν). However, an analysis of the instances in the New Testament in which οὐδέ joins two infinitives shows that two separate, although closely related, ideas are meant.[31] Thus the best rendering of the construction is "to teach [a man] or to exercise authority over a man."

But how do teaching and exercising authority relate to one another? A central issue in verses 11–15 is authority and submission. It seems that teaching is a subset of holding authority. Paul wrote about a situation in which some women were violating God's pattern of authority and submission, which was made clear in the pattern of creation (as vv. 13–14 demonstrate). Some women in Ephesus were violating God's pattern by teaching men in the worship assembly.

Paul completed this section (vv. 11–12) with the phrase, "but to be in quietness." He used the same phrase in verse 11 (ἐν ἡσυχίᾳ , "in quietness") both to provide a positive contrast to the negative prohibition in the first half of the verse and to underscore the positive directive in verse 11 that women should learn in a quiet and submissive manner.[32]

Summary. In verse 12, then, Paul explained that women are permitted neither to teach men nor to exercise authority over men in the worship assembly. Instead, as he had already directed in verse 11, they are to receive instruction with an inner attitude of quietness and submission to the truth of God's Word (and His chosen teachers).

VERSE 13

Paul continued his discussion by giving two reason why he instructed women in the worship assembly to learn in a quiet and submissive manner rather than to hold a position of teaching and exercising authority over a man. Though it is grammatically possible for the γὰρ ("for") which begins verse 13 to be either explanatory or causal, the latter sense is preferable for two reasons. First, the explanatory use of γὰρ is rare, and definite contextual evidence would be needed to argue for an explanatory sense.[33] Second, it is usual in Paul's letters for γὰρ to be causal when it follows a verb or idea of command or prohibition.[34]

Reference to Genesis 2 and 3. In verses 13 and 14 Paul referred to the Genesis accounts of the creation and Fall of mankind. This is clear both from the general content of each verse and from the specific verbal links with the Septuagint version of Genesis 2 and 3. The word ἐπλάσθη ("formed") in verse 13 corresponds to ἔπλασε(ν) in Genesis 2:7, 15. In 1 Timothy 2:14 the word ἠπατήθη ("deceived") corresponds to the word ἠπάτησε in Genesis 3:14. It is important to note that Paul was not simply referring to two verses taken from Genesis 2 and 3. Instead, he was using a common rabbinic method of referring to the Old Testament, a method known as summary citation.[35] That is, he used the summary statement in 1 Timothy 2:13 to point the reader to the entire pericope describing the creation of man and woman (Gen. 2:4–24), and in 1 Timothy 2:14 he referred back to the entire pericope detailing the Fall (Gen. 3:1–25). Paul was not limiting his focus to two specific, isolated thoughts; rather, he was drawing on two complete narratives.[36]

Chronological primacy. Paul was a Pharisee (Acts 23:6; 26:5; Phil. 3:5) who had been trained by Gamaliel the Elder (Acts 22:3).[37] The apostle freely employed rabbinic methods of Old Testament interpretation commonly used in his day.[38] In typical rabbinic fashion, Paul was making an analogical application based on the Genesis text.[39] He was stating that according to the Genesis 2 account, Adam was first created; and the implication is that Adam's chronological primacy in creation carried with it some degree of authority.

The Genesis 2 text does not spell out the manner in which this is true, but the Old Testament concept of primogeniture may provide some explanation. In the Old Testament the firstborn son received a number of specific privileges. First, he succeeded his father as head of the family and leader of the family worship (Deut. 21:15–17).[40] Second, he received a "double portion" of the inheritance (v. 17). When Paul appealed to Adam's chronological priority, he was possibly asserting that Adam's status as the oldest carried with it the leadership fitting for a firstborn son.[41]

Summary. Paul was not saying that the Genesis account teaches the ontological superiority of the male over the female. Nor was he stating that his prohibition on women teaching is found in the Genesis account. As Ross has noted, "His ruling would stand as authoritative whether he connected it to creation or not; but he shows how his instruction harmonizes with the design of the Creator in this world."[42] The unstated application of Paul's argument, then, is that just as in creation the final authority rested with the man, so in the church this order should be maintained.

VERSE 14

In verse 14 Paul used the same line of argumentation, that is, argument by analogy. In this case, however, he referred to the Genesis 3 account of the Fall of mankind. First Timothy 2:14 states, "And it was not Adam who was deceived, but the woman being quite deceived, fell into transgression." In this verse Paul was not suggesting that women are more easily deceived than men or that women are less intelligent. Both Scripture and history witness repeatedly to the ease with which both men and women may be deceived, especially with regard to doctrine.[43] Paul was actually referring here to the entire account of the Fall, and so he used the word "deceived" to draw attention to the connection with Genesis 3.

Reversal of roles. In Genesis 3, the serpent tempted the woman to disobey God by eating of the fruit that had been forbidden to her. The serpent deceived her and she ate. Immediately after her own fall into sin she offered the forbidden fruit to her husband. He willingly ate and also fell into sin. In this scene a reversal of roles has occurred.[44] The ultimate responsibility before God rested with Adam, who allowed himself to be led astray by his wife.

That God considered Adam ultimately responsible, rather than Eve, is clear not only from Romans 5:12, which states that "through one man sin entered into the world," but also by the fact that the all-knowing God first asked not Eve but Adam to explain his actions. Further, in Genesis 3:17, God told Adam that the curse would come on the earth "because you have listened to the voice of your wife, and have eaten from the tree about which I commanded you, saying, 'You shall not eat from it.'" The term "listened to" means "obeyed" in this case, as it often does in the Hebrew Old Testament.[45]

Summary. Paul's point is that this role reversal that caused such devastation at the beginning must not be repeated in the church. The woman must not be the one who leads the man in obedience to her. Thus when the teaching of the Word of God in the assembly occurs, a qualified male elder should fill the role of teacher.

VERSE 15

Possible interpretations. Many interpretations have been suggested for verse 15.[46] These include the following. (1) Women will be delivered (physically) through childbirth.[47] (2) Women will be saved (spiritually) even though they must bear physical children.[48] (3) Women will be saved (spiritually) through the Childbearing (i.e., the birth of Christ).[49] (4) Women will be saved (spiritually) equally with men through fulfilling their God-given role in the home just as men fulfill theirs in public church leadership.[50] (5) Women will be kept safe from seizing men's roles in the worship assembly by fulfilling their God-given role in the home.[51] (6) Women will be saved (spiritually, with the focus on eschatological salvation) through faithfulness to their proper role, exemplified in motherhood.[52]

An analysis of these six interpretive statements reveals that four key grammatical and lexical issues are involved in understanding this verse. These are the meaning of σωθήσεται ("she shall be saved"), the force of διά ("through"), the force of τῆς ("the") before τεκνογονίας ("childbearing"), and the meaning and use of τεκνογονίας. An interpretation that satisfies the grammatical and lexical problems and that also fits the larger context is the sixth option. That is, women will enter into eschatological salvation, with its accompanying rewards, through faithfulness to their proper role, exemplified in motherhood and in godly living generally.

Role of δέ. The verse begins, literally, "Yet she shall be saved through childbearing." The δέ ("yet") is a mild adversative that serves, first, to provide a contrast with the preceding verse, in which Paul referred to the results of the reversal of roles in Genesis 3. The δέ also introduces a final, concluding statement about the results of women fulfilling their God-given roles.

Meaning of σώζω. The verb σώζω in the New Testament may refer to physical deliverance from some peril (Matt. 14:30; 27:40; Acts 27:20), to physical healing (Mark 5:34; Luke 17:19; 18:42; Acts 4:9; 14:9), to deliverance from demonization (Luke 8:36), and, very commonly, to spiritual salvation. In this latter sense salvation has an essential eschatological component regardless of whether that is the focus of a particular Scripture passage.[53] Salvation may be pictured as a trajectory that has justification as its beginning point and sanctification as the route of the trajectory.[54] Both justification and sanctification will be consummated at a future time when believers will be in their glorified state.[55]

Justification and sanctification have both a present and a future aspect. Justification begins the moment a person receives Christ as Savior, but this vindication is consummated in the believer's end-time glorification (Rom. 5:9–10; cf. 8:31–39).[56] Sanctification, which begins at the moment of justification and is dependent on it, is a positional truth with an experiential component. Positionally, Christians belong to God; they are set apart as His people (Rom. 15:16; 1 Cor. 1:2; 2 Thess. 2:13).[57] As those who have been set apart, however, they are exhorted to experience sanctification through Spirit-empowered, holy living (Rom. 6:19; Gal. 5:16; Phil. 2:12–13; Col. 1:10; 1 Thess. 4:7). As motivation to live a sanctified life, Paul wrote of the future time when believers' works will be judged and rewards will be given (Rom. 14:10; 2 Cor. 5:10; cf. 1 Cor. 3:10–15).[58] The goal of sanctification is eschatological: to be presented to God in complete purity (Eph. 5:26–27; Col. 1:22; 1 Thess. 3:13; 5:23).[59]

In 1 Timothy 2:15 Paul focused on the future aspects of a

woman's salvation.[60] This is underscored by his choice of the future tense of the verb. In particular, he stressed the necessity of her consistently living a life characterized by holiness and obedience, one worthy of future rewards. In other words he was referring here to salvation as the consummation of the process of sanctification. As he did elsewhere (e.g., Col. 1:21–23; 1 Thess. 5:8–9), Paul used the hope for attaining the fullness of salvation as a motivation to faithful Christian living.[61]

Use of διά. The preposition διά may refer to ultimate cause,[62] to efficient cause, or to attendant circumstance.[63] Either of the latter two senses would fit here, but attendant circumstance seems preferable, given the contextual stress on the process of sanctification. More specifically, "childbearing" is one of the good works that is to be part of the lifestyle of a godly woman (cf. v. 10).

Use of the definite article. Some commentators consider the use of the definite article before "childbearing" to be par excellence (i.e., it is the most important of all instances of childbearing). This makes possible the interpretation "the Childbearing" as a reference to the birth of Christ. It is equally possible, however, to consider its use to be generic (i.e., it describes the whole process of "childbearing"),[64] and this sense fits the flow of Paul's argument better.

Meaning of τεκνογονία. The literal meaning of the noun τεκνογονία is certainly "childbearing." The question is whether it is used literally or figuratively in this passage. A literal view seems improbable here, since not all women bear children.[65] Further, τεκνογονία may refer not only to childbearing but also to child-rearing.[66] This suggests that a far more probable explanation of the term is that it serves as a synecdoche of the part for the whole. That is, childbearing represents "the general scope of activities in which a Christian woman should be involved."[67]

In Paul's day this was an appropriate figure to use, since a woman would commonly be married and involved in child-rearing in much if not all of her adult life.[68] Further, these were activities of surpassing social worth for a first-century woman.[69] Support for this position comes from 1 Timothy 5:14, in which Paul stated that he desired young widows to marry and to "bear children" (τεκνογονεῖν).

Qualities worthy of eternal rewards. Carrying out activities is not enough, however, to participate in the rewards that may accompany eschatological salvation. The inner qualities of a Christlike character must also be present, and so Paul mentioned four of them.

Verse 15 is actually a conditional sentence whose protasis, "if they remain" (ἐὰν μείνωσιν), comes at the end of the sentence. The verb, meaning "remain, continue, abide," has the sense of not leaving the realm or sphere in which one find oneself.[70] The change from third person singular ("she shall be saved") to third person plural ("they remain") is awkward, but can be understood by noting that in verses 9–15 Paul referred to women either with the plural noun (v. 9: γυναῖκας) or with the singular, generic noun (vv. 11–12: γυνή).[71] Thus in verse 15 Christian women are in view in both parts of the sentence; an understood generic noun is used in the first part with a singular verb, and a plural form is understood with the plural verb in the second part.

Next, Paul specified that Christian women are to remain "in faith and love and holiness." These nouns are used without the definite article to stress the qualities involved. "Faith" (πίστει) is active, personal faith in Christ (cf. Eph. 1:15).[72] He is also the source of that faith (1 Tim. 1:14; 2 Tim. 1:13), and its result is practical activity (1 Thess. 1:3). "Love" (ἀγάπη) is love that reaches out to serve others (1 Cor. 13:4–7; Eph. 5:2; Phil. 1:15–16). "Holiness" (ἁγιασμῷ) refers to the daily process of sanctification and "it is always assumed that it is accomplished on the basis of the state of sanctification attained in the atonement."[74] The condition of holiness that results stresses the active process of being sanctified.[75]

The final phrase, "with discretion" (μετά σωφροσύνης), serves as the closing bracket for Paul's instructions concerning women in the worship assembly in 1 Timothy 2:9–15. The word σωφροσύνης also occurs in verse 9, where women are exhorted to adorn themselves with decency and discretion. The term carries with it the ideas of good judgment, moderation, and self-control,[76] and in verse 15 the term underscores the moderation and self-control Christian women are to demonstrate as they participate in the process of progressive sanctification.

Summary. In verse 15 Paul summarized his discussion of how women are to act in the worship assembly, and he stated the expected result: They will experience salvation in the eschatological sense, which includes the judgment of works and receiving of rewards. Women are to fulfill their proper role in life, a concept summarized by "childbearing." This figure of speech refers to the general scope of activities in which Christian women are to be involved.

In addition to these outward activities, women should have the inner adornment of Christian character, typified by faith, love, and holiness, accompanied by discretion. Together these activities and attitudes combine to exemplify the "good works" of verse 10 with which a woman is to adorn herself. These works are the result of God's working in the life of the believer (Phil. 2:13) and are worthy of eschatological rewards. Therefore in the fullness of eschatological salvation ("she shall be saved"), women will receive rewards commensurate with the good works they have done (2 Cor. 5:10).

Conclusion

First Timothy 2:11–15 is a key passage in understanding the New Testament's teaching on women in ministry. In seeking to provide a consistent exegesis of this passage, this chapter has sought to determine how the original audience—Timothy and those in the Ephesian church—would have understood the Apostle Paul's directives to them.

In 1 Timothy 2 Paul addressed four problem areas in the worship assemblies at Ephesus and gave directives for correcting them. First, believers should offer prayer in the assembly for all individuals, especially government officials (vv. 1–7). Second, the men must pray with cleansed consciences, free from the stain of interpersonal conflicts (v. 8). Third, the women, rather than dressing ostentatiously, should adorn themselves with modest clothing and attitudes and with deeds worthy of eschatological reward (vv. 9–10).

Fourth, the women should learn with an attitude of quiet submissiveness, rather than be involved improperly in teaching and leading men in the worship assembly (vv. 11–15). More specifically, Paul directed women to learn in the worship assembly with a quiet and submissive attitude rather than to teach or have authority over a man in that context. He gave two reasons for this directive. First, the pattern of male headship was established in creation and Paul wanted to see this principle affirmed in the church. Second, the principle of male headship was violated through the reversal of authority roles in the Fall with devastating consequences, and Paul wanted the believers to avoid such a role reversal and its consequences in the church. Despite the results of this reversal of roles in the Garden of Eden, women who fulfill their God-ordained roles as women and who have the inner adornment of a godly character may expect to receive future perfection of salvation with its accompanying rewards.

CHAPTER 18

Perimeters of Corrective Church Discipline

Ted G. Kitchens

The church has often wrestled with the question, What specific sins in believers call for disciplinary action? In the Reformation, Luther threatened to excommunicate a person who intended to sell a house for 400 guilders that he had purchased for 30. Luther suggested 150 guilders and labeled the offender as one in need of discipline because of unbridled greed.[1]

It has been the practice to compile lists of sins deserving church discipline. Jescke writes,

> Numerous writers in the history of Christianity have attempted to compile a catalog of sins that offers a reliable guide for initiating church discipline. Some have even sought to establish a graduated scale of sins that rather automatically triggers the appropriate response from the church—perhaps from mild admonition through public censure to full excommunication. When a given act is committed, it needs only to be classified in order for church machinery, set for the proper cycle, to be set in motion.[2]

Puritans in the time of Cotton Mather considered a broad range of sins worthy of discipline: "swearing, cursing, sabbath-breaking, drunkenness, fighting, defamation, fornication, unchastity, cheating, stealing, idleness, lying, and 'such Heresies as manifestly overturn the Foundations of the Christian Religion and of all Piety.'"[3] Other lists of discipline-inducing offenses have included matters of political and social evil: slave-holding, participation in the civil government, involvement in the military and in war, child labor, excessive profits, collaboration with oppressive governments, usury, racial discrimination, smuggling, cockfighting, bull-baiting, tax evasion, and rioting.[4]

According to Matthew 18:15 the process of church discipline begins with the simple notice, "If your brother sins . . ." (cf. Luke 17:3). But this phrase is general and offers little specific guidance. Does if mean all sin, every sin? How narrow or broad are the perimeters for church discipline set forth by Christ?

A list, in itself useful enough, can nevertheless become a rule-book that quickly replaces the Word and Spirit of God for needed guidance in matters of church discipline. Lists can engender legalism and can also produce blind spots, that is, preoccupation with some sins while others go unattended. As Jescke observes, "When seventy-five percent of a Church's list of excommunications has to do with clothes, there is something woefully wrong."[5]

Thus there is danger in establishing rigid boundaries by means of lists. Yet, being aware of the dangers should not abort the responsibility to face the question, Which sins should be dealt with? Barth wrestled with this issue and concluded that lists, if updated and kept under the scrutiny of the gospel, may benefit an alert church.[6]

The New Testament does set forth several lists of sins that call for church discipline. Eight other passages in the New Testament also illustrate how the early church handled certain infractions (Matt. 18:17; 1 Cor. 5:5, 11; 2 Cor. 2:5–11; 2 Thess. 3:14; 1 Tim. 1:20; Titus 3:10). Determining which sins to discipline demands that one start with these critical New Testament texts to formulate proper biblical parameters for church discipline.

Discipline in the Gospels

MATTHEW

The seminal passage on the exercise and procedure for church discipline is Matthew 18:15–20. In verse 15, Jesus commanded, "And if your brother sins, go and reprove him in private." He went on to speak of dealing with sins in the context of community discipline. However, no specific sins worthy of reproof are stated.

Jesus' teachings emphasized the righteousness of the heart with the inner character that underlies outward conduct. In Matthew 5:21–22 Jesus linked murder and anger to demonstrate the seriousness not only of outward conduct but also of inner attitude. The Law condemned adultery, but Jesus condemned a lustful appetite. Obviously Jesus was concerned foremost with the origin of sin and not primarily with the form in which it manifested itself.

MARK

Mark recorded Jesus' only direct reference to specific sins needing church discipline. However, as was true in the Matthean account, His emphasis was less on the acts themselves than on the origin of the evil, namely, man's heart. "That which proceeds out of the man, that is what defiles the man. For from within, out of the heart of men, proceed the evil thoughts, fornications, thefts, murders, adulteries, deeds of coveting and wickedness, as well as deceit, sensuality, envy, slander, pride and foolishness. All these evil things proceed from within and defile the man" (Mark 7:20–23). Jesus seems to have been demanding a perfect inner righteousness or pure character. Again, Jesus addressed sins that stem from the heart.

The Disciplinary Perimeters in the Epistles

The writings of the Apostle Paul stand as the greatest New Testament resources for establishing perimeters for church discipline.

DISCIPLINE AT CORINTH

First Corinthians 5:9–13 is the premiere Pauline example of how a local church responded to sin. After addressing the heinous sin of an incestuous relationship ("someone has his father's wife," 1 Cor. 5:1), he proceeded to clear up a misunderstanding created by his first letter to Corinth. Then he stated how Christians should respond to a situation in which a member of the church resolutely maintained a condition of moral turpitude.

In verse 11, six sins are labeled as worthy of discipline: immorality, covetousness, idolatry, reviling, drunkenness, and swindling. Paul told the believers not even to associate with the practitioners of such activities.[7] The implication is clear that what the world practices should never be practiced by believers.

The major thrust of Paul's teaching on discipline is not made by the list in verse 11 but by his artful usage of scriptural allusion in verse 13 to Deuteronomy 13:5*b*, 17:7*b*, 12*b*, 19:19*b*, 21:21, 22:21*b*, and 24:7*b* to teach the Corinthians their error. Paul's argument sheds much-needed light on the meaning and purpose for his list of sins.

The apostle argued from the specific to the more general to impress on the church the distinctions between how one should treat sinners in the world and how one should treat Christians who are sinning in the church. To accomplish this, Paul used a word play between πορνεία ("immorality") in verse 1 and πονηρός ("immoral") in verse 11. That is, he wrote specifically of the sin of incest and more generally of immorality.[8] He concluded the chapter

with the words, "But those who are outside, God judges. Remove
the wicked man [τὸν πονηρόν] from among yourselves" (v. 13).
"In this pericope the purity of the community is the goal of the
command."[9] When these sins of the world come into the church
without repentance, the church must deal with them in a disciplinary
fashion.

When Paul said in verse 13, "Remove the wicked from among
yourselves," he had in part already defined "wicked" and the sins
that warrant discipline with the list in verse 11. This command
cites an excommunication formula (ἐξάρατε τὸν πονηρόν ἐξ
ὑμῶν αὐτῶν) that occurs six times in the Septuagint translation of
Deuteronomy.[10] Malan states that Paul applied the Deuteronomic
law of holiness to the congregation, though the means of application
shifted from Old Covenant capital punishment for religio-ethical
offenses to New Covenant spiritual and social punishment for the
same offenses.[11]

Therefore the scriptural allusion functions as a fitting conclusion
to Paul's condemnation of the incestuous brother and of
πορνεία/πονηρία in general, and to the apostle's emphasis on the
need to keep the community of brethren separate from the sins
and influence of the outside world.[12] The list was not foremost in
Paul's thinking; however, the reality of sin in the church was
indeed central.

Besides addressing specific sins deserving punishment,
1 Corinthians 5 calls attention to sins that constitute obvious
worldly compromise in the lives of believers. Jescke clarifies
Paul's intentions.

> Discipline-worthy sin is any deed which represents a reversion from that
> life in the Spirit in which the Christian's activity is motivated by the
> grace of God back to life in the flesh. It represents a usurpation by man
> of that control of his life which belongs properly to God—man's rejection
> of the reign of God in his life.[13]

"Paul's purpose is not to give a list. This is supported by
unevenness of the list and the absence of definition."[14] Rather, a
contrast is being made as to how absurd it is for a believer, a "so-
called brother" (1 Cor. 5:11), to practice the sins pagans routinely
embrace. The sins Paul mentioned were certainly typical of the
ungodly pagan world around the church. "Paul is tossing out
examples of everyday sins of unchurched non-Christians to show
the absurdity of mixing apples with oranges."[15] The church is
called to be separated from such compromising sins (6:9–11).

DISCIPLINE AT ROME

In Romans 16:17 Paul wrote, "Now I urge you, brethren, keep your eye on those who cause dissensions and hindrances contrary to the teaching which you learned, and turn away from them." The warning in this verse lists offenses (divisions and hindrances), and then verse 18 justifies that warning, for it describes the character of those who were causing the offenses (slaves to their own appetites and smooth of speech). Whatever the content of their teaching, it was contrary to what Paul taught. And because their teaching was false, they led others astray who believed them and abandoned true fellowship in the church.

By what actions are these offenders to be identified? What did Paul mean by "dissensions" and "hindrances"? How should one define these offenses that warrant the command, "turn away from them"?

"Dissensions" (διχοστασίας) is an old word used only here and in Galatians 5:20 for "standing apart" or "cleavages."[16] The use of the article ("the dissensions") denotes dissensions that were well known to the Roman fellowship. On the other hand Paul used the word "hindrances" (σκάνδαλα) or "hindrance" (σκάνδαλον) throughout the epistle. In 14:13, it takes the meaning of "a trap" or "cause for stumbling" in the life of a brother or sister. In 11:9 Paul quoted Psalm 69:22, which used the word οκάνδαλον in the Septuagint. In that psalm David asked God to place "hindrances" or "stumbling blocks" before his adversaries. The broadest understanding of Paul's usage is that of an "offense or trap" that causes a Christian to be detoured or to stumble in either practice or belief.

In Romans 16:17 διχοστασίας and σκάνδαλα are separate yet related offenses, suggested by the fact that a definite article precedes each of these two nouns. Godet believed that the first term refers to ecclesiastical divisions while the second refers to "moral disorders which had so often accompanied them."[17] Murray points out that this verse refers to teachers who by their false teaching cause divisions.[18] Shedd notes that "the reference is to differences in both doctrine and practice, because the latter originates in the former."[19]

To ascertain the precise relationship of διχοστασίας and σκάνδαλα is difficult. In other passages οκάνδαλα seems to denote the occasion or causes of the διχοστασία (Rom. 11:9; 14:13), and it is difficult to determine which precedes the other. However, διχοστασίας seems best understood as a schism or division in the sense of an eroding disunity, whereas σκάνδαλα emphasizes more the practice in one's life of false doctrines or a hindrance to what a believer previously embraced. Neither is seen by Paul as the disease, but rather the symptom.

In summary, any believer who teaches contrary to the apostolic (biblical) fundamentals, thereby causing dissension, is an offender. One who propagates a theological position that leads another believer to stumble (hindrance) in daily practice is to be disciplined. There is debate on what constitutes a false teaching, but certainly at minimum it includes anything contrary to the basic elements of faith. Paul emphasized, however, the results of incorrect doctrine (dissensions and hindrances). Anyone who teaches a doctrine that brings disunity and confusion into the church or an individual believer's life is pushing the perimeters of corrective discipline.

DISCIPLINE AT GALATIA

In Galatians 6:1 Paul commented, "If a man is caught in any trespass, you who are spiritual, restore such a one." The trespasses are identified in preceding verses (5:16–26). The list of sins in verses 19– 21 illustrates "the deeds of the flesh" (v. 19), while verses 22–23 speak of "the fruit of the Spirit." Paul contrasted these two lists, one of the Spirit and the other of the flesh, to illustrate the conflict in verse 17 and to emphasize the command in verses 13–15.

Galatians 5:19–21 includes five categories of vice, all internal in nature, that could be committed by a Christian. In each of Paul's lists of sins, the items seem to be carefully chosen and placed in groups, and the groups are arranged to form a statement concerning sins that are discipline-worthy.

The first list of vices are sexual sins (v. 19). The apostle's use of πορνεία is common and refers to prostitution, harlotry, and all types of illicit sexual conduct (Matt. 15:19; Mark 7:21; 1 Cor. 5:1–5). The second word, ἀκαθαρσία, is normally given a broader meaning than πορνεία. Lenski includes in its definition not only sexual aberrations but also all that leads to them. The whole mass of immoral filth is certainly included in its meaning.[20] Finally, lewdness (ἀσέλγεια) is generally defined as lasciviousness and wantonness, entailing the abandonment of all moral restraints. It is noteworthy that sexual sins and idolatry seem to be linked.

The second category in Galatians 5 includes two sins that pertain to false doctrine and worship. In ancient pagan society both idolatry and sorcery were mingled with the sexual. Φαρμακεία is used also in Revelation 18:23, and a closely related word appears in Revelation 9:21, where it is associated with pagan worship and charms of superstition, as well as murder, immorality, and theft. "The word was used so as to include all magic and sorcery and is most probably paired with idolatry (Acts 19:18–20)."[21]

The third and fourth categories deal with vices committed in the context of personal relationships. "Enmities, strife, jealousy, and outbursts of anger" (Gal. 5:20) were types of personal animosity. Personal hatred, discord, and strong emotional explosions are noted. Enmity and jealousy are the motives, strife and anger the product.

The next four sins (vv. 20b–21a) refer to partiality and clashes between members of the church. "Disputes" (ἐριφεῖαι) means rivalries or factions; that is, conflicts arising from a partisan spirit.[22] The word suggests mercenary motives behind the splintering. Διχοστασίαι ("dissensions"), used in Romans 16:17, means splits, divisions, or sunderings in the church. This is usually connected with false teachings in the fellowship. The Greek word "factions" is αἱρέσεις, from which the word "heresy" is derived. "Sects" is a helpful translation. In 2 Peter 2:1 it is used of any false teachings (heresies) that destroy the unity of the church. It is also rendered "factions" in 1 Corinthians 11:19. It refers to a group of people who have chosen a position for themselves based on heretical teaching. "Envyings" (φθόνοι) is used in Matthew 27:18 and Philippians 1:15 to denote feelings of ill will. Envying leads to church splits.

The fifth category of sins in Galatians 5:19–21 are sins of disorderliness—drunkenness and carousing. These are mentioned in Romans 13:13 and Luke 21:34, where excessive drinking is in view, and in 1 Peter 4:3 they are listed along with drinking parties.

The last element in the list—"and things like these" (Gal. 5:21)—indicates that the list is not exhaustive. The sins in Paul's list, though not exhaustive, are activities that have their source in the flesh (v. 16).[23] The apostle's instruction in 6:1 demands that those guilty of operating in the flesh should be approached and gently restored by a brother who is living by the Spirit.

DISCIPLINE AT CRETE

In Titus 3:10–11, Paul told Titus how to deal with a divisive person: "Reject a factious man after a first and second warning, knowing that such a man is perverted and is sinning, being self-condemned." Discerning what the apostle meant by "factious" gives further clarification to the issue of the perimeters of corrective discipline.

A "factious" man (αἱρετικὸν) can refer to a "heretic." The verb αἱερτίξω means "to choose."[24] The verb previously meant to choose in reference to matters of opinion, especially bad opinions. The related noun ἅρεσις then came to refer to the opinion held, and αἱρετικόν to a person holding the opinion. Such a person has the power of choice, and thus he and others, as a self-chosen party or sect, teach self-chosen teachings or heresy.

In the Epistles the plural word "heresies" (αἱρέσεις) is used in only three passages, each with reference to a negative demeanor (1 Cor 11:19; Gal. 5:20; 2 Peter 2:1). Schlier points out that the word seems to have developed a special "Christian" meaning early in church history, and therefore in Titus 3:10 the adjective with the noun "man" denotes "the adherent of a heresy."[26]

However, even though there is support for αἱρετικὸν taking the meaning of "heresy," most lexicographers and commentators hold to the meaning of "factious" or "causing divisions."[27] Kelly argues for the idea of "factious" rather than "heresy" since the word ἅιρεσις did not acquire the meaning of "heretical" until the second century.[28] The idea that this individual is a "separatist" causing division in the body is the probable sense. Though either sense is possible from the context, "factious" seems preferable. Taking both nuances into consideration, Plummer puts the meaning of this term into perspective.

> In all spheres of thought and action, and especially in matters of belief, a tendency to choose of oneself, and to pursue one's own way independently, almost of necessity leads to separation from others, to divisions and factions. And factions in the Church readily widen into schisms and harden into heresies.[29]

The sin in Titus 3:10 is best identified as that of causing splits or divisions in the fellowship, possibly with the divisions resulting from the teaching of false doctrines.

Paul urged Titus to deal with this sin promptly with a first and second "warning" (νουθεσίαν). This word presupposes an opposition that must be overcome. It seeks to correct the mind, to put right what is wrong, to improve the spiritual attitude.[30]

This offender, guilty of causing division in the fellowship at Crete, was "perverted" and was "self-condemned" in his sin. This posed a serious problem to Titus.

> Paul's point is that, since he [the guilty man] has been solemnly warned by the church authorities, he must know what he is doing wrong and his own better judgment must therefore condemn him. Nothing can be done with a man who willfully persists in dividing the church's unity.[31]

Any man who is willfully causing factions in the local fellowship and demonstrating a spirit of rebellion needs disciplinary action.

THE REST OF THE NEW TESTAMENT

First Timothy 1:19–20 and 3 John 9–10 also discuss sins to be dealt with in the church. Hymenaeus was guilty of teaching a false doctrine, which resulted in division and upset the faith of some (1 Tim. 1:19–20; 2 Tim. 2:17–18). Considering him a factious man, Paul "delivered" him "over to Satan" for his offense (1 Tim. 1:20; cf. 1 Cor. 5:5). In 3 John 9–10, the sin of Diotrephes falls in the same category. However, he was guilty of causing factions because of ambition. This "church boss"[32] established himself against Gaius (v. 1) and the elder by ignoring the plea to accept traveling ministers. Diotrephes also forbade others in the church to accept them and even removed (ἐκβάλλει) from the fellowship members who showed hospitality to the travelers (v. 10).[33] As a result, this individual caused a "faction" in the fellowship and imperiled its church government. His attitude and action precipitated discipline.

Other New Testament texts reveal infractions or classes of offenders. In 2 Timothy 3:1–5, Paul listed 19 kinds of people to avoid "in the last days." Their sins are centered in the selfish and undisciplined character of man. He admonished Timothy to "avoid such men as these" (v. 5). Certainly, if such sins became manifest inside the body of Christ, Paul would have pressed for disciplinary action.

In 2 Thessalonians 3:6 the church was facing the dereliction of an unruly life, an unnecessary burden on the local assembly. Idleness and meddlesome conduct disrupt any society (1 Cor. 15:33). "The members of the church should mark . . . the man who has gained a reputation as a parasite and busybody and stay away from him lest they become infected with ideas and actions that hurt the witness of the church."[34] Idleness is therefore a new class of infraction and should be added to the other perimeters already discussed.

Categories of Sins Calling for Church Discipline

The passages discussed suggest four major categories of sins that call for church discipline. These perimeters embrace both the spirit (flexibility) and law (rigidity) essential for the purity of the church. These divisions meet the demands of the New Testament and the needs of the church to be seasonally relevant. They cover all Christian behavior, both public and private, dealing with sin as it relates to Christian love, unity, standards, and truth.[35]

PRIVATE AND PERSONAL OFFENSES THAT VIOLATE CHRISTIAN LOVE

Jesus commanded His disciples, "Love your neighbor as yourself" (Matt. 22:39). This commandment is to be protected and upheld in the church (Gal. 5:13; 1 Peter 4:8; 1 John 4:7). Matthew 5:23–24 and 18:15 are given to help guard the church in this respect. Paul reflected this in Galatians 5:20 when he warned against unloving offenses, including "strife, jealousy, [and] outbursts of anger." Jesus prescribed the method of discipline in such cases in Matthew 18:15–18. Refusal to repent and be reconciled is a severe aggravation of the sin involved and a continued breach of Christian love.

DIVISIVENESS AND FACTIONS THAT DESTROY CHRISTIAN UNITY

Peace and unity in the local church are essential. Church leaders are responsible to note "those who cause dissensions . . . contrary to the teaching" and avoid them (Rom. 16:17). Paul warned believers that the deeds of the flesh such as rivalries, divisions, sects, and envies will not be allowed in the kingdom of God. Churches are to avoid association with "a reviler" (1 Cor. 5:11). Likewise John purposed to discipline a disorderly church leader (3 John 9–10). Those who destroy peace and unity must be watched, rebuked, and, if necessary, removed.

MORAL AND ETHICAL DEVIATIONS THAT BREAK CHRISTIAN STANDARDS

Christian standards are violated by those who lead scandalous lives. Believers should not keep company with a so-called brother who is a fornicator or a drunkard. Paul wrote in Ephesians 5:11, "Do not participate in [literally, 'do not have fellowship with'] the unfruitful deeds of darkness but instead even expose or reprove them." Second Thessalonians 3:6 commands, "Keep aloof from every brother who leads an unruly life." Paul was stressing that violation of the standard of proper Christian conduct was not to go undisciplined in the church.

TEACHING FALSE DOCTRINE

In Titus 1:9–11 Paul wrote that an elder is to be "holding fast the faithful word which is in accordance with the teaching, that he may be able both to exhort in sound doctrine and to refute those who contradict." And in 3:10 he urged, "Reject a factious man after a first and second warning." Several other passages also speak to this matter (1 Tim. 1:19–20; 6:3–5; 2 John 7–11). Of course the perimeter does not mean that Christians should be censured for failing to understand and receive every doctrine revealed in the Bible, for all Christians are learning and growing. Rather, this refers to those who knowingly reject doctrines the church considers essential. For pastors and church elders the standard is more rigid, since they are especially responsible to teach and defend "the whole purpose of God" (Acts 20:27). They are to maintain all the doctrines of the Scriptures (especially as embodied in their church's creed), and are liable to discipline if they fail to do so (1 Tim. 3:2,9; Titus 1:9; James 3:1).

Conclusion

The New Testament presents for the church a code of purity with perimeters. This code for the community in Christ demands that all unrepented sin that is visible be disciplined. Jesus desired self-discipline from His followers (Matt. 5:22–23; Mark 7:14–23), but when self-discipline fails, then the Christian community is responsible to exercise discipline lovingly. The sins that call for discipline include personal offenses, divisiveness, moral deviations, and false teaching. While boundaries are essential, flexibility must be maintained in determining which current sins call for discipline.

Scientific and medical changes in the 20th century are a case in point. How should the church handle biogenetics and any negative impact it might bring to society and the church? The AIDS epidemic is presenting unique problems. Should the church exercise punitive measures on one who has transmitted the disease? Should discipline be exercised if a church member rejects another person because of the disease? Infanticide, drug abuse, euthanasia, divorce, and abortion should also be discussed. The church of the future may have a more complicated struggle than even churches today. Without disciplinary boundaries that are clear yet pliable, the church cannot become a covenant community, separate from the world and not a captive of the culture. The four categories suggested meet the changing problem of leaven in the body of Christ.

In each of these four perimeters, both the sin as an act and the spirit of sin are dealt with. In this regard, Jescke notes, "In the problem of sin in the Church, as with sin anywhere, we are dealing with both spirit and act. On the one hand sin definitely involves an event or act. On the other hand, it is not merely an act, but an act springing from a very specific motivating spirit."[36] These classifications deal with a person's heart attitude toward God as well as outward sin.

As Bangs states, boundaries that allow the Holy Spirit to participate are much needed. "The work of discipline must be a spiritual work, first and foremost. It must move beyond rational ethics or the calculation of strategy and be borne along by something which gives it life."[37]

Ultimately the spirit of unrepentance keeps a person in violation of these boundaries.

> There is always only one sin that excludes from the fellowship of God's people, and that is not the specific sin that first evokes our concern. It is rather the sinning brother's unwillingness to "hear" the pleas and admonitions of his brethren, the sin of persisting on the sinful course and of refusing to come to repentance.[38]

The New Testament teaches that no sin is tolerable to those whom Christ has redeemed. No Christian should be allowed to embrace unrepented sin and move in and out of the church at will.

Difficult as it may be, the contemporary church must follow the mandate that any sin, whether seemingly insignificant (e.g., gluttony) or harsh (e.g., incest), must be approached in the spirit of Christ. Recognizing this responsibility will propel the church into a regular program of discipline. If the code of purity is accepted by a congregation, the impact on unrepented sin will be significant. Tragically, the church today has almost altogether abandoned this mandate.

CHAPTER 19

Court Involvement in Church Discipline, Part 1

Jay A. Quine

These two chapters attempt to curb the fear of lawsuits against local churches and church leaders who exercise church discipline. Because several recent judicial decisions have been determined in part on whether the church has clearly articulated its church discipline policy to the disciplined member, the purposes, causes, and methods of church discipline are briefly reviewed in this first article.[1] The major legal theories and defenses used in church discipline cases are examined to help church leaders avoid unnecessary conduct that tends to increase the risk of a lawsuit. The second article presents a historical overview of church discipline cases and guidelines for church leaders to enable them to remain beyond legal liability while being scriptural in their discipline procedures. An inventive case narrative in the second article demonstrates how a common church situation can raise many of these legal issues.

The Biblical Basis for Church Discipline

Church leaders should have a clear understanding of the necessity, purpose, causes, and method of biblical church discipline. Explaining these principles of church discipline to the congregation is a large step toward avoiding a lawsuit.

THE NECESSITY OF CHURCH DISCIPLINE

Many passages in Scripture call for discipline of erring church members. These passages lead to the inevitable conclusion that church discipline is as much the function of a local church as the preaching of the "pure doctrine of the gospel," and "the administration of the sacraments as instituted by Christ."[2] "Discipline in the church is not optional but mandatory—it is an absolute necessity if we are . . . to be obedient to the Scriptures."[3]

215

Matthew 18:15–20 and 1 Corinthians 5:1–5 clearly proclaim this necessity. In view of the procedure in Matthew 18:15–20 with the present imperative ὕπαγε ("go"),[4] church discipline is not merely suggested; it is required. First Corinthians 5:1–5 confirms its necessity in addressing a specific situation requiring church discipline.[5]

First Thessalonians 5:14 requires warning the disobedient; 2 Thessalonians 3:6–15 suggests warning and, if necessary, withdrawing from a brother; Titus 3:10 commands withdrawing from one causing division; and 1 Timothy 5:20 advises public rebuke of those who persistently sin.[6] Given these commands and exhortations, it is unequivocal that church discipline is not an option.

THE PURPOSE OF CHURCH DISCIPLINE

Three purposes for church discipline are given in the New Testament: to restore and reconcile the sinner (Matt. 18:15; 2 Cor. 2:5–8); to maintain church purity (1 Cor. 5:6–7); and to serve as a deterrent from sin (1 Tim. 5:20).

Restoration is the foremost purpose. As Jesus said, "If he hears you, you have gained[7] your brother" (Matt. 18:15). Paul encouraged the church to "forgive," "comfort," and "reaffirm [their] love" toward the disciplined brother (2 Cor. 2:7–8).[8] As Hughes writes,

> Now, however, the punishment has proved sufficient, for the reason that it has successfully effected the primary end for which all discipline within the Christian community should be exercised, namely, the reformation and thereupon the restoration of the guilty person. Discipline which is so inflexible as to leave no place for repentance and reconciliation has ceased to be truly Christian; for it is no less a scandal to cut off the penitent sinner from all hope of re-entry into the comfort of the fellowship of the redeemed community than it is to permit flagrant wickedness to continue unpunished in the Body of Christ.[9]

Reconciliation with the local assembly is not warranted until there is a turning of the heart of the one disciplined. In 2 Thessalonians 3:14 Paul wrote, "And if anyone does not obey our instruction in this letter, take special note of that man and do not associate with him, so that he may be put to shame," or "so that he may be turned."[10] The discipline is not to humiliate or shame the offender"[11] but to encourage him to repent and be reconciled.[12]

The second purpose for discipline is to benefit the local

congregation. Paul warned the Corinthians that the "leaven" in their midst would permeate the entire "lump" unless they "remove the wicked man" (1 Cor. 5:7, 13). Church discipline is to maintain purity in the local church.

A third purpose of discipline is to deter others from sin. "Those who continue in sin," Paul instructed the elders in Ephesus, "rebuke in the presence of all, so that the rest also may be fearful" (1 Tim. 5:20). Deterrence was the result of the discipline of Ananias and Sapphira, for "great fear came upon the whole church" (Acts 5:11).

THE REASONS FOR CHURCH DISCIPLINE

There are general and specific causes of church discipline. Jesus spoke of the causes for discipline in general terms. In Matthew 16:15–20 He began His discourse on discipline, saying, "If your brother sins against you. . . ."[13] Ἁμαρτάνω, the common word "to sin," means to miss the mark by offending the moral law of God.[14] As Lenski wrote,

> Jesus has in mind graver sins such as all brethren would be compelled to consider too serious and too dangerous to allow them to pass without plain evidence of repentance. Sins of this kind often involve more than the offense against one brother; they may wrong several brethren, all of them seeing and knowing about the deed.[15]

While it is reasonable to state that Jesus referred to serious sin, He did not distinguish any degree of sinfulness.

Paul frequently wrote in general terms about causes of discipline. He said, "Those who continue in sin, rebuke in the presence of all" (1 Tim. 5:20). He cautiously advised believers to "restore . . . in a spirit of gentleness" one who "is caught in any trespass" (Gal. 6:1). In these passages Paul did not describe the sin, and, like Jesus, he may have been referring to a continued propensity,[16] leaving it up to those involved to decide when discipline should be pursued.

In addition to general causes for discipline, Paul also wrote of specific ones. In 1 Thessalonians 5:14 he told church leaders to "admonish the unruly," or more literally, those "out of step or rank."[17] This depicts the disorderly behavior of an idler,[18] which fits the context, for from verse 12 Paul encouraged appreciation for those who had been diligent. Use of this word in 2 Thessalonians 3:6–15 makes it clear that slothfulness requires separation.[19] For idleness, "Paul counsels them all to take steps to end this state of affairs."[20]

Divisiveness is a specific cause for discipline. Paul wrote, "Reject a factious man after a first and second warning" (Titus 3:10). Given the context, this is likely one who causes division by doctrinal heresy.[21] Thus doctrinal unfaithfulness causing divisiveness in the congregation is a specific cause for discipline.

Sexual immorality is also a cause for discipline. A case of vile sexual immorality ($\pi o \rho \nu \epsilon i a$)[22] was continuing, unhindered by the Corinthian leadership. Apparently, a member of the Corinthian church (was) committing incest with his stepmother, or literally, "the report is 'that a man has his father's wife'" (1 Cor. 5:1). After addressing their lax and even boastful attitude regarding this sin, Paul wrote, "Deliver such a one to Satan for the destruction of his flesh" (v. 5)[24] and "remove the wicked man from among yourselves" (v. 13).[25] Thus continued sexual immorality requires church discipline.

In 1 Corinthians 5:11 Paul cited other specific causes for discipline: immorality, covetousness, idolatry, slanderousness, drunkenness, and swindling. More must be intended than common struggle with these sins. Fee writes, "Paul is not advocating that only the sinless can be members of the Christian community; rather, he is concerned about those who persist in the very activities from which they have been freed through the sacrifice of the Pascal Lamb (v. 7)."[26] He adds, "Those who persist in that former way of life, not those who simply struggle with former sins, do not belong to this new community. By their own actions they have opted out; the community must distance itself from such people for its own sake."[27]

Given these general and specific causes, it appears that to a great extent the application of the requirement for church discipline is up to the local church. Jesus mentioned only general causes, and the specific causes referred to by Paul do not specify as to quality, quantity, or seriousness. The local assembly is apparently given latitude to decide when discipline is necessary. This seems right, since it is they who will know the seriousness, frequency, and potential hazard of the offense. However, the lack of specific parameters can make it difficult for a local church to demonstrate legally that there was no caprice or illegitimate motive involved. Since disciplined members have become more litigious, the fact that Scripture gives local churches broad power must be explained to all members.

THE METHOD OF CHURCH DISCIPLINE

In Matthew 18 Jesus outlined four steps to be followed in implementing church discipline. Though Paul did not give such an outline, his writings add guidance for at least three of the four steps.

Step one: Private corrective summons. In describing the method for discipline, Jesus began with private rebuke as the first step. "If your brother sins, go and reprove him in private" (Matt. 18:15). This word "reprove" (ἐλέγχω) means more than merely "to prove" or "to convince someone of sin," but "to set right," and "to point away from sin." It implies educative discipline and a summons to repentance.[28] A corrective goal is implied in the method. It seems reasonable that Paul intended such a private corrective summons when he wrote, "If a man is caught in any trespass, you who are spiritual, restore such a one in a spirit of gentleness" (Gal. 6:1).[29] The initial step is not to expose the sin openly, but to confront the individual gently with a view to repentance.

Step two: Group corrective summons. If a private corrective summons does not result in a response of repentance, then, as Jesus said, "Take one or two more with you, so that by the mouth of two or three witnesses every fact may be confirmed" (Matt. 18:16). Thus before any action is taken, the individual is given another opportunity to turn from his sinful behavior. Paul's language is similar: "Reject a factious man after a first and second warning" (Titus 3:10). Jesus and Paul both affirmed that one is to be privately addressed at least twice before any public disciplinary action is to be taken.

Step three: Public corrective summons. If the two private corrective summons fail to engender a response of repentance, then the offender is to be summoned to a public hearing before the church. Jesus said, "If he refuses to listen to them, tell it to the church" (Matt. 18:17). Though it is unlikely that the disciples understood ἐκκλησία to refer to a local church when they heard these words, it seems that Jesus was looking ahead to a New Testament assembly. Toussaint rightly applies these words to a local church context.

> This is the second and last occurrence of the word "church" (ἐκκλησία) in the gospels. It is used in a different sense here from that in Matthew 16:18. In the earlier occurrence it has reference to the body of Christ composed of those who are baptized by the Holy Spirit into Christ (1 Corinthians 12:13). Here it speaks of the local assembly, a body of believers gathered together as a fellowship. Both times the Lord uses the

term He is anticipating the future when the church age would intervene
between His first and second comings.

Another factor indicates that the Lord is looking ahead to a new age. In
verse twenty He states, "Where two or three have gathered together in
My name, there am I in their midst." This clearly implies a time when He
will be absent from them, a time in which the church would exist.[31]

Jesus, looking forward to this age, advised a summons before the
local assembly while pursuing the restoration of the erring brother.

Step four: Public corrective exclusion. If the accused still does not
turn from his sin, then he is to be excluded from the church. Jesus said,
"If he refuses to listen even to the church, let him be to you as a Gentile
and a tax-gatherer" (Matt. 18:17). Lenski explains, "If all the brotherly
effort of the church fails, then the church must consider the sinner self-
expelled and must take due note of the fact and act accordingly. This is
the so-called ban or excommunication—the man's membership
ceases."[32] He adds, "By his sin the sinner thus makes himself 'one who
is not a sheep, nor wants to be sought, but intends to be completely
lost,' Luther using the imagery of v. 12–13."[33]

Similarly Paul advised exclusion from the church. He instructed
the assembly in Thessalonica to "keep aloof from every brother
who leads an unruly life and not according to the tradition which
you received from us" (2 Thess. 3:6). He also advised them, "And
if anyone does not obey our instruction in this letter, take special
note of that man and do not associate with him, so that he may be
put to shame" (3:14). Thus Paul advocated "withdrawing from,
refusing to fellowship with, withdrawing friendship"[36] and refusing
"close fellowship" or "interchange"[37] with the individual.

There can be no doubt as to Paul's advice to exclude the erring
individual in the specific situation that occurred in the Corinthian
assembly. If he were personally in Corinth, he said, he would have
"already judged" (1 Cor. 5:3) that the incestuous fornicator be
delivered "to Satan for the destruction of his flesh, that his spirit
may be saved in the day of the Lord Jesus" (v. 5). Speaking
metaphorically, he directed them to "clean out the old leaven,"
and later he straightforwardly commanded, "Remove the wicked
man from among yourselves" (vv. 7, 13). Thus after sufficient
warning Paul regarded public corrective action necessary.

CONCLUSION

It is important that church leaders understand the basis for
church discipline and explain its basis to the congregation. To

assist in the successful defense of a lawsuit, church leaders should be able to demonstrate that the grieved member understood the necessity of discipline as mandated by Scripture, its purpose, what actions call for church discipline, and what procedures will be taken by the assembly in carrying out church discipline. As one court wrote, "Elders had a right to rely on Parishioner's consensual participation in the congregation when they disciplined her as one who had voluntarily elected to adhere to their doctrinal precepts."[38]

Legal Theories and Defenses in Church Discipline Cases

Invasion of privacy, outrage (intentional infliction of emotional distress), and defamation are the three main legal theories used in lawsuits against local church leadership. By understanding these legal theories, unnecessary conduct that would contribute to a lawsuit can be avoided. The following analysis of these theories is not to circumvent the mandates of Scripture, but to encourage church leaders to consider legal parameters in carrying out discipline.[39]

INVASION OF PRIVACY

Most lawsuits include a claim "for the giving of publicity to private facts"[40] when church leaders have taken the matter before the congregation. To prove a legally culpable invasion of privacy the plaintiff must establish that (a) there was a public disclosure, (b) of private facts, (c) that were highly offensive to a reasonable person, and (d) that were of no legitimate concern to the public. An announcement read at a Sunday morning service advising the congregation to break fellowship with a disciplined member, coupled with a reading of the Scripture she violated, was deemed a "public disclosure."[41] Showing that the disclosure concerns facts not generally known to the public usually establishes the "private facts" requirement. Thus the first two requirements of invasion of privacy may be easily proved.

A plaintiff must also show that the public disclosure of private facts was "highly offensive to a reasonable person"—a culturally sensitive determination made by evaluating the content and environment in which the disclosure was made.[43] It must further be shown that the disclosure was not of legitimate concern to those who heard it.[44] These determinations are made on a case-by-case basis, which gives rise to the possibility of defense against this claim.

Apart from not having committed the four steps, a church can defend its position by appealing to privileged communication against invasion of privacy.[45] The following is a general rule applied to a church (a "religious association").

> The common interest of members of religious . . . associations . . . is recognized as sufficient to support a privilege for communications among themselves concerning the qualifications of the officers and members and their participation in the activities of the society. This is true whether the defamatory matter relates to alleged misconduct of some other member that makes him undesirable for continued membership, or the conduct of a prospective member.[46]

For example in *Redgate v. Roush*[47] it was held that a congregation did have legitimate concern when the elders announced withdrawing fellowship from a pastor preaching sermons that contravened church doctrine.

Most cases confirm a continuing common interest even if the member being disciplined has been asked to leave or has left before making the matter public.[48] However, it is precisely the fact that a member withdrew her membership in the midst of the disciplinary procedure that swayed one court to conclude that at that moment the common interest of the congregation ceased.[49] This decision has not received favorable response. One writer commented as follows:

> If religious liberty means anything, it must allow for the church to expel its members for reasons that others regard as arbitrary, foolish, prudish, or "no business of the church." The autonomy of religious societies as to matters of membership requires that actions such as *Bates* and *Guinn* be qualifiedly privileged in the law of torts. This privilege can be overcome only upon clear and convincing proof of either fraud motivated by a wholly secular purpose or malicious acts that cause injury beyond the reasonable bounds of any religious interest of the church or its relationship to its members. Thus, in Guinn, the church had a religious interest in announcing the reasons for the expulsion to its congregation, even after Guinn unilaterally resigned.[50]

Though a church may utilize this privilege, it is limited to actions that are not a result of fraud (motivated by a secular purpose), or malice (motivated by personal vengeance). Only action resulting from religious conviction is within the scope of this defense.

OUTRAGE (Intentional Infliction of Emotional Distress)

Fairly new on the legal scene, this theory is defined as "one who by extreme and outrageous conduct intentionally or recklessly causes severe emotional distress to another is subject to liability for such emotional distress."[51] "Extreme and outrageous conduct" occurs

> where conduct has been so outrageous in character, and so extreme in degree, as to go beyond all possible bounds of decency, and to be regarded as atrocious, and utterly intolerable in a civilized community.
> The liability clearly does not extend to mere insults, indignities, threats, annoyances, petty oppressions or other trivialities.[52]

"Emotional distress" has been variously defined, but it includes "all highly unpleasant mental reactions such as fright, horror, grief, shame, humiliation, embarrassment, anger, chagrin, disappointment, worry, and nausea. It is only when it is extreme where liability arises."[53]

Therefore if it is determined that in the course of administering church discipline "extreme and outrageous conduct resulting in emotional distress" occurred, a church can be liable under this theory.

The best defense to the claim of outrage is to avoid even the appearance of being within its parameters. In all procedures and at every stage of the disciplinary process care must be taken to appear and be reasonable. The best defense is to follow the instruction in Galatians 6:1, "Restore such a one in a spirit of gentleness."

DEFAMATION

Whether in the form of libel or slander, a communication is defamatory if "it tends to harm the reputation of another as to lower him in the estimation of the community or to deter third persons from associating or dealing with him."[54]

Against a claim of defamation, truth is an absolute defense.[55] Horrible statements made public cannot be held to be defamatory if true. Even false statements do not automatically result in a successful lawsuit, for a church and its leadership still have the privileged communication defense.[56] Yet this defense is limited. In *Brewer v. Second Baptist Church of Los Angeles*— the court looked at the privileged communication defense and confirmed the limitation of malice.[58] If malice is found, the defendant has gone beyond the privilege.

CONSENT

This ecclesiastical defense has its roots in contract law. It was reasoned that by implied or express consent a church member voluntarily agreed to conform to the church's canons or rules and to submit to the authority of the church. "By becoming a member an individual approves the rules provided by the government of the society and agrees to be governed by its usages and customs."[59] In 1883 a court held that the basis for church membership was voluntary consent, which entailed submission to the acts of its tribunals, that communications in the course of discipline were privileged (if no malice were present), and that announcement of the excommunication to the congregation and recording action in the book of minutes were within the scope of church discipline.[60]

Though no longer couched in terms of contract law, this defense of privilege by consent is still found today. In 1987 the Montana Supreme Court utilized this defense in dismissing a suit brought by a disfellowshiped couple who were wed contrary to church doctrine. The couple sued for defamation against the church and overseers, stating to the congregation that they had been disfellowshiped "for conduct unbecoming Christians," and that "we got the filth cleaned out of the congregation [and] now we will have God's spirit."[61] The court stated, "We find the defendant's statements to be privileged. It is firmly established that statements of church members made in the course of disciplinary or expulsion proceedings, in the absence of malice, are protected by a qualified privilege."[62]

Though this defense is still available, it is limited. It certainly does not protect statements made maliciously. Furthermore many courts have also indicated that just as consent is given, consent can be withdrawn.[63] Language from the Gibson case illustrates this point.

> As the proposition is stated, it is uncontestable so far as the individual defendants are concerned. Their right, individually or collectively, to withdraw themselves from the parent Church is protected to the fullest extent by the Constitution of this State. Individually, or as a congregation, the members of the Church may not be compelled to attend any religious worship, or to contribute to the maintenance of any ministry, against their free will and consent.[64]

Since the First Amendment of the U.S. Constitution is now applicable to state action through the Fourteenth Amendment,[65] courts tend to apply a constitutional privilege under the "free exercise" or "establishment" clauses in church discipline cases.

CONSTITUTIONAL PRIVILEGE

The constitutional standard involving religious issues is the separation of church and state.[66] Generally the First Amendment requires that government maintain neutrality, neither aiding nor opposing religion.[67] The First Amendment has two clauses protecting religious practice. The first prevents the establishment of a state religion, and the second protects an individual's exercise of religion from state interference. The Amendment states, "Congress shall make no law respecting an establishment of religion, or prohibiting the free exercise thereof." While the legal history and theory of these two clauses are distinctly different,[68] the results of their application to church discipline cases are similar. Usually courts utilize the "free exercise" clause and state as follows:

> Nor is it in the competence of courts under our constitutional scheme to approve, disapprove, classify, regulate or in any manner control sermons delivered at religious meetings. Sermons are as much a part of a religious service as prayers. They cover a wide range and have as great a diversity as the Bible or other Holy Book from which they commonly take their texts. To call the words which one minister speaks to his congregation a sermon, immune from regulation, and the words from another minister an address, subject to regulation, is merely an indirect way of preferring one religion over another.[69]

Another court said, "In the present case, this court would be violating defendant's right to free exercise of religion if we were to find defendant's statements actionable under state defamation law."[70]

While churches and church leaders can generally depend on this constitutional privilege, the defense is limited. For instance, "when churches enter into the secular world they lose their privilege."[71]

Also, regarding the establishment clause, the privilege is said to be absolute, unless the action by the church is clearly a "threat to public safety, peace, and order," or "some grav[e] abuse, endangering paramount interests, give[s] occasion for permissible limitation."[72] A church discipline case that involved shunning, for example, was found not to be such a threat: "Harms caused by shunning (are) clearly not the type that would (require) the imposition of tort liability. Without society's tolerance of offenses to sensibility, the protection of religious differences mandated by the First Amendment would be meaningless."[73]

At least one court has found another limitation to the constitutional privilege. Finding the right to withdraw from fellowship constitutionally unqualified, the Oklahoma Supreme

Court went on to say, "The constitutionally protected freedom to impose even the most deeply felt, spiritually inspired disciplinary measure is forfeited when the object of 'benevolent' concern is one who has terminated voluntary submission to another's supervision and command."[74] Although unusual, it is possible other courts may follow this reasoning.

Conclusion

Through an understanding of the legal defenses and their limitations, churches and church leaders can do much to prevent adverse judgments against them. Such understanding enables church leaders to practice church discipline faithfully as articulated in Scripture and still remain outside the scope of legal liability.

CHAPTER 20

Court Involvement in Church Discipline, Part 2

Jay A. Quine

This chapter presents a historical overview of court involvement in church discipline cases through the 1980s. Based on this and the examination of the legal theories most commonly used in such cases (presented in part one of this two-part series), guidelines and parameters for church leaders to consider in their practice of church discipline are suggested. These guidelines are not given to replace the mandates of Scripture, but to assist in the practice of church discipline within the bounds of legal impunity. An illustrative scenario is examined to demonstrate how the law might apply in a situation many churches and church leaders may experience.

Historical Overview of Court Involvement in Church Discipline

EARLY HISTORY

The filing of lawsuits by disciplined church members, though currently on the rise, is not new. In 1850 a woman sued her church and minister for libel after he announced during a worship service that she had "violated the seventh commandment." He declared,

> The church does now as always bear its solemn testimony against the sin of fornication and uncleanness, as an unfruitful work of darkness, eminently dishonorable to the God of purity and love; polluting to the souls of men and fearfully prejudicial to the welfare of society and the world.[1]

Following the established rule of common law, the Massachusetts Supreme Court held that this public reading of the resolution was privileged. The court dismissed the claim, stating, "Maintenance of church order and discipline are amongst the church's long recognized powers, including hearing complaints of misconduct and administering punishment if found to be true."[2]

The case of *Watson v. Jones*[3] is used by both plaintiffs and

227

defendants in church discipline cases. Even though the case involved the conveyance of property, the court said much regarding church discipline. Plaintiffs often quote the following language: "In this country the full and free right to entertain any religious belief, to practice any religious principle, and to teach any religious doctrine which does not violate the laws of morality and property, *and which does not infringe on personal rights*, is conceded to all."[4]

Using the theories of invasion of privacy and outrage, plaintiffs argue that church discipline infringes on their personal rights. Yet this court also said,

> The right to organize voluntary religious associations of any religious doctrine, and to create tribunals for the decision of controverted questions of faith within the association, and for the ecclesiastical governing of all individual members, congregations and officers within the general association, is unquestioned.
>
> It would be vain consent and would lead to the total subversion of such religious bodies, if anyone aggrieved by one of their decisions could appeal to the secular courts and have them reversed.[5]

Churches defending lawsuits also cite *Watson v. Jones*. The failure to distinguish clearly between internal ecclesiastical matters and secular personal rights is also seen through three additional statements of this court:

> "This court," says Chief Justice, "having no ecclesiastical jurisdiction cannot reverse or question ordinary acts of church discipline. We cannot decide who ought to be members of the church, nor whether the excommunicated have been justly or unjustly, regularly or irregularly cut off from the body of the church."[6]

And further, in support of church autonomy in discipline,

> The judicial eye cannot penetrate the veil of the church for the forbidden purpose of vindicating the alleged wrongs of excised members; when they became members they did so upon the condition of continuing or not as they and their churches might determine, and they thereby submit to the ecclesiastical power and cannot now invoke the supervisory power of the civil tribunals.[7]

Yet as if to say there are occasions when courts will interfere, the court stated, "When a civil right depends upon an ecclesiastical matter, it is the civil court and not the ecclesiastical which is to decide."[8]

Apparently the court found it difficult to distinguish clearly between an ecclesiastical matter and a civil matter. Because of the relative infrequency of church discipline cases, this lack of clarity was not a serious matter until more recently.

RECENT CASES

Several church discipline cases arose in the 1960s and 1970s. The United States Supreme Court attempted to draw a line between ecclesiastical and secular matters when it said, "Only the gravest abuses, and endangering paramount interests, give occasion for permissible limitation [of religious practice]."[9] Thus a developing rule was clarified and confirmed. Only when there is conduct that imposes some substantial threat to public safety, peace, and order will secular courts get involved. The court cited a case involving polygamy[10] and one involving religious snake-handling[11] as examples warranting secular judicial involvement.

In an important case involving expulsion of a deacon, the New Jersey Supreme Court added a church's failure to follow its own procedures as the kind of case warranting secular involvement. The court reasoned,

> There is no question of spiritual matters of church doctrine in the present case. We cannot, however, accept the proposition that civil courts lack jurisdiction to determine whether established procedures of a religious organization, as approved, have been followed where a member is expelled from that organization.[12]

The court added that there are "many cases which granted judicial review to ousting where churches failed to follow their own procedures."[13] Because the court looked to the procedure of the vote taken, and not the religious reasons behind the vote to excommunicate the plaintiff, it felt it was not looking at a doctrinal or ecclesiastical matter. The New Jersey court also seemed to suggest other situations besides the breaking of a church's own procedure where it felt courts could interfere in church discipline cases. It stated,

> We believe expulsion from a church or other religious organization can constitute a serious emotional deprivation which, when compared to some losses of property or contract rights, can be far more damaging to an individual. The loss of the opportunity to worship in familiar surroundings is a valuable right which deserves the protection of the law where no constitutional barrier exists.[14]

Unfortunately this court did not explain what it considered a "constitutional barrier" that would prohibit civil interference. It gave no example that would limit judicial involvement. If the "loss of opportunity to worship in familiar surroundings" is considered a property right, then in what kind of case would such a right be enforced? Perhaps this statement is only dicta,[15] since the court did not examine the deacon's "loss of opportunity to worship in familiar surroundings." This court's language is at best imprecise and is certainly confusing.

Perhaps the Pennsylvania Supreme Court has helped eliminate this confusion. The court indicated that in certain cases it would be inclined to entertain cases where churches are sued by disciplined members. It explained, "Certain interests of the state may be invaded by 'shunning,'[16] such as interference with marriage and family relationships, alienation of affection, and tortuous interference with business relationships."[17] This court reversed a motion to dismiss and ordered a trial to determine whether any such state interest was "invaded."

CASES IN THE 1980s

Litigation by disciplined members has seen unprecedented frequency in the 1980s. Continuing legal education courses are now offered to plaintiff attorneys to guide them in their lawsuits against churches.[18] With such legal resources committed to pursue lawsuits against churches, it is imperative for church leaders to be aware of certain issues in order to avoid unnecessary adverse judgments.

The most famous church discipline case of the 1980s was *Guinn v. Church of Christ of Collinsville*.[19] The church leadership was meticulous in following the procedures outlined in Scripture and in following their own policy as established by prior practice. The plaintiff was a member of the church. She was fully aware of the church's disciplinary policy and had seen it administered in a previous case in the church. When the church leaders approached her privately about her adulterous relationship, she denied it. Nearly a year later she was again approached by the elders and questioned about her immorality. She then admitted to having an affair and seemed remorseful. She agreed no longer to see her partner.

Approximately two months later she was confronted by the elders on her arrival home with her lover late one night. The elders told her that if she did not repent and publicly acknowledge her sin to the church, they had no alternative but to withdraw fellowship from her. In a letter they warned her that if she did not make public repentance of her sin, fellowship would be withdrawn. On advice from her attorney, she wrote back a letter withdrawing membership from the church. At the next Sunday service the elders announced to the congregation their concern for her and requested the members to contact her and pray for her. The elders explained that if she refused to repent, they would have no choice but to withdraw fellowship from her. The reason for pursuing discipline in this manner was their belief that such procedure is required by Scripture.

The plaintiff sued the church and its elders for invasion of privacy, and outrage.[20] The court refused to dismiss the case and a trial was held. The jury awarded the plaintiff $390,000 in damages. On appeal, the church again argued religious privilege, consent, and public interest as defenses.[21] In affirming the trial court's decision and jury verdict, the Oklahoma Supreme Court said, "Because the controversy in the instant case is concerned with the allegedly tortuous nature of religiously motivated acts and not with their orthodoxy vis-á-vis established church doctrine, the justification for judicial abstention is nonexistent and the theory does not apply."[22]

The court also stated, "By continuing to discipline her as though she were a practicing Church of Christ member (after she withdrew membership), the Elders are alleged to have invaded her privacy and caused her emotional distress."[23] The court concluded,

> When parishioner withdrew her membership from the Church of Christ and thereby withdrew her consent to participate in a spiritual relationship in which she had implicitly agreed to submit to ecclesiastical supervision, those disciplinary actions thereafter taken by the Elders against parishioner, which actively involved her in the church's will and command, were outside the purview of the First Amendment protection and were proper subject of state regulation.[24]

Therefore the Oklahoma Supreme Court ordered a new trial to determine the amount of damages attributable to actions occurring after the plaintiff revoked her membership.[25]

Potentially enormous implications arise from this case. If church discipline following biblical mandates, without malice on behalf of the church leadership, consistent with church policy, following prior incidents and policy, and with implied if not explicit prior consent by the disciplined member is not considered a doctrinal or ecclesiastical matter warranting constitutional privilege, then what action in church discipline matters will courts allow? If all a member about to be disciplined need do to sustain a lawsuit is state that he or she withdraws his or her membership, then the courts have essentially prohibited discipline by churches and have effectively decided the ecclesiastical merits of discipline. The Oklahoma Supreme Court effectively decided that Matthew 16 and the other discipline passages cannot be practiced by churches in its state.

Fortunately *Guinn v. Church of Christ of Collinsville* is not the only or the last word on the matter. In *Kaufman v. Sheehan*[26] an appellate court affirmed the granting of a summary judgment by a trial court. Here the plaintiff was a priest who sued his archbishop for invasion of privacy and breach of confidentiality for sending a letter expressing concern regarding the priest's psychological condition to a church where he was seeking employment. The court judged it a religious matter and therefore the First Amendment demanded separation.

In *Chavis v. Rowe*[27] the New Jersey Court instructed the trial court to grant summary judgment in favor of the church. Here a deacon was dismissed and sued the church for failure to follow church procedures. The court examined the church policy and noted, "There were no procedures spelled out for removal of deacon in mid term, but generally all matters of discipline would be under the jurisdiction of the deacons and pastor."[28] The court considered such matters inherently ecclesiastical and therefore out of bounds for civil judiciaries.

In *Van Schaick v. Church of Scientology of California*[29] the court affirmed that if a disciplinary action was in accord with church policy, the secular courts were to stay out of disciplinary matters.

Regarding interference with civil rights, it should be noted that in *Nunn v. Black*[30] a West Virginia trial court's decision granting summary judgment was upheld, dismissing the case of an expelled member where the member alleged violation of his civil rights.

In the State of Washington, in *Paul v. Watchtower Bible Society*,[31] the court clearly yielded to church autonomy and separation in discipline matters.[32] On appeal the Ninth Circuit Federal Court of Appeals agreed, stating, "When the imposition of liability would result in the abridgment of the right to free exercise of religious beliefs, recovery in tort is barred."[33] The court went on further to say,

Imposing tort liability for shunning on the church or its members would in the long run have the same effect as prohibiting the practice, and would compel the church to abandon part of its religious teachings. In sum, a state tort law prohibition against shunning would directly restrict the free exercise of the Jehovah Witnesses' religious faith.[34]

It is significant that this court also determined that this action of discipline by a church did "not constitute a sufficient threat to the peace, safety, or morality of the community to warrant state intervention." Such intangible or emotional harms, the court concluded, cannot ordinarily serve as a basis for maintaining a tort cause of action against a church for its practices."[35]

CONCLUSION

Even though there are no "bright line" rules, this body of church discipline case law lends itself to some suggestions to be followed to help churches limit their liability if sued.

Suggested Guidelines and Parameters

OVERALL ANALYSIS

Though uncertainty remains regarding church discipline cases, some general guidelines, if followed, would tend to limit a lawsuit's success against a local church and its leaders. While these are not absolute and they provide no guarantee against adverse judgments, they represent conclusions from the cases presented in these two chapters.

First and foremost, church leaders must follow the guidelines found in Scripture. Regardless of the legal consequences, churches should recognize that the authority of the legal system of the United States stands under God's authority. As Paul commanded, "Let every person be in subjection to the governing authorities" (Rom. 13:1). Churches are obligated to obey civil authority; yet when that authority calls for action contrary to Scripture, obedience to God takes precedence. As Peter said, "We must obey God rather than men" (Acts 5:29). Fortunately following Scripture in the area of church discipline will rarely result in a conflict with the law.

Courts tend to require that church policies for discipline be articulated carefully and followed consistently. No court has dictated such a policy, so passages such as Matthew 18 can be used as a church's disciplinary procedure. Since it is Scripture, the requirement that the church's procedure be followed consistently should not be a problem. If a church is guilty of malice or fraud, this would be contrary to Scripture and would result in legal liability.

In light of the tendency of courts to require churches to have a policy for discipline, it is advisable for churches to have such a policy stated in their bylaws. These bylaws should be publicly reviewed at regular intervals (such as the church's annual meetings). This should satisfy the frequent reference to "consent" made by many courts. By a public review, members would be on notice of the church's policy regarding discipline.

Another principle derived from the cases discussed is that in every step of the discipline process the leaders must be reasonable. This too is consistent with Scripture, for church discipline should be carried out with a calm mind and gentle spirit (Gal. 6:1). This requirement is perhaps best met if the church leaders put themselves in the shoes of the one disciplined, respecting the Lord's words, "love . . . your neighbor as yourself" (Luke 10:27). The requirement of reasonableness is not to deter engagement in the practice of discipline, but to help ensure scriptural practice as well as limit legal liability.

If it becomes necessary for a church to break fellowship with the member being disciplined, certain principles should be kept in mind. One is that the breaking of fellowship should not involve the alienation of the affection and relationship of those within the immediate family of the disciplined member.[36] Thus the spouse and children should not be encouraged to break all association with a spouse or parent under discipline. A related application pertains to business associations. Contractual obligations between the disciplined member and other members of the church must be honored.[37] While church leadership might encourage no new contracts or other business associations, they may incur legal liability if they suggest the breaking of existing ones.

Even though a church has authority over its members, its authority is limited. Hodge wrote, "Fifthly, the Scriptures clearly teach that no human authority is intended to be unlimited. Such limitation may not be expressed, but it is always implied."[38] With respect to the church, Hodge added,

> The visible Church being organized for a definite purpose, its power being derived from God, and its prerogatives being all laid down in the Scriptures, it follows not only that its powers are limited within the bounds thus prescribed, but also that the question, whether its decisions

and injunctions are to be obeyed, is to be determined by every one concerned, on his own responsibility. If the decision is within the limits to which God has confined the action of the Church, and in accordance with the Scriptures, it is to be obeyed. If it transcends those limits, or is contrary to the word of God, it is to be disregarded. . . . All this is included in the principle that we must obey God rather than man.[39]

These potential legal limits on church authority with respect to immediate family associations and existing legal obligations seem consistent with principles of Scripture.

Though the principles declared by courts are often harmonious with those found in Scripture, in some cases language is found that may be contrary. In most cases the courts speak of the disciplined person as a "member." The Oklahoma Supreme Court even articulated a difference between disciplining members and those who had withdrawn their membership from the church.[40] While not the practice of all churches, it may be wise for a church to maintain a current membership roll should another court make this distinction.

The following scenario is given to illustrate these principles. The situation may easily be one in which a church and its leaders could find themselves.

ILLUSTRATIVE SCENARIO

Local Community Church began with four families who had the common desire to start a church in which the Scriptures would be taught. They first met in their homes, but as other families joined, they rented an old church building in town. After four years of itinerant preaching by students from a nearby seminary, the church had grown in size sufficiently so that they were able to hire a full-time pastor. This was Pastor Steve's first pastorate.

The church wanted to remain "sensitive to the leading of the Spirit of God," and so they had no bylaws or constitution; they had only a single page statement of faith. Because "anyone who accepts Jesus Christ as his personal Savior is a member of His church," they had no roster of church membership. Though the church was growing, for various reasons people came and went, occasionally without much word to others. The church had never exercised discipline toward any member.

Dirk, age 35, had been attending the church for about a year. He was currently living with his mother and his two preschool children of whom he had custody. Dirk began attending the Local

Community Church after being removed from fellowship at another church in a nearby town for sexual impropriety with a deacon's 18-year-old daughter. When Pastor Steve heard of it, he questioned Dirk. Dirk confirmed the truth of the allegations and said he fully acknowledged his guilt, had repented of the sin, and was no longer seeing Candice. Dirk was visibly angry at the leaders of his former church for disfellowshiping him as part of their disciplinary action.

Dirk worked from job to job as a mechanic and roofer. To earn a skill in hopes of someday getting different work, Dirk began taking computer program courses at the community college in the evenings. Dirk began missing Wednesday evening prayer meetings and more and more church services on Sunday. Pastor Steve was unable to contact him at home.

Sometime over the course of his first year Pastor Steve preached a series of sermons on marriage, divorce, and remarriage. He admitted that the Bible's position on divorce and remarriage is difficult (he believed it taught at a minimum that God disapproves of divorce except in the case of adultery, and in any case did not allow for remarriage). He ended the series with a message on acceptance of one another regardless of current marital status, "for we are all united as one in the body of Christ."

As the church continued to grow, it became apparent that some kind of organization was needed. The church had no designated elders or deacons. So they started the process of careful selection of church leadership.

In the midst of this process, Pastor Steve learned that Candice had moved out of her home and was living with Dirk and his two children. He questioned one of the men of the church who admitted he suspected it. Dirk's mother confirmed these suspicions. Pastor Steve felt something must be done.

Steve knew the hazards involved in discipline. He felt it was to be carried out by mature men of the faith. However, the church was still in the process of selecting elders. Steve presented the problem of Dirk to one of the founders of the church, who felt it "too sticky of a mess for me to get involved in." Each founder thought something should be done but did not know what to do or how to go about it.

With hesitance and much prayer Steve went to Dirk privately. At first Dirk was defensive, accusing Steve of spying; he claimed Steve had no right to get involved in his private life. Though his mother continued to attend church, he declared that he was not going to church much anyway. He wanted the children to have a "mother figure" around, and so he had asked Candice to move in with him. He said he considered marrying her. There was no remorse or repentance for what he was doing.

Again Steve contacted the church founders and discussed the problem. Together they read and discussed Scripture that spoke of church discipline. Finally one of the men agreed to go with Steve and talk to Dirk again.

When Dirk saw them, he bristled. He accused them of being "self-righteous, no-good busybodies" and "people with nothing better to do than to judge and upset others." Steve asked if they could pray together, and he prayed. He turned to Dirk and told him he was willfully violating the mandates of Scripture and was pursuing a course contrary to the teaching of the church. Dirk was visibly upset and replied, "Well, do what you have to do."

Dirk was not present at church the next Sunday or the next. Rumors began to spread. Steve announced that the following Sunday the issue of discipline would be addressed.

The congregation was unusually quiet and attentive that next Sunday. Steve read Matthew 18:15–20; 1 Corinthians 5:1–5; and other passages. He stressed that the purpose of church discipline was for restoration of an erring brother. He then briefly explained that Dirk was willfully violating Scripture and the church's teaching, and continued to be involved in an extramarital sexual relationship. He instructed the congregation to approach Dirk, call him, pray with him, and encourage him to repent.

The next week several members of the congregation had contact with Dirk. Each one mentioned the announcement made by the pastor and encouraged Dirk to confess his sin, turn from it, and come back to church. With each successive conversation Dirk became more and more agitated, feeling that the whole world knew about his private affairs. He worked himself up to a rage, felt that this had to stop, and wanted to get even. He called an attorney.

ANALYSIS OF THE ILLUSTRATIVE SCENARIO

Several things are to be noted about this incident at the Local Community Church. First, they had young leadership. Though they were looking for elders, they had no history of eldership or established record of authority. The church had gone on for several years without the kind of leaders or base of authority courts look for to establish a pattern of doctrine, rule, and obedience from members.

However, the church also had no "members." Though their position on the church as a body was noble, courts focus on membership as a guide to determine who is under the authority of the leaders. Because people came and went, it was difficult to determine when someone was a part of the church. Was Dirk still a "member," an ongoing part of the local assembly? What if he had not attended for four or six months? Could the church still discipline him? An active membership role establishing parameters when an attendant becomes inactive would have eliminated this problem.

The church also had no written policy regarding discipline and no previous incident of church discipline. Were the members aware that the church might actively pursue a disciplinary course of action? One defense that courts tend to rely on to dismiss a case is prior consent from the members. But members cannot give consent to something of which they are not aware.

Was Steve's teaching on marriage and divorce sufficient to establish church doctrine, deviation from which would warrant discipline? Could his messages be used as a policy or guide for discipline? Were they enough of a basis for discipline so that contacting Dirk would not appear arbitrary or malicious? Was Steve being reasonable in assuming Dirk was aware of this position of the church?

Was Steve reasonable in communicating what he learned about Dirk to the church leaders, even though they were not yet recognized as elders? They all admitted they did not want to get involved. Was Steve possibly acting on his own for some hidden motivation, perhaps even a fraudulent political purpose to be advantageously used in the ongoing process for the church's selection of elders? Was Steve in a power struggle using Dirk's situation as an opportunity to prove his control and authority in the church? Steve and the leaders knew Dirk was upset. Was it then reasonable to contact him again, knowing the likelihood that Dirk would get more upset? Did that action appear as shocking and outrageous conduct?

Steve gained private information about Dirk's personal life. Then one Sunday he spread that information to the entire congregation. Was he invading Dirk's privacy by telling his fellow churchgoers about his private life?

A small local church can quickly appear to be a malicious

monster. However, most of these issues are easily avoidable. Some written policy or bylaws that include a section on church discipline would satisfy the consent requirement. If the church had at least some membership or attendance roll with a procedure by which to follow up those who stop coming (as with a telephone call or letter), this would satisfy the membership issue. These two items alone may be enough to change the entire outcome of a lawsuit.

SPECIFIC SUGGESTIONS

If invasion of privacy is claimed in a lawsuit, the plaintiff must show that there was a public disclosure of private facts. It would therefore be advisable to hold a special service, perhaps a Sunday evening service for "members only" if it becomes necessary to make an announcement about a discipline matter to the congregation. This would limit the "public" nature of the announcement. Also at such a meeting a comment about the disciplinary action being a local church family matter would help prevent further public disclosure.

To show that the facts were not so "private," reference should be made as to how the sin was discovered, perhaps even to the point of mentioning the witnesses involved. This would tend to minimize the private nature of the information revealed.

To be liable for publicly disclosing private facts, the disclosure must be highly offensive and of no legitimate concern to the hearers. In addressing the congregation the pastor should establish a mood of seriousness. He should not be vulgar or flippant, but brief and reasonable, taking great care not to be offensive. Reference could be made to the church as a living body in which the entire body suffers if one part is not functioning well (1 Cor. 12:12–31). This demonstrates that every member of the congregation has a legitimate concern in the matter.

Since it is also likely that a claim of defamation could be included in a lawsuit, a pastor's remarks to the congregation should include reference to human sinfulness and to the fact that every believer struggles with sin to some degree. The veracity and accuracy of all statements made to the congregation must be confirmed. There is no better defense to defamation than truth.

Church leaders must examine themselves and the witnesses to ensure that they are pure in motive. If malice or personal vengeance is suspected, then that must be addressed before another step is taken in the disciplinary process.

Many churches today are involved in affairs other than traditional ecclesiastical matters. If the event occurs in a secular context, then there is no constitutional defense to a lawsuit. For example if the lawsuit stems from an employee matter at the church's local bookstore, the courts will not likely recognize such an issue as a matter of church discipline.

All actions taken should be demonstrably based on Scripture. Besides involving obedience to God this will help establish the sole motive and basis of the disciplinary process as ecclesiastical. Church leaders must genuinely believe that the disciplinary action would never be taken were it not for the mandates of Scripture. Any policy formulated or acknowledged must then be consistently followed in every church discipline case.

Conclusion

If a disciplined church member files a lawsuit against a local church, it is important that the leaders respond immediately to assist the church's attorney in every way possible. The church should not hesitate to expend great effort at the beginning of the lawsuit. If a case is allowed to be fully tried, juries usually find the church liable.[41] However, in the preliminary hearings (before an actual trial takes place) judges can become educated in this area of law, and in the vast majority of cases dismiss the lawsuit on the basis of one or more of the legal defenses. Therefore the church being sued must concentrate great effort long before the trial actually begins.

While there is no guarantee against a church being sued, following these guidelines and suggestions will help minimize the possibility of an adverse judgment while allowing a church to be faithful to the Word of God.

Chapter Notes

Chapter 1

1. Trevor Beeson, *Discretion and Valour* (London: Collins, 1974), p. 24.
2. Theodore Roszak, *Where the Wasteland Ends* (1972; reprint, New York: Anchor, 1973), pp. xxi, 22, 66–67, 70, 227–28.
3. Alvin Toffler, *The Third Wave* (London: Collins, 1980).
4. *The Economist*, November 25, 1978.
5. Carlos Castaneda, *The Teachings of Don Juan* (1968; reprint, New York: Penguin, 1970), p. 182.
6. Fedor Dostoevski, *The Possessed*, cited in Ernest Gordon, *Miracle on the River Kwai* (London: Collins, 1963), p. 159.
7. Arnold Toynbee, *Experiences* (Oxford: Oxford University Press, 1969), cited in *Times* (London), April 5, 1969.
8. Desmond Morris, *The Naked Apple* (London: Jonathan Cape, 1967).
9. Victor Frankl, *Man's Search for Meaning* (New York: Washington Square, 1963), p. 154.
10. Ibid., pp. 164–165.
11. Mel White, *Deceived* (Old Tappan, NJ: Revell, 1979), pp. 19, 184.
12. Stephen C. Neill, *Christian Faith Today* (New York: Penguin, 1955), pp. 171, 174.

Chapter 2

1. The title "slave of Yahweh" belongs uniquely to Israel in the Old Testament (Deut. 32:36; Pss. 34:22; 89:50; 90:13, 16; 102:28; 105:25; 135:14), and is given to the great men of faith: Abraham (Gen. 26:24; Ps. 105:42), Isaac (Gen. 24:14), Jacob (Gen. 32:10), Moses (Num. 12:6–8; Josh. 14:7; Ps. 105:26), Joshua (Josh. 14:29; Judg. 2:18), David (2 Sam. 3:18; 1 Kings 8:24–26; 14:8; Pss. 78:70–71; 89:3), and the prophets (2 Kings 17:23; Amos 3:7).
2. Anthony T. Hansen, *The Church of the Servant* (London: SCM, 1962), p. 41.
3. *The New International Dictionary of New Testament Theology*, s.v. "Serve, Deacon, Worship," by K. Hess, 3:544.
4. *Theological Dictionary of the New Testament*, s.v. "διακονέω, διακονία, διάκονος," by H. W. Beyer, 2:82–83.
5. *The New International Dictionary of New Testament Theology*, 3:545.

241

6. Διακονεω occurs 37 times in the New Testament, διακονία 34 times, and διάκονος 29 times.
7. Cited in William B. Lane, *Commentary on the Gospel of Mark*, New International Commentary on the New Testament (Grand Rapids: Eerdmans, 1974), p. 339, n. 40.
8. William Barclay, *The Gospel of Mark* (Edinburgh: Saint Andrew, 1956), p. 231.
9. Leon Morris, *The Gospel According to St. Luke*, Tyndale New Testament Commentaries (Grand Rapids: Eerdmans 1974), p. 309.
10. T. W. Manson, *The Church's Ministry* (London: Hodder and Stoughton, 1948), p. 27.
11. Ray S. Anderson, ed., *Theological Foundations for Ministry* (Grand Rapids: Eerdmans, 1979), p. 715.
12. John R. W. Stott, *The Preachers Portrait* (Grand Rapids: Eerdmans, 1961), pp. 104–5.
13. W. H. Griffith Thomas, *Ministerial Life and Work* (Grand Rapids: Baker, 1974), p. 82.
14. James Denney, *The Second Epistle to the Corinthians*, The Expositor's Bible (New York: Armstrong & Son, 1894), p. 216.
15. *The New International Dictionary of New Testament Theology*, 3:544.

Chapter 3

1. Leroy Eims, *Be the Leader You Were Meant to Be* (Wheaton, IL: Victor, 1975), p. 7.
2. Howard E. Butt, Jr., *The Velvet-Covered Brick* (New York: Harper & Row, 1973), p. 50.
3. Ibid.
4. Ibid., p. 71.
5. Ibid. p. 73.
6. Howard G. Hendricks, "How to Lead, Part I," cassette tape set, Vision House Publishers.
7. Private conversation with Howard G. Hendricks.
8. "Vision Key Trait of 'Superleaders,' Researcher says," *The Dallas Morning News*, November 23, 1982.
9. J. Oswald Sanders, *Paul the Leader* (Colorado Springs: NavPress, 1984), p. 39.
10. Warren Bennis and Burt Nanus, *Leaders* (New York: Harper & Row, 1985), p. 5.
11. C. K. Barrett, *A Commentary on the First Epistle to the Corinthians* (New York: Harper & Row, 1968), pp. 283–84.
12. Leon Morris, *The First Epistle of Paul to the Corinthians* (Grand Rapids: Eerdmans, 1958), p. 170.
13. For a secular discussion of these elements, see Bennis and

Nanus, *Leaders*, pp. 19–86; for such thinking from a Christian perspective, see Fred Smith, *Learning to Lead* (Waco, TX: Word, 1986), pp. 32–44.

14. Sanders, *Paul the Leader*, p. 41.
15. J. Oswald Sanders, *Spiritual Leadership* (Chicago: Moody, 1978), p. 19.
16. Ibid., p. 20.
17. Smith, *Learning to Lead*, p. 29.
18. D. Edmond Hiebert, *Mark: A Portrait of the Servant* (Chicago: Moody, 1974), p. 257.
19. Ibid., p. 261.
20. Smith, *Learning to Lead*, p. 29 (italics his).
21. William L. Lane, *The Gospel According to Mark* (Grand Rapids: Eerdmans, 1974), p. 382.
22. *Theological Dictionary of the Greek New Testament*, s.v. προΐστημι, by Bo Reicke, 6:700.
23. Walter Bauer, William F. Arndt, and F. Wilbur Gingrich, *A Greek-English Lexicon of the New Testament and Other Early Christian Literature* (Chicago: University of Chicago Press, 1957), p. 714.
24. *Theological Dictionary of the Greek New Testament*, s.v. προΐστημι, by Bo Reicke, 6:701.
25. Ibid.
26. Ibid., p. 702.
27. Ibid.
28. Smith, *Leaning to Lead*, p. 23.
29. F. Duane Lindsey, "The Call of the Servant in Isaiah 42:1–9," *Bibliotheca Sacra* 139 (January-March 1982): 28, n. 14.
30. Butt, *The Velvet-Covered Brick*, p. 11.
31. Philip Edgcumbe Hughes, *Paul's Second Epistle to the Corinthians* (Grand Rapids: Eerdmans, 1962), pp. 267–68.
32. Smith, *Learning to Lead*, p. 25.
33. Kenneth Blanchard and Spencer Johnson, *The One-Minute Manager* (New York: Morrow & Co., 1982).
34. Thomas J. Peters and Robert H. Waterman, *In Search of Excellence* (New York: Harper & Row, 1982).
35. Bennis and Nanus, *Leaders*.
36. Kenneth O. Gangel, *Competent to Lead* (Chicago: Moody, 1974), p. 10.
37. Butt, *The Velvet-Covered Brick*, p. 16.

Chapters 4

1. R. C. H. Lenski, *The Interpretation of St. Paul's Epistles to the Colossians, to the Thessalonians, to Timothy, to Titus, and to Philemon* (Minneapolis: Augsburg, 1961), p. 790.

2. N. A. Woychuk, *An Exposition of Second Timothy, Inspirational and Practical* (Old Tappan, NJ: Revell, 1973), p. 41.
3. E. K. Simpson, *The Pastoral Epistles* (Grand Rapids: Eerdmans, 1954), p. 130.
4. William Barclay, *The Letters to Timothy, Titus, and Philemon*, The Daily Study Bible (Edinburgh: Saint Andrew, 1956), p. 182.
5. J. N. D. Kelly, *A Commentary on the Pastoral Epistles*, Harper's New Testament Commentaries (New York: Harper & Row, 1963), p. 171.
6. Alfred Plummer, *The Pastoral Epistles, An Exposition of the Bible* (Hartford, CT: Scranton, 1903), p. 469.
7. Woychuk, *Exposition of Second Timothy*, pp. 44–45.
8. Walter Lock, *A Critical and Exegetical Commentary on the Pastoral Epistles*, International Critical Commentary (Edinburgh: Clark, 1924), p. 94.
9. Simpson, *The Pastoral Epistles*, p. 132.
10. J. J. Van Oosterzee, *The Pastoral Epistles, Commentary on the Holy Scriptures, Critical, Doctrinal, and Homiletical*, ed. John Peter Lange, trans. Edward Abiel Washburn and Edwin Harwood (Grand Rapids: Zondervan, n.d.), p. 94.
11. Woychuk, *Exposition of Second Timothy*, p. 49.
12. John R. W. Stott, *Guard the Gospel: The Message of 2 Timothy* (Downers Grove, IL: InterVarsity, 1973), p. 57.
13. Plummer, *The Pastoral Epistles*, p. 475.
14. Kelly, *The Pastoral Epistles*, p. 183.
15. E. F. Stott, *The Pastoral Epistles*, Moffatt New Testament Commentary (London: Hodder & Stoughton, 1936), p. 109.
16. William Hendriksen, *Exposition of the Pastoral Epistles*, New Testament Commentary (Grand Rapids: Baker, 1957), p. 262.
17. Simpson, *The Pastoral Epistles*, p. 137.
18. Walter Bauer, William F. Arndt, and F. Wilbur Gingrich, *A Greek-English Lexicon of the New Testament and Other Early Christian Literature* (Chicago: University of Chicago Press, 1957), p. 584.
19. Patrick Fairbairn, *Commentary on the Pastoral Epistles, I and II Timothy, Titus* (1874; reprint, Grand Rapids: Zondervan, 1956), p. 344.
20. Barclay, *Timothy, Titus, and Philemon*, p. 206.
21. Woychuk, *Exposition of Second Timothy*, p. 91.
22. Barclay, *Timothy, Titus, and Philemon*, p. 208.
23. Lenski, *St. Paul's Epistles*, p. 826.
24. Barclay, *Timothy, Titus, and Philemon*, p. 208.

Chapter 5

1. For an excellent portrayal of the historical setting of the book of

Jeremiah, see John Bright, *Jeremiah*, Anchor Bible (Garden City, NY: Doubleday, 1965), pp. xxvii–liv.
2. Cf. Ronald F. Youngblood, "The Prophet of Loneliness," *Bethel Seminary Quarterly* 13 (May 1965): 3–19.
3. Cf. James Muilenburg, "The Intercession of the Covenant Mediator (Exodus 33:1a, 12–17)," in *Words and Meanings*, ed. Peter R. Ackroyd and Barnabas Lindars (London: Cambridge University Press, 1968), pp. 159–81; also see the literature cited there in footnotes on pp. 177–80.
4. Francis Brown, S. R. Driver, and Charles A. Briggs, *A Hebrew and English Lexicon of the Old Testament* (Oxford: Clarendon, 1955), p. 873.
5. Ibid., p. 680.
6. For the etymology and meaning of "prophet," see William F. Albright, *From the Stone Age to Christianity*, 2d ed. (Baltimore: Johns Hopkins, 1957), p. 303; and Hobart E. Freeman, *An Introduction to the Old Testament Prophets* (Chicago: Moody, 1968), pp. 37–40.
7. Brown, Driver, and Briggs, *A Hebrew and English Lexicon of the Old Testament*, p. 394.
8. Ibid., p. 655.

Chapter 6

1. Mark Twain, *The Adventures of Huckleberry Finn* (1884; reprint, Eureka, CA: Mad River, 1968), p. 347.
2. Richard Baxter, *The Reformed Pastor* (1656; reprint, London: Epworth, 1939), pp. 121–22.
3. Ibid., p. 24.

Chapter 7

1. William G. Schutz, "The Ego, FIRO Theory and the Leader as Completer," in *Leadership and Interpersonal Behavior*, ed. Luigi Petrullo and Bernard M. Bass (New York: Holt, Rinehart, and Winston, 1961), p. 49.
2. Ibid., pp. 50–54.
3. Ibid., p. 61.
4. Ibid., p. 62.
5. Ibid.
6. Jay Adams, "Making Preaching a Pleasure," *Journal of Pastoral Practice 3* (1979): 161.

Chapter 8

1. Peter Drucker, "The Art of Doing the Important," *Christian Ministry*, September 1972, p. 6.

2. Marcus Dods, "The Book of Genesis," in *The Expositor's Bible* (London: Hodder & Stoughton, 1907), 1:131.
3. Ezra Earl Jones, *Strategies for New Churches* (New York: Harper & Row, 1978), p. 17.
4. De Vern F. Fromke, *Ultimate Intention* (Mount Vernon, MO: Sure Foundation, 1961), p. 10.
5. Paul W. Witte, "Can Catholics Learn Anything from Evangelical Protestants?" *Christianity Today*, December 18, 1970, p. 14.
6. Alexander Whyte, *Lancelot Andrews and His Private Devotions* (London: Oliphant, Anderson & Ferrier, 1896), p. 103.
7. See Robert Coleman, *The Master Plan of Evangelism* (Old Tappan, NJ: Revell Co., 1963), for amplification of these ideas.
8. See Raymond C. Ortlund, *Lord, Make My Life a Miracle* (Glendale, CA: Regal, 1974), and Raymond C. Ortlund, *Intersections* (Waco, TX: Word, 1979), pp. 69–87.

Chapter 9

1. Robert H. Fife, *The Revolt of Martin Luther* (New York: Columbia University Press, 1957), p. 359.
2. Merrill F. Unger, *Principles of Expository Preaching* (Grand Rapids: Zondervan, 1955), p. 89.

Chapter 10

1. Franklyn S. Haiman, "An Experimental Study of the Effects of Ethos in Public Speaking," *Speech Monographs* 16 (1949): 190–202.
2. Since the Haiman experiment, more research has been done on the topic of ethos than on any other single concept specifically related to communication. For a summary of the research, see Kenneth Andersen and Theodore Clevenger, Jr., "A Summary of Experimental Research in Ethos," *Speech Monographs* 30 (1963): 59–78.
3. James C. McCroskey. *An Introduction to Rhetorical Communication* (Englewood Cliffs, NJ: Prentice-Hall. 1968), pp. 59–61.
4. Judson Mills and Elliot Aronson, "Opinion Change as a Function of the Communicator's Attractiveness and Desire to Influence," *Journal of Personality and Social Psychology* 1 (1965): 173–77.
5. Gerald R. Miller and Murray A. Hewgill, "The Effect of Variations in Nonfluency on Audience Ratings of Source Credibility," *Quarterly Journal of Speech* 50 (1964): 36–44.
6. A study by Bettinghaus likewise confirms that "effectiveness in delivery contributes not only to the credibility of the speaker, but also to the persuasiveness of the speaker in achieving acceptance of his message." (Erwin P. Bettinghaus, "The

Operation of Congruity in an Oral Communication Situation,"
Speech Monographs 28 [1961]: 142).
7. Harry Sharp, Jr. and Thomas McClung, "Effects of
Organization on the Speaker's Ethos," *Speech Monographs*
33 (1966): 182–83.
8. Ibid., p. 183.
9. To "restate" is to say immediately the same thing using different words.
It is using other terms and phrases to convey the concept just stated. It
is expressing right away the same truth in different language. (The
preceding three sentences in this note are an example of "restatement,"
which is used in preaching to highlight, to emphasize, and to give
"handles" to major concepts so that the listener can retain them.)
10. Erwin P. Bettinghaus, *Persuasive Communication*, 3d ed. (New
York: Holt, Rinehart and Winston, 1980), p. 169.
11. Ibid.
12. The necessity for character even beyond competency was revealed
during the primary contests in the 1980 national election for the
United States presidency. As the networks interviewed voters
exiting from the polls, they asked such questions as, "Which
candidate do you think could handle the economy better? Who do
you feel has the best grasp of foreign affairs? Who do you think
could best work with Congress to get things done? Which candidate
did you vote for?" A great majority of the voters would give one
candidate's name to the first three questions, but the other
candidate's name to the fourth. When asked to explain their vote,
their answers invariably pointed to such things as "morals,"
"integrity," "trustworthiness," and "character."
13. Aristotle, *Rhetoric* 1.2, trans. W. Rhys Roberts (New York: Random
House, 1954).
14. Henry Winthrop, "Effect of Personal Qualities on One-Way
Communication," *Psychological Reports 2* (1956): 323–24.
15. Albert Mehrabian and Morton Wiener, "Decoding of Inconsistent
Communications," *Journal of Personality and Social Psychology*
6 (1967): 109–14.
16. Albert Mehrabian and Susan R. Ferris, "Inference of Attitudes
from Nonverbal Communication in Two Channels," *Journal of
Consulting Psychology 31* (1967): 248–52.
17. Ibid., p. 252.
18. John Knox, *The Integrity of Preaching* (New York: Abingdon,
1957), p. 59.

Chapter 11

1. John Naisbitt and Patricia Aburdene, *Megatrends 2000* (New York:
Morrow, 1990), p. 12.

2. Reginald W. Bibby, *Fragmented Gods: The Poverty and Potential of Religion in Canada* (Toronto: Irwin, 1987), pp. 259–71.

3. Ibid., p. 111.

4. They are independent as a result of abandoning God, insignificant as a result of losing themselves in the machine of production, and isolated as a result of consuming as a means and end of existence.

5. John R. W. Stott, "The World's Challenge to the Church," *Bibliotheca Sacra* 145 (April–June 1988): 123–32.

6. Ibid., p. 132.

7. Carl F. H. Henry, *Twilight of a Great Civilization: The Drift Toward Neo-Paganism* (Westchester, IL: Crossway, 1988), pp. 54–56; Ronald A. Dworkin, "'Natural' Law Revisited," *University of Florida Law Review* 34 (Winter 1982): 165–88.

8. Bibby, *Fragmented Gods: The Poverty and Potential of Religion in Canada*, pp. 138–39. Also see Richard M. Weaver, *Ideas Have Consequences* (Chicago: University of Chicago Press, 1948), chap. 3, "Fragmentation and Obsession," pp. 52–59, and chap. 4, "Egotism in Work and Art," pp. 70–91.

9. Bibby, *Fragmented Gods: The Poverty and Potential of Religion in Canada*, p. 264; and Weaver, *Ideas Have Consequences*, chap. 5, "The Great Stereopticon," pp. 92–112.

10. Henry, *Twilight of a Great Civilization*, p. 170.

11. Henry, for example, has criticized American Christianity for failing to "relate biblical verities to crucial contemporary concerns" (ibid., p. 164).

12. Bibby, *Fragmented Gods: The Poverty and Potential of Religion in Canada*, p. 254.

13. Ibid., p. 258.

14. Ibid., pp. 270, 175.

15. Sidney Greidanus, *The Modern Preacher and the Ancient Text: Interpreting and Preaching Biblical Literature* (Grand Rapids: Eerdmans, 1988), pp. 2, 9.

16. Haddon W. Robinson, *Biblical Preaching* (Grand Rapids: Baker, 1980), p. 18. Invention of arguments, not truth, is the work of the preacher. Arguments for truth and applications of truth vary from context to context, but the propositional truth is divine.

17. Walter C. Kaiser, Jr., *Toward an Exegetical Theology: Biblical Exegesis for Preaching and Teaching* (Grand Rapids: Baker, 1981), p. 155.

18. Allen P. Ross, *Creation and Blessing* (Grand Rapids: Baker, 1988), p. 47.

19. Care must be taken to distinguish between a mere recitation of the details of the text (preaching the text) and preaching the idea of

the text in a proper way. It is not necessary or even possible for the preacher to identify and explain every textual detail. The expositor makes choices as to which points he will cover in order to convince his listeners that the "theological idea" is indeed derived from this particular text.

20. Ross, *Creation and Blessing*, p. 46.
21. Ibid., p. 47.
22. James D. Smart, *The Strange Silence of the Bible in the Church: A Study in Hermeneutics* (Philadelphia: Westminster 1970), pp. 29, 34.
23. David J. Hesselgrave and Edward Rommen, *Contextualization: Meanings, Methods, and Models* (Grand Rapids: Baker, 1989). Also Greidanus wrote, "Without genuine relevance there is no sermon. . . . one cannot select a text, formulate a sermon theme, and select a sermon form without an eye to the congregation" (*The Modern Preacher and the Ancient Text*, p. 157).
24. Stott has argued that "unless believers listen attentively to the voices of secular society and struggle to understand people's misunderstandings of the gospel, unless Christians feel with people in their frustration, alienation, and even despair, and weep with those who weep, they will lack authenticity as the disciples of Jesus of Nazareth. They will run the risk . . . of answering questions nobody is asking, scratching where nobody is itching, supplying goals for which there is no demand . . . of being totally irrelevant" ("The World's Challenge to the Church," p. 124).
25. Hesselgrave and Rommen reveal that despite the varying nuances of evangelical definitions of contextualization, all are sensitive to the demands of the context in which the message is to be delivered. The three definitions they present urge adaptation to one's specific audience. (1) "We understand the term to mean making concepts or ideals relevant in a given situation" (Byang H. Kato). (2) "[Contextualization is] the translation of the unchanging content of the Gospel of the kingdom into verbal form meaningful to the peoples in their separate culture and within their particular existential situations" (Bruce J. Nicholls). (3) "Contextualization properly applied means to discover *the legitimate implications* of the gospel in a given situation" (George W. Peters) (Hesselgrave and Rommen, *Contextualization: Meanings, Methods, and Models*, pp. 34–35).
26. "One of the dominant features of contemporary society is that [successful religious organizations] like their secular counterparts, are having to contend with highly individualized patterns of consumption. . . . the consumption of belief, practice, and service

fragments—versus identifiable commitment—is considerably more prevalent among [the] younger. . . . As the population ages, the consumption segment of the population can accordingly be expected to increase" (Bibby, *Fragmented Gods: The Poverty and Potential of Religion in Canada*, pp. 126, 234).

27. Tozer argues that "Bible teaching without moral application could be worse than no teaching at all and could result in positive injury to the hearers. What is generally overlooked is that truth as set forth in the Christian Scriptures is a moral thing; it is not addressed to the intellect only, but to the will also. It addresses itself to the total man, and its obligations cannot be discharged by grasping it mentally. Truth engages the citadel of the human heart and is not satisfied until it has conquered everything there" (Warren W. Wiersbe, comp., *The Best of A. W. Tozer* [Grand Rapids: Baker, 1978], pp. 140–41).

28. Jay E. Adams's book, *Truth Applied: Application in Preaching* (Grand Rapids: Zondervan, 1990), addresses this critical question. Adams begins, "When Haddon Robinson wrote, 'Many homileticians have not given application the attention it deserves [and] no book has been published devoted exclusively, or even primarily to the knotty problems raised by application,' he was expressing the felt need that brought forth this volume" (p. 9).

29. Phillips Brooks, *The Joy of Preaching* (reprint, Grand Rapids: Kregel, 1989), pp. 51–52.

30. John R. W. Stott, *Between Two Worlds* (Grand Rapids: Eerdmans, 1982) p. 144.

31. Ibid.

32. Brooks, *The Joy of Preaching*, pp. 25–26, 38.

33. Ibid., pp. 39–40. See also Bill Hybels, "Speaking to the Secular Mind," *Leadership* 9 (Summer 1988): 28–34.

34. Motl argues that "if communications is the theological specialty to which the other areas of theological study lead, it is surely not far-fetched to suggest that homiletics be considered as a crucial element in the integration of a theological curriculum" (James R. Motl, "Homiletics and Integrating the Seminary Curriculum," *Worship* [January 1990]: 24–30). Not a few seminary students have had difficulty expressing how their various theological skills fit together in preaching. True integration seems missing. Kaiser argues that "a gap of crisis proportions exists between the steps generally outlined in most seminary or biblical training classes in exegesis and the hard realities most pastors face . . . as they prepare their sermons. Nowhere in the total curriculum of theological studies has the student been more deserted and left to his own devices than in bridging the

yawning chasm between understanding the content of Scripture as it was given in the past and proclaiming it with . . . relevance in the present" (*Toward an Exegetical Theology*, p. 18).

35. It is readily acknowledged that Paul's writings are letters, not sermons (see James D. Hester, "The Use and Influence of Rhetoric in Galatians," *Theologische Zeitschrift* 42 [1986]: 386–408). Still the nature of the epistles is both New Testament and sermonic, more so than other biblical genres. For contrasting views on Paul's rhetorical strategies, see Hans D. Betz, "The Literary Composition and Function of Paul's Letter to the Galatians," *New Testament Studies* 21 (1975): 353–79, and Joop Smit, "The Letter of Paul to the Galatians: A Deliberative Speech," *New Testament Studies* 35 (1989): 1–26.

36. See Kaiser's and Greidanus's books for fuller statements of the issues involved in interpreting the ancient biblical text for contemporary audiences.

37. Anthony C. Thiselton, *The Two Horizons: New Testament Hermeneutics and Philosophical Description* (Grand Rapids: Eerdmans, 1980), p. 445.

38. Stott, *Between Two Worlds*, pp. 137, 144.

39. Ibid., p. 178.

40. Kaiser says, "Traditionally this is the very place where theological education has failed in its program. None of the theological departments has been specifically charged with assisting the student in the most delicate maneuver of transferring the results of the syntactical-theological analysis of the text into a viable didactic or sermonic format. In fact, everyone has assumed that this is so very obvious to anyone who has spent hours analyzing the biblical text, that it would be a work of supererogation to even delve into the matter at all" (*Toward an Exegetical Theology*, p. 149).

41. Robinson, *Biblical Preaching*, p. 52.

42. The following paradigm takes into account preaching models and theories past and present but seeks to fill in gaps that still exist. The author is indebted not only to those who have contributed publicly to the question, but also to his colleagues, especially Ramesh P. Richard and Timothy S. Ralston, for their perceptive insights.

43. Based on inspiration.

44. Based on the changing circumstances of the audience.

45. Scripture is the result of the process of inspiration. Two issues are noteworthy here. God superintended the process in order to guarantee its accuracy and authority, and the process was completed with the writing of revelation. Inspiration has preceded preaching

and claims absoluteness, whereas preachers must recognize their fallibility in presenting God's Word.

46. The exegetical product may be viewed as a *re-cognition* of the truth expressed in the text, the theological product as a *re-presentation* of the universal principle, and the homiletical as a *re-lation* of that truth to the contemporary audience. Since one claims inspiration for neither the exegesis nor the theologizing nor the preaching, he must recognize that his conclusions in these areas will be faulty at points.

47. One certainly must distinguish between the Revelational (capital R) product which is the result of the process of inspiration, and the revelational (small r) process of making God known through righteous living. In 2 Corinthians 2:14–16; 3:18; and 4:6–12 Paul argued that the glory of God and the life of Jesus are revealed in Christians' mortal bodies. The increasingly obedient Christian is not an inspired and infallible Word but is a witness to and of the glory of God.

48. See, for example, Matthew 5:16; 2 Corinthians 3:18; and Phillippians 3:12–14.

49. See Milton S. Terry, *Biblical Hermeneutics* (Grand Rapids: Zondervan, 1964); J. Edwin Hartill, *Principles of Biblical Hermeneutics* (Grand Rapids: Zondervan, 1947); L. Berkhof, *Principles of Biblical Interpretation* (Grand Rapids: Baker, 1950); A. Berkeley Mickelsen, *Interpreting the Bible* (Grand Rapids: Wm. B. Eerdmans Publishing Co., 1963); Bernard Ramm, *Protestant Biblical Interpretation* (Grand Rapids: Baker, 1970); Henry A. Virkler, *Hermeneutics: Principles and Processes of Biblical Interpretation* (Grand Rapids: Baker, 1981); Gordon D. Fee and Douglas Stuart, *How to Read the Bible for All Its Worth* (Grand Rapids: Zondervan, 1982); and Roy B. Zuck, *Basic Bible Interpretation* (Wheaton, IL: Victor, 1991).

50. See John Warwick Montgomery, "The Theologian's Craft," *Concordia Theological Monthly* 37 (1966): 67–98, in which retroductive reasoning is contrasted with both inductive and deductive approaches to understanding. Whereas induction argues formally that something certainly is, and deduction proves formally that something must be, retroduction seeks to demonstrate informally that something may be by proposing what is probable and then testing and adjusting that proposal until the final suggestion "fits the available facts."

51. "Proposition" means the concept, theme, or idea consisting of subject (What am I talking about?) and complement (What am I saying about what I am talking about?). See Robinson, *Biblical Preaching*, pp. 31–41.

52. Kaiser points out the vital ministry of the Spirit throughout the preaching process in a much-welcomed chapter, "The Exegete/Pastor and the Power of God," *Toward an Exegetical Theology*, pp. 235–47. Kaiser explains that the Spirit of God provides knowledge (for understanding the text) as well as wisdom (for applying), utterance (for declaring), and holiness (for living) to those who seek divine power through dependent prayer. See also Roy B. Zuck, "The Role of the Holy Spirit in Hermeneutics," *Bibliotheca Sacra* 141 (April–June 1984): 120–30, and id., *Teaching with Spiritual Power* (reprint, Grand Rapids: Kregel, 1993).

53. For a helpful discussion on the interplay between the objective, subjective, and divine aspects of interpretation, see Montgomery, "The Theologian's Craft," pp. 87–97.

54. Hermeneutical bracketing, like mathematical bracketing, brackets (or parenthesizes), not in order to eliminate, but merely to place out of question for the time being. Attention is narrowed to the essential problem at hand, disregarding or ignoring the superfluous or misleading. This temporary suspension of judgment purposes to grasp the meaning of the original text untainted by the influence of either a more fully developed theology or any contemporary cultural significance. For an introductory discussion of hermeneutical bracketing, see David Stewart and Algis Mickunas, *Exploring Phenomenology* (Chicago: American Library Association, 1974), pp. 23–27, 45–48.

55. Greidanus, *The Modern Preacher and the Ancient Text*, p. 260 (italics added).

56. David L. Wolfe, *Epistemology: The Justification of Belief* (Downers Grove, IL: InterVarsity, 1982), p. 15.

57. Tests for reasonableness determine whether the conclusions are based on circumstance, consequence, analogy, or principle. Tests for rationalness determine whether the conclusions are sufficient, relevant, complete, probable, and coherent. For a more detailed discussion of validation, see Timothy S. Warren, "Rhetorical Strategies for Biblical Hermeneutics" (PhD diss., Ohio State University, 1987), pp. 111–23.

58. "It is the biblical message alone that provides the irreducible *Gegenstande* or theological theorizing—the 'foot' which all theological theories must 'fit'" (Montgomery, "The Theologian's Craft," p. 81).

59. Charles Caldwell Ryrie, *Biblical Theology of the New Testament* (Chicago: Moody, 1959), p. 11.

60. Kaiser, *Toward an Exegetical Theology*, pp. 136, 140.

61. Montgomery, "The Theologian's Craft," p. 73.

62. "Science and theology form and test their respective theories in the same way; the scientific theorizer attempts objectively to formulate conceptual gestalts (hypotheses, theories, laws) capable of rendering nature intelligible, and the theologian endeavors to provide conceptual gestalts (doctrines, dogmas) which will 'fit the facts' and reflect the norms of Holy Scripture" (ibid., pp. 85–86).

63. Ross, *Creation and Blessing*, p. 38.

64. This is "not a reading into the text of theological doctrines and theories, but a reading from the text of the fullness of meaning required by God's complete revelation" (Greidanus, *The Modern Preacher and the Ancient Text*, p. 111).

65. Ramesh P. Richard, "Application Theory in Relation to the New Testament," *Bibliotheca Sacra* 143 (July–September 1986): 207.

66. Ross, *Creation and Blessing*, p. 45.

67. Ibid., p. 46.

68. Kaiser, *Toward an Exegetical Theology*, p. 162.

69. Ross, *Creation and Blessing*, pp. 23-24.

70. Montgomery, "The Theologian's Craft," p. 79.

71. "There is no single step in speech preparation that deserves more careful attention than the analysis of the particular audience to which the particular message is to be presented. Each new sermon requires a fresh assessment of the congregation's relationship to a subject" (J. Daniel Baumann, *An Introduction to Contemporary Preaching* [Grand Rapids: Baker, 1972], p. 54). Litfin illustrates the principle that "the need for a given idea will vary with the audience" and "the need of a given audience will vary with the subject matter" (A. Duane Litfin, *Public Speaking* [Grand Rapids: Baker, 1981], pp. 118–23).

72. Hesselgrave and Rommen, *Contextualization: Meanings, Methods, and Models*, p. 203.

73. Ibid., p. 211.

74. Robinson, *Biblical Preaching*, pp. 77–96.

75. Quintilian concludes that "we must therefore accept the view of the authorities followed by Cicero, to the effect that there are three things on which inquiry is made in every case: we ask whether a thing is, what it is, and of what kind it is" (*The Institutio Oratoria*, trans. H. E. Butler [London: William Heinemann, 1921], p. 451).

76. Aristotle defined rhetoric as "the faculty of discovering in the particular case what are the available means of persuasion" and identified three such means: the ethical, the emotional, and the logical (*The Rhetoric of Aristotle*, trans. Lane Cooper [New York: Appleton-Century-Crofts, 1932], pp. 7–9). For a contemporary view of rhetorical strategies see Steven Toulmin, Richard Rieke, and

Allan Janik, *An Introduction to Reasoning* (New York: Macmillan, 1978).

77. It is a devaluation of the developmental questions to see exegesis as answering the first question ("What does the text mean?"), theology as answering the second ("Is that meaning true?"), and homiletics the third ("What difference does that meaning make?"). All three questions must be asked after the theological process has been completed and while homiletics is being done. The developmental questions are the distinctively homiletical element of the preaching process.

78. Preaching has been characterized as "quadruple-think," or "thinking out what I have to say, then thinking out how the other man will understand what I say, and then rethinking what I have to say, so that, when I say it, he will think what I am thinking!" M. A. C. Warren, *Crowded Canvas* [Kent, England: Hodder & Stoughton, 1974], p. 143).

79. Kaiser, *Toward an Exegetical Theology*, p. 236.

80. Jay E. Adams, *Preaching with Purpose: The Urgent Task of Homiletics* (Grand Rapids: Zondervan, 1982), p. 19.

81. The author takes issue with Kaiser's statement, "The whole objective of what we are here calling 'textual expository preaching' is to let the Scriptures have the major, if not the only, role in determining the shape, logic, and development of our message" (*Toward an Exegetical Theology*, p. 160). The shape, logic, and development of contemporary communication must meet the demand of the contemporary audience, though without violating the theological proposition expressed in the text.

82. "The basic purpose of expository preaching is the basic purpose of the Bible. It takes place so that through it the Holy Spirit may change men's lives and destinies" (Haddon W. Robinson, "What Is Expository Preaching?" *Bibliotheca Sacra* 131 [January–March 1974]: 59).

83. Greidanus, *The Modern Preacher and the Ancient Text*, p. 121.

84. Adams, *Truth Applied: Application in Preaching*, p. 39.

85. The goal here is "not to deny the reality of the fuller sense but to insist that that fuller sense be established only as an extension of the original sense and solely on the basis of subsequent biblical revelation" (Greidanus, *The Modern Preacher and the Ancient Text*, p. 112).

86. Richard makes the point that "the literal sense refers to what the author intended 'in' not 'by' what he said" (Ramesh P. Richard, "Selected Issues in Theoretical Hermeneutics," *Bibliotheca Sacra* 143 [January–March 1986]:16).

87. "Any expression has a range of meaning. Since the Bible consists of many 'expression complexes,' the meaning of the passage goes beyond what is explicitly affirmed. That is, there is a field of meaning around each statement" (Ramesh P. Richard, "Levels of Biblical Meaning," *Bibliotheca Sacra* 143 [April–June 1986]: p. 126).

88. Ibid., p. 126.

89. Ibid., p. 128. Greidanus argues that sermons must be "in line with" the biblical purpose (*The Modern Preacher and the Ancient Text*, p. 120).

90. "[Extratextual research] must be considered. This information helps answer questions pertaining to the original audience: What would the communication have meant to them? and, How did they understand it? Answers to these questions help in arriving at the literal meaning" (Richard, "Levels of Biblical Meaning," p. 123).

91. See Richard, "Application Theory in Relation to the New Testament," pp. 207–14. Though his discussion focuses on epistolary literature, the concepts of audience-reference and audience-trait are useful in authorizing application in any genre.

92. Adams, *Truth Applied: Application in Preaching*, p. 48. Greidanus states that "in its context, every passage has a purpose since every passage seeks a response from the audience. . . . The response sought indicates past relevance. Once a passage's relevance for the early church has been established, that relevance can be transferred to the contemporary church via the analogies [audience-reference and audience-trait] that exist between the church then and the church today" (*The Modern Preacher and the Ancient Text*, pp. 308–9).

Chapter 12

1. Ken Parker, "Seven Characteristics of a Growing Church," in *The Pastor's Church Growth Handbook*, ed. Win Arn (Pasadena, CA: Church Growth, 1979).

2. Robert Schuller, "Three Characteristics of a Successful Pastor," in *The Pastor's Church Growth Handbook*, pp. 92–94.

3. Charles Mylander, "How to Build High Morale in Your Church," in *The Pastor's Church Growth Handbook*, pp. 85–91.

4. Donald A. McGavran, *Understanding Church Growth* (Grand Rapids: Eerdmans, 1970), p. 119 (italics added).

5. Win Arn, "How to Find a Pastor Who Fits Your Church," in *The Pastor's Church Growth Handbook*, p. 12 (italics added).

6. Bob Smith, *When All Else Fails . . . Read the Directions* (Waco, TX: Word, 1974), p. 58 (italics added).

7. Haddon W. Robinson, "Leadership Forum: Power, Preaching, and Priority," *Leadership* 1 (Winter 1980): 17.
8. D. Martyn Lloyd-Jones, *Preaching and Preachers* (Grand Rapids: Zondervan, 1971), p. 92.
9. Ibid., p. 138.
10. Robinson, *Biblical Preaching* (Grand Rapids: Baker, 1980), p. 27.
11. Ibid., p. 20.
12. Lloyd-Jones, *Preaching and Preachers*, p. 92.
13. Robinson, *Biblical Preaching*, p. 21.

Chapter 13

1. Walter Bauer, William F. Arndt, and F. Wilbur Gingrich, *A Greek-English Lexicon of the New Testament and Other Early Christian Literature*, 2d ed., rev. F. Wilbur Gingrich and Frederick W. Danker (Chicago: University of Chicago Press, 1979), p. 699.
2. Henry George Liddell and Robert Scott, *A Greek-English Lexicon*, rev. ed. (Oxford: Clarendon Press, 1968), p. 1462.
3. *Theological Dictionary of the New Testament*, s.v. "πρέσβυς," by Günther Bornkamm, 6:652.
4. Bauer, Arndt, and Gingrich, *A Greek-English Lexicon of the New Testament and Other Early Christian Literature*, p. 700.
5. Merrill C. Tenney, *New Testament Survey* (Grand Rapids: Eerdmans, 1985), p. 121.
6. Bauer, Arndt and Gingrich, *A Greek-English Lexicon of the New Testament and Other Early Christian Literature*, p. 345.
7. Meyer argued that He was probably 31 or 32 (Heinrich A. W. Meyer, *Meyer's Commentary on the New Testament*, 22 vols. [reprint, Peabody, MA: Hendrickson, 1983], 2:300).
8. A. T. Robertson, *Word Pictures in the New Testament*, 6 vols. (Nashville: Broadman, 1930), 2:45.
9. Tenney, *New Testament Survey*, p. 249.
10. Francis Brown, S. R. Driver, and Charles A. Briggs, *A Hebrew and English Lexicon of the Old Testament* (Oxford: Clarendon Press, 1972), p. 278.
11. Ibid.
12. *Theological Wordbook of the Old Testament*, s.v. "זָקֵן," by Jack P. Lewis, 1:249.
13. *Theological Dictionary of the New Testament*, s.v. "πρέσβυς," by Günther Bornkamm, 6:655.
14. Ibid.
15. Tenney, *New Testament Survey*, p. 40.
16. G. Adolf Deissman, *Bible Studies*, trans. Alexander Grieve (reprint, Winona Lake, IN: Alpha, 1979), p. 156.

17. *Dictionary of the Apostolic Church*, 2 vols., (Edinburgh: Clark, 1926), s.v. "Church Government," by Alfred Plummer, 1:210.
18. John Calvin, *Calvin's Commentaries*, vol. 19: *Commentary on the Acts of the Apostles* (reprint, Grand Rapids: Baker, 1981), p. 44.
19. Fenton John Anthony Hort, *The Christian Ecclesia* (London: Macmillan, 1898), pp. 65–66.
20. Most scholars agree that πρεσβύτερος and ἐπίσκοπος refer to the same office or officers. This is also the view of this writer (cf. Acts 20:17, 28).
21. Philip Carrington, *The Early Christian Church*, 2 vols. (Cambridge: University Press, 1957), 1:269.
22. Ed Glasscock, "'The Husband of One Wife' Requirement in 1 Timothy 3:2," *Bibliotheca Sacra* 140 (July–October 1983): 244–58.
23. Bauer, Arndt, and Gingrich, *A Greek-English Lexicon of the New Testament and Other Early Christian Literature*, p. 172.
24. In 1 Timothy 3:2 and Titus 1:7 the singular τὸν ἐπίσκοπον is found but since in neither case is the overseer identified with a particular local church the plural rule of eldership in local churches is not affected. The article is used in the generic sense and thus represents the noun ἐπίσκοπος as a class or group identified by certain characteristics rather than as an individual.
25. *Encyclopedia Judaica*, s.v. "Elder," by Moshe Weinfeld, p. 478.
26. George Park Fisher, *History of Christian Doctrine* (Edinburgh: Clark, 1949), p. 77.
27. Polycarp, *To the Philippians* 5.

Chapter 14

1. The word has received various spellings in English: diacon, diacne, diakne, daecne, dekne, deken, deeken, deakon, decoun, deacone, deacon (*Oxford English Dictionary* [Oxford: University Press, 1971], 3:56).
2. Ten Greek terms occur in the Greek New Testament, each conveying some aspect of the "servant" theme.
3. The noun λατρεὺς and λάτρις do not occur in the New Testament: the cognate verb λατρεύω and the noun λατρεία do occur.
4. Richard Chenevix Trench, *Synonyms of the New Testament* (reprint, Grand Rapids: Eerdmans, 1947), p. 125.
5. Herman Cremer, *Biblico-Theological Lexicon of New Testament Greek*, trans. William Urwick (reprint, Edinburgh: Clark, 1954), p. 763.
6. Nigel Turner, *Christian Words* (Nashville: Nelson, 1982), p. 280.

7. J. Stegenga, *The Greek-English Analytical Concordance of the Greek-English New Testament* (Grand Rapids: Zondervan, 1963), p. 424.

8. Trench calls it "a mere fanciful derivation, and forbidden by the quality of the antepenultima in diakonos" (*Synonyms of the New Testament*, p. 32).

9. Henry George Liddell and Robert Scott, *A Greek-English Lexicon*, 7th ed. (Oxford: Clarendon, 1890), p. 369.

10. Cremer, *Biblico-Theological Lexicon*, p. 177; Liddell and Scott, *A Greek-English Lexicon*, p. 348; Trench, *Synonyms of the New Testament*, p. 32.

11. For a concordance of the Greek terms, see W. F. Moulton and A. S. Geden, *A Concordance to the Greek Testament*, 3d ed. (Edinburgh: Clark, 1950), pp. 202–3. For their renderings in the King James Version, see George V. Wigram and Ralph D. Winter, *The Word Study Concordance* (Pasadena, CA: William Carey Library, 1978), pp. 144–45; Robert Voting, *Analytical Concordance to the Bible*, 25th ed. (New York: Funk & Wagnalls, n.d.), page 64 of *Index-Lexicon to the New Testament*. For the renderings in the NASB see Robert L. Thomas, ed., *New American Standard—Exhaustive Concordance of the Bible, Hebrew-Aramaic and Greek Dictionaries* (Nashville: Holman, 1981), p. 1642.

12. The Greek text is literally, "Women in like manner . . ." and is capable of either interpretation. The KJV rendering "Even so must their wives . . ." introduces the former meaning into the text; and the NIV does the same. The ASV and the NASB render the words literally and leave the question open. See D. Edmond Hiebert, *First Timothy* (Chicago: Moody, 1957), pp. 70–71; and Ronald A. Ward, *Commentary on 1 & 2 Timothy & Titus* (Waco, TX: Word, 1974), pp. 60–61. Also see Robert M. Lewis. "The 'Women' of 1 Timothy 3:11," *Bibliotheca Sacra* 135 (April–June 1979): 167–75.

13. *Dictionary of the Apostolic Church*, s.v. "Deacon, Deaconess," by Alfred Plummer, 1:285.

14. C. H. Dodd, *The Epistle of Paul to the Romans*, Moffatt New Testament Commentary (New York: Ray Long & Richard R. Smith, 1932), p. 235.

15. Cremer, *Biblico-Theological Lexicon*, p. 178; D. Edmond Hiebert, *Personalities around Paul* (Chicago: Moody, 1973), pp. 198–200; R. C. H. Lenski, *The Interpretation of St. Paul's Epistle to the Romans* (Minneapolis: Augsburg, 1961), pp. 899–901; William Kelly, *Notes on the Epistle of Paul, the Apostle, to the Romans* (n.p.: Hammond, 1873), pp. 274–75. In favor of the nonofficial view see John Murray, *The Epistle to the Romans*, New

International Commentary on the New Testament, 2 vols. (Grand Rapids: Eerdmans, 1965), 2:226.

16. R. C. H. Lenski, *The Interpretation of St. Paul's Epistles to the Colossians, to the Thessalonians, to Timothy, to Titus and to Philemon* (Minneapolis: Augsburg, 1961), pp. 208–9; E. F. Scott, *The Epistles of Paul to the Colossians, to Philemon and to the Ephesians*, Moffatt Commentary (London: Hodder & Stoughton, 1930), p. 93; Curtis Vaughan, "Colossians," in *The Expositor's Bible Commentary* (Grand Rapids: Zondervan, 1978), 11:225.

17. *Theological Dictionary of the New Testament*, s.v. "διαχονέω, διαχονία, διάχονος," by Hermann W. Beyer, 2:84.

18. *The New International Dictionary of New Testament Theology*, s.v. "Serve, Deacon, Worship," by K. Hess, 3:547.

19. Ibid., p. 548.

Chapter 15

1. Robert Webber, *Worship—Old and New* (Grand Rapids: Zondervan, 1982), p. 11.

2. Ibid., p. 20.

3. Cited by James F. White, "Where the Reformation Was Wrong on Worship," *Christian Century*, October 27, 1982, p. 1077.

4. Langdon Gilkey, *How the Church Can Minister to the World without Losing Itself* (New York: Harper & Row, 1964), p. 108.

5. Leslie B. Flynn, *Worship: Together We Celebrate* (Wheaton, IL: Victor, 1983).

6. Justin Martyr, "The First Apology of Justin the Martyr," *Early Christian Fathers*, ed. Cyril Richardson (Philadelphia: Westminster, 1953), p. 287.

7. Wilfred Funk, *Word Origins and their Romantic Stories* (New York: Bell, 1960), p. 257.

Chapter 16

1. William H. Willimon and Robert L. Wilson, *Preaching and Worship in the Small Church* (Nashville: Abingdon, 1980), p. 7.

2. Rick Danielsen, "Worship in the Small Church," *Church Administration*, April 1982, p. 21.

3. Willimon and Wilson, *Preaching and Worship in the Small Church*, pp. 19–20.

4. Carl S. Dudley, *Making the Small Church Effective* (Nashville: Abingdon, 1978), p. 20.

5. Ibid., p. 23.

6. Lyle E. Schaller, *The Small Church Is Different* (Nashville: Abingdon 1982), pp. 12–13.

7. David R. Ray, *Small Churches Are the Right Size* (New York: Pilgrim, 1982), p. 45.
8. *Church Planning: A Manual for Use in the United Church of Christ* (New York: United Church of Christ Office for Church Life and Leadership, 1976), pp. C1–C2.
9. Schaller, *The Small Church Is Different!*, pp. 130–35.
10. Paul O. Madsen, *The Small Church—Valid, Vital, Victorious* (Valley Forge, PA: Judson, 1975), pp. 111–12.
11. Willimon and Wilson, *Preaching and Worship in the Small Church*, p. 25.
12. Alan T. Hansell, "Life in the Small Membership Church," *Brethren Life and Thought* 27 (Autumn 1982): 234–35.
13. Willimon and Wilson, *Preaching and Worship in the Small Church*, p. 27.
14. Danielsen, "Worship in the Small Church," pp. 21–22.
15. Willimon and Wilson, *Preaching and Worship in the Small Church*, p. 108.
16. Carolyn C. Brown, *Developing Christian Education in the Smaller Church* (Nashville: Abingdon, 1982), p. 96.
17. Willimon and Wilson, *Preaching and Worship in the Small Church*, p. 69.
18. Dudley, *Making the Small Church Effective*, p. 5.
19. Ray, *Small Churches Are the Right Size*, p. xiv.
20. Shaller, *The Small Church Is Different!*, p. 57.
21. Ibid., pp. 135–36.
22. Ibid., p. 185.
23. Willimon and Wilson, *Preaching and Worship in the Small Church*, pp. 27–28.

Chapter 17

1. The occasional nature of the Epistles and the "task theology" they contain is discussed by Gordon D. Fee and Douglas Stuart in *How to Read the Bible for All Its Worth* (Grand Rapids: Zondervan, 1982), pp. 44–46,70–71.
2. James B. Hurley, *Man and Woman in Biblical Perspective* (Grand Rapids: Zondervan, 1981), p. 202; Homer A. Kent, Jr., *The Pastoral Epistles*, rev. ed. (Chicago; Moody, 1982), pp. 107–9; J. N. D. Kelly, *A Commentary on the Pastoral Epistles* (New York: Harper & Row, 1961; reprint, Peabody, MA: Hendrickson, 1987), p. 68.
3. Bruce Barron, "Putting Women in Their Place: 1 Timothy 2 and Evangelical Views of Women in Church Leadership," *Journal of the Evangelical Theological Society* 33 (December 1990): 451–59; Catherine C. Kroeger, "1 Timothy 2:12—A Classicist's View,"

in *Women, Authority and the Bible*, ed. Alvera Mickelson (Downers Grove, IL: InterVarsity, 1986), pp. 225–44; Philip B. Payne, "Libertarian Women in Ephesus: A Response to Douglas J. Moo's Article: '1 Timothy 2:11–15: Meaning and Significance,'" *Trinity Journal* n.s. 2 (1981): 183; David M. Scholer, "1 Timothy 2:9–15 and the Place of Women in the Church's Ministry," in *Women, Authority and the Bible*, p. 204.

4. Aida Besançon Spencer, *Beyond the Curse* (Peabody, MA: Hendrickson, 1985), p. 84; Richard and Joyce Boldrey, *Chauvinist or Feminist? Paul's View of Women* (Grand Rapids: Baker, 1976), pp. 62–64.

5. Gordon D. Fee, *1 and 2 Timothy, Titus* (Peabody, MA: Hendrickson, 1984), pp. 7–8, 39–40. The false teachers' identity as Ephesian elders is supported by their self-designation as "teachers of the Law" (1:7), which was an elder's responsibility (5:17; cf. 3:2); by the excommunication of Hymenaeus and Alexander by Paul (1:19–20) rather than by the church (2 Thess. 3:14; 1 Cor. 5:1–5); and by Paul's emphasis on the elders' qualifications (1 Tim. 3:1–7) and discipline (5:19–25).

6. This was a Jewish custom (1 Kings 8:22; Pss. 28:2; 63:4; 141:2; 143:6; Lam. 3:41; 2 Macc. 14:34; Philo, *de Hum.* 2) that Christians also practiced at times (1 Clem. 2:3; 29:1; Clement of Alexandria, *Strom.* 7:7; Tertullian, *Apol.* 30; *de Orat.* 11). A more complete discussion and bibliography may be found in C. Spicq, *Les Épitres Pastorales*, 4th rev. ed., 2 vols. (Paris: Gabalda, 1969), 1:372–73.

7. The term translated "holy" (ὁσίους) carries the idea of "devout," "holy," and "pleasing to God" in both secular and Christian writing of the period. While the phrase "holy hands" is unique in the New Testament, the idea is present in: Genesis 20:5; Job 17:9; 22:30; Psalm 24:3–4; and James 4:8. The general idea is that of a cleansed conscience (Martin Dibelius and Hans Conzelmann, *The Pastoral Epistles*, trans. Philip Buttolph and Adela Yarbro [Philadelphia: Fortress, 1972], p. 44, ns. 2, 3; *Theological Dictionary of the New Testament*, s.v. "ὅσιος," by F. Hauck 5 [1967]: 492; Spicq, *Les Épitres Pastorales*, pp. 373–74).

8. Scholer, "1 Timothy 2:9–15 and the Place of Women in the Church's Ministry," p. 201–2.

9. Kelly, *A Commentary on the Pastoral Epistles*, p. 66; P. Dornier, *Les Épitres Pastorales*, (Paris: Gabalda, 1969), p. 55.

10. Herman Ridderbos, *Paul: An Outline of His Theology*, trans. John R. DeWitt (Grand Rapids: Eerdmans, 1975), p. 462, n. 107.

11. Douglas J. Moo, "1 Timothy 2:11–15: Meaning and Significance," *Trinity Journal* n.s. 1 (1980): 64.

12. *Theological Dictionary of the New Testament*, s.v. "μανθάνω," by

K. Rengtorf, 4:410; Walter Bauer, William F. Arndt, and F. Wilbur Gingrich, *A Greek-English Lexicon of the New Testament and Other Early Christian Literature*, 2d ed., rev. F. Wilbur Gingrich and Frederick W. Danker (Chicago: University of Chicago Press, 1979), p. 490.

13. Moo notes that these meanings occur with equal frequency in the Septuagint, Josephus, and Philo ("1 Timothy 2:11–15: Meaning and Significance," p. 64, n. 15). See the discussions in Stephen B. Clark, *Man and Woman in Christ* (Ann Arbor, MI: Servant, 1980), p. 195; Spencer, *Beyond the Curse*, 80; and J. Keir Howard, "Neither Male nor Female: An Examination of the Status of Women in the New Testament," *Evangelical Quarterly* 55 (January 1983): 31–42. Clark and Howard argue for the meaning "quietness," and Spencer argues for the meaning "silence." The word σιγάω means "remain silent," as seen in 1 Corinthians 14:28, 34.

14. For example in 1 Corinthians 14:26–40 Paul gave instructions to both men and women concerning vocal participation in the assembly. Fee has pointed out that Paul used the vocative "brothers" (ἀδελφοί) many times in 1 Corinthians and other epistles. Women were certainly part of the worship community and would have been included in his instructions to the "brothers." Philippians 4:1–3 is especially noteworthy because Paul refers to "my beloved brethren" and then immediately addresses two women by name in the next sentence (Gordon D. Fee, *The First Epistle to the Corinthians* [Grand Rapids: Eerdmans, 1987], pp. 52, n. 22; 690).

15. Clark, *Man and Woman in Christ*, p. 92.

16. Walter Lock, *A Critical and Exegetical Commentary on the Pastoral Epistles* (Edinburgh: Clark, 1924), p. 32; Kent, *The Pastoral Epistles*, p. 108.

17. Dibelius and Conzelmann, *The Pastoral Epistles*, p. 47.

18. Walter Kaiser, "Paul, Women and the Church," *Worldwide Challenge* (September 1976), p. 11. He suggests, but offers no supporting evidence, that this is used in the same sense as Paul's statement that "I wish that all men were even as I myself," that is, unmarried (1 Cor. 7:7). A more substantial attempt to limit the meaning of ἐπιτρέπω to personal preference is offered by Payne, "Libertarian Women in Ephesus," pp. 170–73.

19. George A. Knight III, *The Role Relationship of Men and Women*, rev. ed. (Chicago: Moody, 1977), p. 19, n. 4; Clark, *Man and Woman in Christ*, pp. 199–200.

20. The context of 1 Corinthians 14:34 is concern for orderly behavior in the Corinthian church. Paul had already enjoined silence on the one who spoke in tongues without interpretation (v. 28) and the

one prophesying who was interrupted by a second person with a prophecy (v. 30). In 1 Corinthians 14:34 he described a third situation in which a group of people were told to be silent in the worship assembly. Various interpretations of this passage abound, but the context (regulation of inspired utterance in the worship assembly) indicates that it may refer to women judging prophecies in that setting. For recent discussions of possible views see J. D. G. Dunn, "The Responsible Congregation (1 Co 14, 26–40)," in *Charisma und Agape (1 Ko 12–14)*, ed. Lorenzo De Lorenzi (Rome: St. Paul vor den Mavern, 1983), pp. 227, 231, 243–44; E. Earle Ellis, "The Silenced Wives of Corinth (1 Cor. 14:34–35)," in *New Testament Textual Criticism: Its Significance for Exegesis*, ed. Eldon Jay Epp and Gordon D. Fee (Oxford: Clarendon, 1981), 213–20; Wayne Grudem, "Prophecy—Yes, but Teaching—No: Paul's Consistent Advocacy of Women's Participation without Governing Authority," *Journal of the Evangelical Theological Society* 30 (March 1987): pp. 20–23.

21. Roy B. Zuck, "Greek Words for Teach," *Bibliotheca Sacra* 122 (April–June 1965): 159–60. He notes that in only three of nearly 100 occurrences does the word refer to the teaching of individuals: John 8:28; Romans 2:21; Revelation 2:14.

22. Harold Mare, "Prophet and Teacher in the New Testament Period," *Bulletin of the Evangelical Theological Society* 9 (Summer 1966): 146; Floyd V. Filson, "The Christian Teacher in the First Century," *Journal of Biblical Literature* 60 (1941): 324.

23. *Theological Dictionary of the New Testament*, s.v. "διδάσκω," by K. Rengstorf 2:146; id.,, s.v. "διδάσκαλος," 2:158; Filson, "The Christian Teacher in the First Century," p. 318; John F. Walvoord, "Contemporary Issues in the Doctrine of the Holy Spirit, Part IV," *Bibliotheca Sacra* 130 (October–December 1973): 316.

24. Significant recent studies include the following: George W. Knight III, "ΑΥΘΕΝΤΕΩ in Reference to Women in 1 Timothy 2:12," *New Testament Studies* 30 (January 1984): 143–57; C. D. Osburn, "ΑΥΘΕΝΤΕΩ (1 Tim. 2:12)," *Restoration Quarterly* 25 (1982): 1–12; Catherine C. Kroeger, "Ancient Heresies and a Strange Greek Verb," *Reformed Journal* 29 (March 1979): 12–15; Armin J. Panning, "ΑΥΘΕΝΤΕΙΝ—A Word Study," *Wisconsin Lutheran Quarterly* 78 (1981): 185–91; Kroeger, "1 Timothy 2:12—A Classicist's View," 229–32; Walter L. Liefeld, "Response," in *Women, Authority and the Bible*, 244–48; Philip B. Payne, "Οὐδέ in 1 Timothy 2:12" (Paper presented at the Evangelical Theological Society Annual Meeting, November 21, 1986), pp. 8–10.

Knight's article is a model word study, but since it is based on only the few occurrences of the term cited by Bauer, Arndt, Gingrich, and Danker, in *A Greek-English Lexicon of the New Testament and Other Early Christian Literature*, it is necessarily incomplete. This is not to say that Knight's conclusions are incorrect; it is simply to say that the same high quality of study now needs to be done on the more than 90 occurrences of the verb and its cognates that are available through the *Thesaurus Linguae Graecae* project of the University of California at Irvine.

Kroeger has argued for the meaning "to proclaim oneself the author or originator of something." In the context of 1 Timothy 2:12 this means that women are not to teach "a mythology similar to that of the Gnostics in which Eve predated Adam and was his creator" (p. 232). Liefeld's response points out some obvious problems (e.g., methodological problems such as lack of dates and full contexts for sources, and a questionable reconstruction of the socioreligious background of the passage ["Response," 245–48]). The earlier article by Kroeger, which argued for the meaning "to engage in fertility practices" (p. 14), has been refuted in the detailed article by Panning.

25. Scholer, "1 Timothy 2:9-15 and the Place of Women in the Church's Ministry," p. 205.
26. Knight, "ΛΥΘΕΝΤΕΩ in Reference to Women," pp. 150–53.
27. Osburn, "ΛΥΘΕΝΤΕΩ (1 Timothy 2:12)," pp. 2–8.
28. Knight, "ΛΥΘΕΝΤΕΩ in Reference to Women," pp. 144–53.
29. Hurley, *Man and Woman in Biblical Perspective*, p. 201.
30. Payne, "Οὐδέ in 1 Timothy 2:12," p. 1.
31. The analysis by Payne, while helpful, does not compare instances of the actual grammatical construction of infinitive—οὐδέ — infinitive. This construction is rare in the New Testament, occurring only in Acts 16:21 and 1 Timothy 2:12. In addition, an identical construction occurs in Revelation 5:3 in which οὔτε rather than οὐδέ is used. (John most probably used οὔτε for stylistic reasons, since the compound subject of the sentence uses οὐδέ correlatively.) Acts 16:21 reads, "[Those men] are proclaiming customs which it is not lawful for us to accept or to observe [παραδέχεσθαι οὐδέ ποιεῖν], being Romans." Revelation 5:3 states, "And no one in heaven, or [οὐδέ] on the earth, or [οὐδέ] under the earth, was able to open the book, or to look into it [ἀνοῖξαι τὸ βιβλίον οὔτε βλέπειν αὐτό]." In both verses the infinitives are closely related, but are not identical. To accept customs or to acknowledge them as correct and to practice those customs are two different things. To open a book and to look into that book are two separate activities. In 1 Timothy 2:12 the ideas of teaching and exercising

authority are likewise closely related, but they denote two activities rather than one.

32. The phrase "in quietness" actually serves as an inclusio, bracketing the chiasm formed by the two verses. The ABB'A' pattern suggested by Fung is simpler and more completely chiastic than the ABCB'A' pattern favored by Moo (Ronald Y. K. Fung, "Ministry in the New Testament," in *The Church in the Bible and the World*, ed. D. A. Carson [Grand Rapids: Baker, 1987], p. 336, n. 186; Moo, "1 Timothy 2:11–15: Meaning and Significance," p. 64). In Fung's model the two positive statements flank the two negative ones, with the emphasis falling on ἐν ἡσυχίᾳ.

A   γυνὴ ἐν ἡσυχίᾳ μανθανέτω ἐν πάσῃ ὑποταγῇ
    B   διδάσκειν δέ γυναικὶ οὐκ ἐπιτρέπω
    B'   οὐδὲ αὐθεντεῖν ἀνδρός,
A'   ἀλλ᾽ εἶναι ἐν ἡσυχίᾳ.

33. Robertson is nearly alone in taking the primary meaning of γὰρ as something other than causal. Dana and Mantey and Blass and Debrunner consider its primary use to be causal; Zerwick's grammar and Bauer, Arndt, Gingrich, and Danker offer only a few instances in which its sense is not causal. Moo offers a detailed summary of information from the grammars ("1 Tim. 2:11–15: A Rejoinder," *Trinity Journal* n.s. 2 [1981]: 202–3). Also see H. E. Dana and J. R. Mantey, *A Manual Grammar of the Greek New Testament* (New York: Macmillan, 1927), p. 243; F. Blass and A. Debrunner, *A Greek Grammar of the New Testament and Other Early Christian Literature*, trans. Robert W. Funk (Chicago: University of Chicago Press, 1961), § 452; and Maximillian Zerwick, *Biblical Greek Illustrated by Examples* (Rome: Pontifical Biblical Press, 1963), § 173.

34. Moo, "1 Timothy 2:11–15: A Rejoinder," p. 203. He offers 21 instances in the Pastorals alone in which this sequence occurs: 1 Timothy 3:13; 4:5, 8, 16; 5:4, 11, 15; 2 Timothy 1:7; 2:7, 16; 3:6; 4:3, 6, 10, 11, 15; Titus 1:10; 2:11; 3:3, 9, 12.

35. If Paul had focused on specific verses taken from the Genesis 2 and 3 account, he would probably have quoted or closely paraphrased specific verses and likely would have used one of the common introductory formulas he used elsewhere. To name only a few of these formulas: "so also it is written" (οὕτῶ καὶ γέγραπται) in 1 Corinthians 15:45; "as it was written" (καθῶ γέγραπται) in 1 Corinthians 1:31; 2:9; 2 Corinthians 8:15; 9:9; "then will come about the saying which is written" (τότε γενήσεται ὁ λόγος) in 1 Corinthians 15:54; "for the Scripture says" (λέγει γὰρ ἡ γραφή) in 1 Timothy 5:18. A thorough

listing of introductory formulas may be found in Bruce Metzger, "The Formulas Introducing Quotations of Scripture in the New Testament and the Mishnah," *Journal of Biblical Literature* 70 (1951): 297–307; Joseph A. Fitzmeyer, "The Use of Explicit Old Testament Quotations in Qumran Literature and in the New Testament," *New Testament Studies* 7 (1960–1): 299–305. Also see Joseph Bonsirven, *Exégèse rabbinique et exégèse paulinienne* (Paris: Beauchesne et ses fils, 1939), pp. 264–65.

36. An example of a single statement recalling an entire pericope is Luke 17:32, "Remember Lot's wife." To understand Jesus' implied warning one must recall the circumstances that caused Sodom's destruction (Gen. 18:22–19:11), the flight of Lot and his family from the city (19:12–25), and the sin of Lot's wife and its results (vv. 17, 26).

37. F. F. Bruce, *New Testament History* (Garden City, NY: Doubleday, 1969), pp. 237–39; Emil Schürer, *The History of the Jewish People in the Age of Jesus Christ* (175 B.C.–A.D. 135), rev. and ed. Geza Vermes, Fergus Millar, and Matthew Black (Edinburgh: Clark, 1979), 2.367–68.

38. Many studies have been done on this topic, including Bonsirven, *Exégèse rabbinique et exégèse paulinienne*; Dan Cohn-Sherbok, "Paul and Rabbinic Exegesis," *Scottish Journal of Theology* 35 (1982): pp. 117–32; E. Earle Ellis, *Paul's Use of the Old Testament* (1957; reprint, Grand Rapids: Baker, 1981), pp. 38–54; Richard N. Longenecker, *Biblical Exegesis in the Apostolic Period* (Grand Rapids: Eerdmans, 1975), pp. 104–32; Anthony J. Hanson, *Studies in Paul's Technique and Theology* (London: SPCK, 1974), pp. 136–257; H. J. Schoeps, *Paul*, trans. Harold Knight (Philadelphia: Westminster, 1961), pp. 37–43.

39. An example of analogical application occurs in 1 John 3:11–15. In teaching the church to "love one another," John used an analogy from Genesis 4 to strengthen his point: Believers should not be "as Cain, who was of the evil one, and slew his brother." He later wrote that "every one who hates his brother is a murderer." This is clearly derived from Genesis, but Genesis does not specifically teach that believers who hate fellow believers are murderers. Rather John built an analogy here. God exhorted Cain to do well, but instead he murdered his (physical) brother. John's analogy is that believers are spiritual brothers who are exhorted by God to love one another. When they hate one another, it is as if they have committed murder.

40. The rights of the firstborn son are clearly explained by Roland de Vaux, *Ancient Israel*, 2 vols. (New York: McGraw-Hill, 1961), 1 :41–

42, 53. The rabbis affirmed this understanding of the firstborn son's rights in the Mishnah (m. *Baba Bathra* 8:4–5; m. *Bechoroth* 8:1, 9–10).

41. Hurley, *Man and Woman in Biblical Perspective*, p. 207.

42. Allen P. Ross, "The Participation of Women in Ministry and Service," in *Exegesis and Exposition* 4 (1989): 77.

43. For example warnings against deception by false teachers are often given to believers (e.g., Rom. 16:17–18; Eph. 5:6; Col. 2:8; 2 Thess. 2:3). Warnings against self-deception are also issued (e.g., 1 Cor. 3:18; James 1:26).

44. Kent, *The Pastoral Epistles*, p. 109. Also see Ross, "The Participation of Women in Ministry and Service," p. 78. It should be noted that while Paul in his analogy focused on the reversal of roles, the Genesis text simply states the fact that Adam obeyed his wife by eating the fruit God had commanded him not to eat (Gen. 3:17; see n. 46 below). Genesis 3 focuses on the couple's blatant, rebellious act of sin as they defied the God who had created them and sought only their highest benefit. They sinned and fell, both as individuals and as a pair: "The eyes of both of them were opened and they knew that they were naked" (v. 7). See Mary K. Evans, *Man and Woman in the Bible* (Downers Grove, IL: InterVarsity, 1983), p. 18.

45. Brown, Driver, and Briggs classify the expression שָׁמַעְתָּ לְקוֹל ("you listened to the voice") in Genesis 3:17 with other texts meaning "obey," such as Exodus 15:26 and Judges 2:20 (Francis Brown, S. R. Driver, and Charles A. Briggs, *A Hebrew and English Lexicon of the Old Testament* [1907; reprint, Oxford: Clarendon, 1977], p. 1034). Harris, Archer, and Waltke give it the meaning "listen to" (along with verses such as 1 Kings 22:19; Ps. 81:11 [12, Heb.]; Prov. 12:15) and state that "this usage shades into that of 'to obey,'" as in Exodus 24:7; Nehemiah 9:16; Isaiah 42:24; and Jeremiah 35:18 (R. Laird Harris, Gleason L. Archer, Jr., and Bruce K. Waltke, *Theological Wordbook of the Old Testament* [Chicago: Moody, 1980], p. 938). Also see Allen P. Ross, *Creation and Blessing* (Grand Rapids: Baker, 1988), p. 147.

46. The most comprehensive discussions, with evaluations of strengths and weaknesses of various views, may be found in Moo, "1 Timothy 2:11–15: Meaning and Significance," pp. 70–73; Kent, *The Pastoral Epistles*, 112–17; and Spicq, *Les Epîtres Pastorales*, pp. 382–84.

47. C. F. D. Mode, *An Idiom-Book of New Testament Greek*, 2d ed. (Cambridge: Cambridge University Press, 1959), p. 56; H. A. Ironside, *Addresses on the First and Second Epistles of Timothy* (New York: Loizeaux Brothers, 1947), p. 72; E. K. Simpson,

The Pastoral Epistles (Grand Rapids: Eerdmans, 1954), p. 24. This view is proven incorrect by the many godly women who have died in childbirth over the centuries. The unacceptable implication of this view is that any woman who dies in childbirth is ungodly.

48. E. F. Scott, *The Pastoral Epistles* (London: Hodder and Stoughton, 1936), p. 28. The implication here is that childbearing is not a consequence of the Fall and thus inherently sinful (contra the false teachers, 1 Tim. 4:3); rather it is a worthy calling. This view has three problems. (1) It requires a rare use of διά with the genitive: "even though," rather than either instrumentality or attendant circumstance. (2) Contextually the focus of the passage is not on bearing children but on the proper role of women in the worship assembly. (3) This view limits the meaning of τεκνογονία to the act of birth (see the discussion below on the meaning of τεκνογονία).

49. This position is argued most ably by Kent, *The Pastoral Epistles*, 114–17. Also see J. Oliver Buswell, *A Systematic Theology of the Christian Religion*, 2 vols. (Grand Rapids: Zondervan, 1962), 1:284, n. 26. Against this view it may be noted that the passage as a whole is about women in general, and not just one woman (Mary as the "new Eve"). Also the general thrust of the passage is women's role in the worship assembly, not Christ's birth. Further, if Christ's birth were what Paul wished to describe, "he could hardly have chosen a more obscure or ambiguous way of saying it" (Donald Guthrie, *The Pastoral Epistles: An Introduction and Commentary* [Grand Rapids: Eerdmans, 1957], p. 78).

50. N. J. D. White, "The First and Second Epistles to Timothy," in *The Expositor's Greek Testament*, ed. W. R. Nicoll, 5 vols. (reprint, Grand Rapids: Eerdmans, 1951), 4:110. The underlying idea here seems to be that, despite what happened in the Fall, women will still experience spiritual salvation; they need only to fulfill their role in the home. While it is true that *both* women and men will be saved despite the Fall, this view fails to note the analogical argument Paul was making in verses 13 and 14 (see explanation above) and instead focuses on the fact rather than on the nature of the sin in the Garden (i.e., that their sin of disobedience to God's command included a reversal of God-ordained roles).

51. S. Jebb, "A Suggested Interpretation of 1 Timothy 2:15," *Expository Times* 81 (1969–70): 221–22; Hurley, *Man and Woman in Biblical Perspective*, pp. 222–23. While this view accurately focuses on the nature of the sin in the Garden (i.e., Adam and Eve's disobedience included a reversal of roles), it fails to give the verb σώζω its usual

sense of spiritual salvation and instead makes it refer to deliverance ("kept safe").

52. Moo, "1 Timothy 2:11–15; Meaning and Significance," pp. 71–73; Fung, "Ministry in the New Testament," p. 203. Also see Spicq, *Les Épîtres Pastorales*, pp. 383–84.

53. Floyd V. Filson, *St. Paul's Conception of Recompense* (Leipzig: Hinrich, 1931), pp. 141–42.

54. Karl P. Donfried, "Justification and Last Judgment in Paul," *Interpretation* 30 (1976): 144.

55. Glorification is the final, concluding phase of salvation. It is commonly associated with a point in time that may be either the believers' transition from earth to glory (2 Cor. 5:8) or the return of Christ (Col. 3:4). In their glorified state believers are at last fully conformed to the image of Christ (Rom. 8:28–29), and they receive their resurrection bodies (1 Cor. 15:38–50; 2 Cor. 5:1–5; Phil. 1:21). It is also in this state that the final judgment of the believers' works will occur and rewards will be given (Rom. 14:10; 2 Cor. 5:10). For further discussion, see Bernard Ramm, *Them He Glorified* (Grand Rapids: Eerdmans, 1963), pp. 62–136; and Charles A. A. Scott, *Christianity According to St. Paul* (Cambridge: Cambridge University Press, 1961), pp. 238–39.

56. Thus Paul could confidently assert in Ephesians 2:8 that "by grace you have been saved" (ἐστε σεσῳσμένοι), with the perfect periphrastic construction emphasizing both the past and present reality of an individual's salvation. At the same time, in Romans 5:9–10 he spoke of salvation—and of the aspects of justification and reconciliation in particular—as being consummated in the future: "we shall be saved" (σωθησόμεθα). See Ramm, *Them He Glorified*, pp. 67–69; and Donfried, *Justification and Last Judgment*," pp. 144–45. Donfried summarizes, "While salvation begins already now in the present (2 Cor. 6:2), its final manifestation is still to be found in the future (Rom. 13:11; 1 Thess. 5:8)" (ibid., p. 147).

57. George E. Ladd, *A Theology of the New Testament* (Grand Rapids: 1974), p. 519; and Ridderbos, *Paul: An Outline of His Theology*, p. 261.

58. Ladd, *A Theology of the New Testament*, pp. 521–22; Filson, *St. Paul's Conception of Recompense*, pp. 98–115, 143–44; and Donald Guthrie, *New Testament Theology* (Downers Grove, IL: Intervarsity 1981), pp. 859–62. For discussions on eschatological rewards, see Samuel L. Hoyt, "A Theological Examination of the Judgment Seat of Christ" (ThD diss., Grace Theological Seminary, 1977), pp. 198–240; and J. Dwight Pentecost, *Things to Come* (Grand Rapids: Zondervan, 1958), pp. 219–26.

59. Ramm, *Them He Glorified*, pp. 69–73; Ladd, *A Theology of the New Testament*, p. 520.
60. *Theological Dictionary of the New Testament*, s.v. "σῴζω," by W. Foerster, 7:995.
61. Ladd explains that "Paul uses the motivation of the final attainment of salvation in the Kingdom of God as a motivation to faithful and devoted Christian living. It is significant that Paul does not use the ethical sanction in any theoretical way that leads him to discuss the possibility of losing salvation; he uses it as a sanction to moral earnestness to avoid having the gospel of grace distorted into Hellenistic enthusiasm, libertinism, or moral passivity" (*A Theology of the New Testament*, p. 522).
62. Moo, "1 Timothy 2:11–15: Meaning and Significance," p. 72; id., "1 Timothy 2:11–15: A Rejoinder," *Trinity Journal* n.s. 2 (1981): 206. For example Galatians 5:6 shows love to be the medium (i.e., the efficient cause) through which faith works.
63. Bauer, Arndt, and Gingrich, *A Greek-English Lexicon of the New Testament and Other Early Christian Literature*, s.v. "δία," p. 180; Blass and Debrunner, *A Greek Grammar of the New Testament*, § 223(3); Moule, *An Idiom-Book of New Testament Greek*, p. 57; Spicq, *Les Épîtres Pastorales*, p. 383; Ridderbos, *Paul: An Outline of His Theology*, p. 309, n. 140; and Georges Didier, *Désinteressement du Chrétien* (Aubier: Montaigne, 1955), p. 195. Examples of its use are in Romans 2:27; 14:20; 1 Corinthians 3:15; 16:3; 2 Corinthians 2:4; 3:11; 6:8; 1 Timothy 4:14; 1 Peter 3:20.
64. Robertson cites the generic use of the article as one of its primary uses (*A Grammar of the Greek New Testament in the Light of Historical Research*, pp. 756–57).
65. Paul, in fact, legitimized and even exalted the position of both single men and single women (1 Cor. 7:25–38). Also he spoke highly of widows, some of whom may have been childless (cf. 1 Tim. 5:3–10).
66. Spicq, *Les Épîtres Pastorales*, pp. 383–84; Moo, "1 Timothy 2:11–15: Meaning and Significance," p. 72, n. 69; id., "1 Timothy 2:11–15: A Rejoinder," pp. 205–6; cf. Hurley, *Man and Woman in Biblical Perspective*, pp. 222–23.
67. Moo, "1 Timothy 2:11–15: Meaning and Significance," 72; cf. Hurley, *Man and Woman in Biblical Perspective*, pp. 222–23.
68. Hopkins's study of Roman tombstones suggests that the median age of death for wives was 34 and for husbands was 46.5. Angel's study of skeletal remains found in Greece during the period of Roman rule suggests that the median age of death was 34.3 for women and 40.2 for men. See Keith Hopkins, "On the Probable

Age Structure of the Roman Population," *Population Studies* 20 (1966): pp. 260–63; and J. Lawrence Angel, "Ecology and Population in the Eastern Mediterranean," *World Archaeology* 4 (1972): pp. 94–95, table 28.

69. Hurley, *Man and Woman in Biblical Perspective*, 222–23; Spicq, *Les Épîtres Pastorales*, pp. 399–400.
70. Bauer, Arndt, and Gingrich, *A Greek-English Lexicon of the New Testament and Other Early Christian Literature*, s.v. "μένω,"pp. 503–4.
71. Kelly, *A Commentary on the Pastoral Epistles*, p. 69; and Spicq, *Les Épîtres Pastorales*, p. 384. Bullinger refers to this as a Hebrew idiom called heterosis of person or number, whose purpose is to call attention to the truth taught by the change (E. W. Bullinger, *Figures of Speech Used in the Bible* [1898; reprint, Grand Rapids: Baker, 1968], p. 525).
72. Bauer, Arndt, and Gingrich, *A Greek-English Lexicon of the New Testament and Other Early Christian Literature*, s.v. "πίστις," p. 663.
73. Ibid., s.v. "ἀγάπη," p. 5.
74. Ibid., s.v. "σωφροσύνης," p. 802; cf. *Theological Dictionary of the New Testament*, s.v. "ἁγιασμός," by O. Proksch, 1:113.
75. Ridderbos, *Paul: An Outline of His Theology*, p. 263.
76. Bauer, Arndt, and Gingrich, *A Greek-English Lexicon of the New Testament and Other Early Christian Literature*, s.v. "σωφροσύνης," p. 802.

Chapter 18

1. Ruth Gotze, *Wie Luther Kirchenzucht Ubte* (Göttingen: Vanderhoeck & Ruprecht, 1958), p. 110.
2. Marvin L. Jescke, "Toward an Evangelical Conception of Corrective Church Discipline" (PhD diss., Northwestern University, 1965), p. 68.
3. Emil Oberholzer, "Saints in Sin: A Study of the Disciplinary Action of the Congregational Churches of Massachusetts in the Colonial and Early National Periods" (PhD diss., Columbia University, 1954), p. 31.
4. Carl D. Bangs, "The Search for the Marks of a Disciplined Church," *Register* 19 (January 1980): 15.
5. Jescke, "Toward an Evangelical Conception of Corrective Church Discipline," p. 76.
6. Karl Barth, *Church Dogmatics*, trans. G. W. Bromiley, vol. 4, 1: *The Doctrine of Reconciliation* (Edinburgh: Clark, 1956), p. 74. Barth says there is a place for church law. The church must give "answers which involve the establishment and execution of

ecclesiastical and congregational ordinances in which one thing is commanded, another forbidden, and a third permitted, or left to free and responsible judgment . . . according to the best of our knowledge and conscience."

7. Συναναμείγνυμι is probably not to be understood as a technical term for avoiding contact with certain people in the church or for discipline. The Corinthians had not understood it in this sense, for Paul had to explain its meaning to them. In the Septuagint the word frequently refers to the Israelites mixing with other people, with the result that the purity of the people of God was compromised (*Theological Dictionary of the New Testament*, s.v. "συναναμείγνυμι," by Heinrich Greeven, 7:852–55).

8. Commandments against πορνεία are the general theme of chapters 5 and 6 of 1 Corinthians. Πορνεία, πόρνοις, πόρνος, πόρνοι, and πόρνης appear in 5:1 (twice), 9–11; 6:9, 13, 15–16, 18 (twice); πόρνος heads the vice catalogs in 5:10–11 and 6:9.

9. F. S. Malan, "The Use of the Old Testament in 1 Corinthians," *Neotestamentica* 14 (1981): 149.

10. Deuteronomy 17:7, of an idolator; 19:19, of a false witness; 21:21, of a disobedient woman caught in adultery; and 24:7, of one who enslaves an Israelite. Paul changed the Septuagint's indicative to the plural imperative ἐξάρατε, to fit the grammar of his sentence better.

11. Malan, "The Use of the Old Testament in 1 Corinthians," p. 149.

12. S. R. Driver, *A Critical and Exegetical Commentary on Deuteronomy*, International Critical Commentary (Edinburgh: Clark, 1902), p. 152. See Gerhard von Rad, *Studies in Deuteronomy*, trans. D. M. Stalker (London: SCM, 1953), pp. 22–23.

13. Jescke, "Toward an Evangelical Conception of Corrective Church Discipline," p. 66.

14. John White and Ken Blue, *Healing the Wounded: The Costly Love of Church Discipline* (Downers Grove, IL: InterVarsity, 1985), p. 106.

15. Ibid., p. 107.

16. A. T. Robertson, *Word Pictures in the New Testament*, 6 vols. (Nashville: Broadman, 1933), 6:428.

17. Frederic Louis Godet, *Commentary on Romans* (reprint, Grand Rapids: Kregel, 1977), p. 496.

18. John Murray, *The Epistle to the Romans*, 2 vols. (Grand Rapids: Eerdmans, 1965), 2:235–36.

19. William G. T. Shedd, *Commentary on the Epistle of St. Paul to the Romans* (Grand Rapids: Baker, 1980), p. 430.

20. R. C. H. Lenski, *The Interpretation of St. Paul's Epistles to the*

Galatians, to the Ephesians, and to the Philippians (Minneapolis: Augsburg, 1961), p. 285.

21. Ibid., p. 288.

22. Ibid.

23. Two other arguments support the view that the sins listed, rather than being exhaustive, are representative of sins demanding discipline. First, in 5:19 the word "which" (ἄτινά) is qualitative and is best translated "of a kind which" rather than simply "which." Second, Paul referred to "some, any" (τινι) trespass in 6:1 to demonstrate that he did not have a particular sin in mind. Paul's list is simply representative of the multiple deeds of the flesh that plague the believer.

24. Walter Bauer, William F. Arndt, and F. Wilbur Gingrich, *A Greek-English Lexicon of the New Testament and Other Early Christian Literature*, 2d ed., rev. F. Wilbur Gingrich and Frederick W. Danker (Chicago: University of Chicago Press, 1979), p. 23.

25. Alfred Plummer, *The Pastoral Epistles*, New International Critical Commentary (Edinburgh: Clark, 1915), p. 458.

26. *Theological Dictionary of the New Testament*, s.v. "αἱρετικός," by Heinrich Schlier, 1:184.

27. Plummer, *The Pastoral Epistles*, p. 458.

28. J. N. D. Kelly, *A Commentary on the Pastoral Epistles*, Thornapple Commentaries (Grand Rapids: Baker, 1981), p. 255.

29. Plummer, *The Pastoral Epistles*, p. 458.

30. In Titus 3:10 νουθεσία "is the attempt to make the heretic aware of the falsity of his position, a pastoral attempt to reclaim rather than a disciplinary measure, though there is place for this if the corrective word is of no avail" (*Theological Dictionary of the New Testament*, s.v. "νουθετέω, νουθεσία," by J. Behm, 4:1022).

31. Kelly, *A Commentary on the Pastoral Epistles*, p. 256; cf. *Theological Dictionary of the New Testament*, s.v. "ἀκατάκριτος," by Friedrich Büchself, 3:952.

32. Robertson, *Word Pictures in the New Testament*, 6:265.

33. There is debate on the exact nature of the offender's actions. A common interpretation is that Diotrephes put out of the church members who wanted to receive the travelers. See C. H. Dodd, *Johannine Epistles* (London: Hodder and Stoughton, 1946), p. 162.

34. James E. Mignard, "Jewish and Christian Cultic Discipline to the Middle of the Second Century" (PhD diss., Boston University Graduate School, 1966), p. 205.

35. Daniel E. Wray, *Biblical Church Discipline* (Carlisle, PA: Banner of Truth Trust, 1978), pp. 8–9.

36. Jescke, "Toward an Evangelical Conception of Corrective Church Discipline," p. 69.
37. Bangs, "The Search for the Marks of a Disciplined Church," p. 20.
38. H. J. A. Bouman, "Biblical Presuppositions for Church Discipline," *Concordia Theological Monthly* 30 (February 1959): 515.

Chapter 19

1. Also see Ted G. Kitchens, "Perimeters of Corrective Church Discipline," *Bibliotheca Sacra* 148 (April–June 1991): 201–13.
2. Belgic Confession XXIX.
3. Don Baker, *Beyond Forgiveness* (Portland, OR: Multnomah, 1984), p. 33.
4. The present imperative ordinarily has the sense of a command or exhortation with a durative aspect (A. T. Robertson, *A Grammar of the Greek New Testament in the Light of Historical Research* [Nashville: Broadman, 1934], pp. 946–47). An iterative use, more like the use here, is suggested by F. Blass, A. Debrunner, and Robert W. Funk, *A Greek Grammar of the New Testament and Other Early Christian Literature* (Chicago: University of Chicago Press, 1961), p. 172.
5. If Paul had been present in Corinth, he would already have disciplined the individual. The perfect κέκρικα, "I have judged" (v. 3), the main verb of the entire passage, supports the requirement of discipline.
6. Baker also offers a list (*Beyond Forgiveness*, pp. 33–34).
7. Κερδαίνω is often used for gaining earthly riches, but it is used figuratively here for gaining someone for benefit of the kingdom of God (cf. 1 Cor. 9:19–22 and see Walter Bauer, William F. Arndt, and F. Wilbur Gingrich, *A Greek-English Lexicon of the New Testament and Other Early Christian Literature*, 2d ed., rev. F. Wilbur Gingrich and Frederick W. Danker [Chicago: University of Chicago Press, 1979], p. 429).
8. In all likelihood this is the happy ending to the incident in 1 Corinthians 5:1–5 (Charles Hodge, *1 and 2 Corinthians* [reprint, Carlisle, PA: Banner of Truth Trust, 1978], p. 412).
9. Philip E. Hughes, *The Second Epistle to the Corinthians* (Grand Rapids: Eerdmans, 1962), pp. 66–67.
10. Ἐντρέπω ("put to shame") may designate a "turn toward, about, or in" (Henry G. Liddell, Robert Scott, Henry S. Jones, and Roderick McKenzie, *A Greek-English Lexicon* [Oxford: Clarendon, 1968], p. 577). Cf. 1 Corinthians 6:4 and Titus 2:8. It is clear that the root τρέπω designates the concept of "turning" (ibid., p. 1813) to which the prefix ἐν is added. Also see John Lineberry, *Vital Word Studies in 2 Thessalonians* (Grand Rapids: Zondervan, 1961), p. 87, who takes this as a turning inward in self-examination.

11. If humiliation or shame were Paul's intention, he could have used the clearer word for "shame," αἰσχύνη.
12. J. Carl Laney, *A Guide to Church Discipline* (Minneapolis: Bethany, 1985), pp. 80–81.
13. While there is some doubt whether the qualifying phrase "against you" (εἰς σε) is part of the original text (see A. F. Brooke II, "A New Testament Theology of Church Discipline" [ThM thesis, Dallas Theological Seminary, 1986], p. 12), it has little influence on the scope of the "sin" to which Jesus is referring.
14. Bauer, Arndt, and Gingrich, *A Greek-English Lexicon of the New Testament and Other Early Christian Literature*, p. 42.
15. R. C. H. Lenski, *The Interpretation of St. Matthew's Gospel* (Minneapolis: Augsburg, 1961), p. 699.
16. Ἁμαρτάνοντα" ("continue in sin") in 1 Timothy 5:20 is in the present tense, taken most naturally in its usually durative aspect. The "trespass" in Galatians 6:1 is nominal and therefore not helpful in this determination.
17. Liddell and Scott, *A Greek-English Lexicon*, 267. Ἀτάκτος was a military term for a soldier marching out of step; it is used metaphorically for general disorderliness.
18. George Milligan, *St. Paul's Epistles to the Thessalonians* (Grand Rapids: Eerdmans, 1953), pp. 152–54. He substantiates the metaphorical use of ἀτάκτος for a slothful or idle person.
19. See John F. Walvoord, *The Thessalonian Epistles* (Findlay, OH: Dunham, n.d.), pp. 152, 155–57.
20. Leon Morris, *The First and Second Epistles to the Thessalonians* (Grand Rapids: Eerdmans, 1989), p. 168.
21. Donald Allen Waite, "An Exegetical Exposition of the Epistle of Paul to Titus" (ThD diss., Dallas Theological Seminary, 1955), pp. 203–7; R. C. H. Lenski, *The Interpretation of St. Paul's Epistles to the Colossians, to the Thessalonians, to Timothy, to Titus, and to Philemon* (Minneapolis: Augsburg, 1961), pp. 941–43; and J. N. D. Kelly, *Commentary on the Pastoral Epistles* (London: Adam and Black, 1963), p. 255.
22. Πορνεία in Pauline literature is a general term, indicating "any kind of illegitimate sexual intercourse" (*New International Dictionary of New Testament Theology*, s.v. "Discipline," by H. Reisser, p. 500).
23. Brooke demonstrates that γυνή πατρός designates a stepmother ("A New Testament Theology of Church Discipline," p. 39). The phrase is found in the Septuagint in Leviticus 18:7–8, which distinguishes between "father's wife" and "mother."
24. The form of discipline entailed is discussed under "Method of Church Discipline." p. 225

25. In all probability Paul concluded the matter of this specific sin with this command. See Gordon Fee, *The First Epistle to the Corinthians* (Grand Rapids: Eerdmans, 1987), p. 226.
26. Ibid., p. 224.
27. Ibid.
28. *Theological Dictionary of the New Testament*, s.v. "ἐλέγχω," by Friedrich Büchsel, 2:474.
29. Ronald Y. K. Fung, *The Epistle to the Galatians* (Grand Rapids: Eerdmans, 1988), p. 286.
30. James M. Boice, "Galatians," in *The Expositor's Bible Commentary* (Grand Rapids: Zondervan, 1976), 10:501.
31. Stanley D. Toussaint, *Behold the King: A Study of Matthew* (Portland, OR: Multnomah, 1980), pp. 217–18.
32. Lenski, *The Interpretation of St. Matthew's Gospel*, p. 702.
33. Ibid., p. 703.
34. The act of "withdrawing from personal fellowship" is suggested by Lineberry (*Vital Word Studies in 2 Thessalonians*, pp. 78–79). Milligan suggests "restrain yourself from association with him" (*St. Paul's Epistles to the Thessalonians*, p. 113).
35. See above for the probable purpose of this disciplinary action.
36. Walvoord, *2 Thessalonians*, pp. 155–56.
37. Leon Morris, *The Epistles of Paul to the Thessalonians*, Tyndale New Testament Commentaries (1956; reprint, Grand Rapids: Eerdmans, 1974), p. 149.
38. *Guinn v. Church of Christ of Collinsville*, 775 P.2d 766, 774 (Okla. 1989).
39. This discussion is a compilation of cases pertaining to church and law across the country. There is no uniform federal or state law (apart perhaps from the First Amendment defense). In each individual case particular state tort law applies. Though a helpful guideline this discussion is not legally binding in any state.
40. *Guinn v. Church of Christ of Collinsville*, Brief of Plaintiff-Appelee, p. 25.
41. *Guinn v. Church of Christ of Collinsville*, 775 P.2d 766, 769. Chapter 20 suggests how the announcement to the congregation could be handled to possibly avoid "public disclosure" designation.
42. Restatement (Second) of Torts, 28A, section 652D (1977).
43. Restatement (Second) of Torts, 28A, section 652D, comment c (1977).
44. Restatement (Second) of Torts, Publicity Given to Private Life section 652D, comment d (1977).
45. This defense is borrowed from the laws of defamation. 41 Am. Jur., *Privacy*, Section 20 (1942), p. 940. See also Restatement (Second) of Torts, section 652G, comment a (1977).

46. Restatement (Second) of Torts, Common Interest, section 596, comment 2 (1977).
47. 59 P. 1050 (Kan. 1900).
48. Following the rule established in *Farnsworth v. Storrs*, 59 Mass. (5 Cush.) 412 (1850); *Landis v. Campbell*, 79 Mo. 433 (1883).
49. See *Guinn v. Church Christ of Collinsville*.
50. Carl H. Esbeck, "Tort Claims against Churches and Ecclesiastical Officers: The First Amendment Considerations," *West Virginia Law Review* 89 (1986): 102.
51. Restatement (Second) of Torts, section 46 (1977).
52. Ibid., note d.
53. Ibid., note j.
54. Restatement (Second) of Torts, Defamatory Communications, Section 559 (1977).
55. Restatement (Second) of Torts, Section 581A (1977).
56. The same defense used for invasion of privacy given above.
57. 197 P.2d 715 (Cal. 1948).
58. "Malice" is defined as "action motivated by hatred or ill will toward the person" (Restatement [Second] of Torts, Section 603 [1977]).
59. W. Torpey, *Judicial Doctrines of Religious Rights in America* (1948) at 126.
60. *Landis v. Campbell*, 79 Mo. 483 (1883).
61. *Rasmussen v. Bennett*, 741 P.2d 755, 56 (Mont. 1987).
62. Ibid., at 58.
63. See *Watson v. Jones*, 20 L. Ed. 666 (1872); *Trett v. Lambeth*, 195 S.W.2d 524 (Mo. App. 1946); *Katz v. Singerman*, 127 So.2d 515 (La. 1961); *Brady v. Reiner*, 198 S.E.2d 812 (W. Va. App. 1973); *Church of God of Decatur v. Finney*, 101 N.E.2d 156 (Ill. App. 1951); *Trustees of Pencader Presbyterian Church v. Gibson*, 22 A.2d 782 (Del. 1941); *St. John's Greek Catholic Church v. Fedak*, 213 A.2d 651 (N. J. 1965).
64. Gibson, 22 A.2d 782, 790.
65. *Cantil v. Connecticut*, 310 U.S. 296, 60 S. Ct. 900, 84 L. Ed. 1213 (1943) incorporated the "free exercise" clause; *Everson v. Board of Education*, 330 U.S. 1, 67 S. Ct. 504 91 L. Ed. 711 (1947), incorporated the "establishment" clause. The application of the Bill of Rights to state as well as federal action progressed over time from the passing of the Amendment.
66. *Zorach v. Clauson*, 346 U.S. 306, 72 S. Ct. 679, 96 L. Ed. 954 (1952).
67. *Abington School District v. Schempp*, 374 U.S. 203, 83 S. Ct. 1560, 10 L. Ed. 2d 844 (1963).
68. In church discipline cases it is clear that the state is prohibited by

the establishment clause from determining, even indirectly, church doctrine or ecclesiastical questions. *Fowler v. Rhode Island*, 345 U.S. 67, 70, 73 S. Ct. 526, 97 L. Ed. 828 (1953). Whether there is a violation of the free exercise clause is established by three tests articulated in *Lemon v. Kurtzman*, 403 U.S. 602, 91 S. Ct. 2105, 29 L. Ed. 2d 745 (1971): (1) The statute must have a secular legislative purpose. (2) Its principal or primary effect must be one that neither advances nor inhibits religion. (3) The statute must not foster an excessive government entanglement with religion to be valid.

69. *Fowler v. Rhode Island*, 345 U.S. 67, 70 (1953).
70. *Rasmussen v. Bennett*, 741 P.2d 755 (Mont. 1987).
71. *United States v. Lee*, 455 U.S. 252, 261, 71 L. Ed. 2d 127, 102 S. Ct. 1051(1982).
72. *Sherbert v. Verner*, 374 U.S. 398, 403, 406 (1963).
73. *Paul v. Watchtower Bible Society*, 819 F.2d 875, 883 (1987).
74. *Guinn v. Church of Christ of Collinsville*, 775 P.2d, 766, 779 (Okla. 1989).

Chapter 20

1. *Farnsworth v. Storrs*, 59 Mass. (5 Cush.) 412, 413 (1850).
2. Ibid., at 413.
3. *Watson v. Jones*, 80 U.S. (13 Wall.) 679, 20 L. Ed. 666 (1872).
4. Ibid., at 676 (italics added).
5. Ibid.
6. Ibid., quoting Shannon v. Frost, 3 B.Mon. 253.
7. Ibid., at 677.
8. Ibid.
9. *Sherbert v. Verner*, 374 U.S. 398, 406, 83 S. Ct. 1790,10 L. Ed. 2d 965 (1963).
10. *Reynolds v. United States*, 98 U.S. 145, 25 L Ed. 244 (1877).
11. *Hill v. State*, 33 Ala. App. 404, 88 So.2d 880 (1956).
12. *Baugh v. Thomas*, 265 A.2d 675, 677 (N. J. 1970).
13. Ibid., at 678, citing *Taylor v. Jackson*, 273 F. 345 (1921); *Walker Memorial Baptist Church v. Saunders*, 35 N.E.2d 42 (1941); *David v. Carter*, 22 S.W.2d 900 (1949); *Randolf v. First Baptist Church*, 120 N.E.2d 485 (1954). See also 20 A.L.R.2d 417, 462–466 (1951).
14. *Baugh v. Thomas*, 265 A.2d. 675, 677 (N. J. 1970).
15. "Dicta" are "expressions in a court's opinion which go beyond the facts before the court and therefore are individual views of the author of the opinion and not binding in subsequent cases" (*Black's Law Dictionary*, 5th ed. [St. Paul: West, 1979], 408).
16. "Shunning" is the practice of totally cutting off the disciplined member

from all church functions and from all association with the assembly and its members with a view to bringing the shunned party to repentance. This practice, sometimes including even shunning by one's own family members, is followed in some Amish and Mennonite churches.

17. *Bear v. Reformed Mennonite Church*, 341 A.2d. 105, 107 (Pa. 1975).

18. One such course was presented by the American Bar Association, Section of Tort and Insurance Practice; Section of Individual Rights and Responsibilities, held in San Francisco, May 4–5, 1989.

19. *Guinn v. Church of Christ of Collinsville*, 775 P.2d 766 (Okla., 1989).

20. She also initially sued for defamation, but this claim was dropped because all statements that were made in public were true.

21. For explanations of these terms, see chapter 19.

22. *Guinn v. Church of Christ of Collinsville*, 775 P.2d, 766, 773 (Okla. 1989).

23. Ibid., at 776 and 777.

24. Ibid., at 777 and 778.

25. However, a new trial was not held, because the parties concluded the matter in an out-of-court settlement.

26. 707 F.2d. 355 (1983).

27. 459 A.2d. 674 (N. J. 1983).

28. Ibid., at 676.

29. 535 F. Supp. 1125 (Ca. 1989).

30. 506 F. Supp. 444 (W. Va. 1989).

31. 819 F.2d. 875 (1987).

32. The church member sued after being "shunned."

33. *Paul v. Watchtower Bible Society*, 819 F.2d 875, 880 (1987).

34. Ibid., at 881.

35. Ibid., at 883.

36. No church discipline case involving the tort of alienation of affection was found, though the potential liability under such a legal theory is certainly present. See comments of the New Jersey Supreme Court in *Baugh v. Thomas*, 265 A.2d 675 (N. J. 1970).

37. The tort of intentional interference with business relations was not examined; yet this could be a legal basis for legal liability. See *Baugh v. Thomas*, 265 A.2d 675 (N. J.1970).

38. Charles Hodge, *Systematic Theology*, 3 vols. (Grand Rapids: Eerdmans, 1981), 3:358.

39. Ibid., p. 361.

40. *Guinn v. Church of Christ of Collinsville*, 775 P.2d 766 (Okla. 1989).

41. It should be noted that every case read by this writer that was allowed to go to the jury was decided against the disciplining church.